THE
UNWANTED
STORIES OF THE SYRIAN REFUGEES

WRITTEN AND ILLUSTRATED BY
DON BROWN

HOUGHTON MIFFLIN HARCOURT

Boston   New York

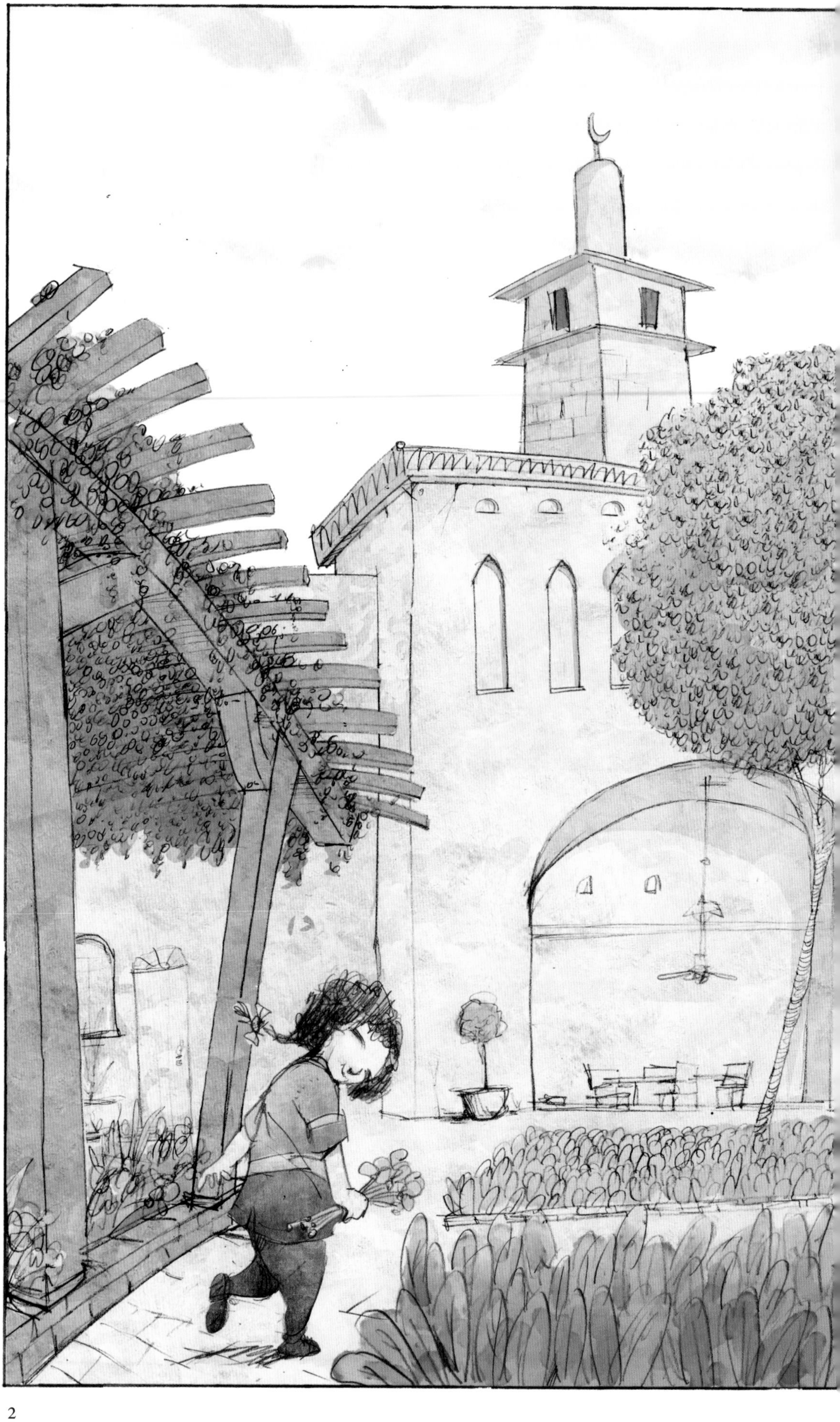

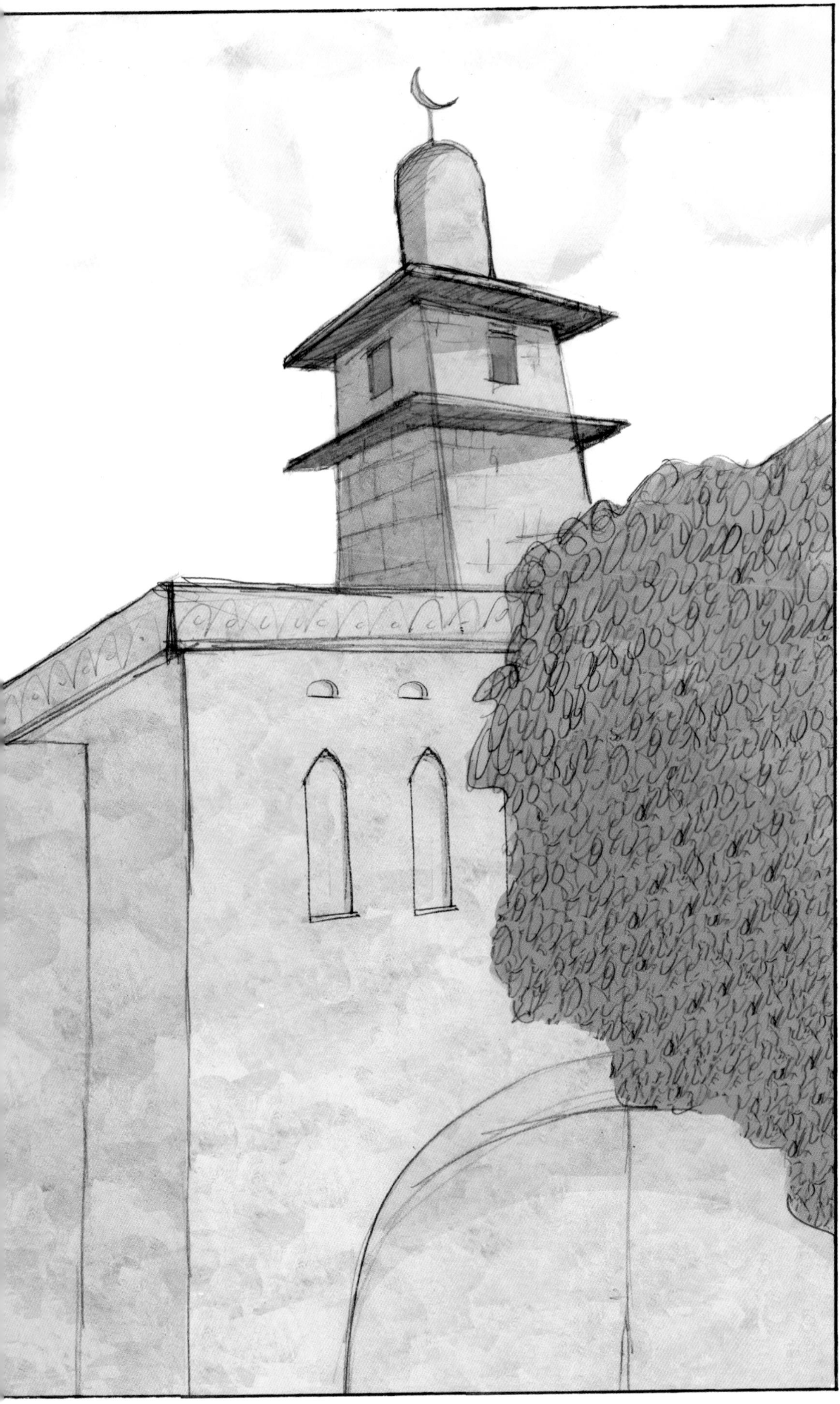

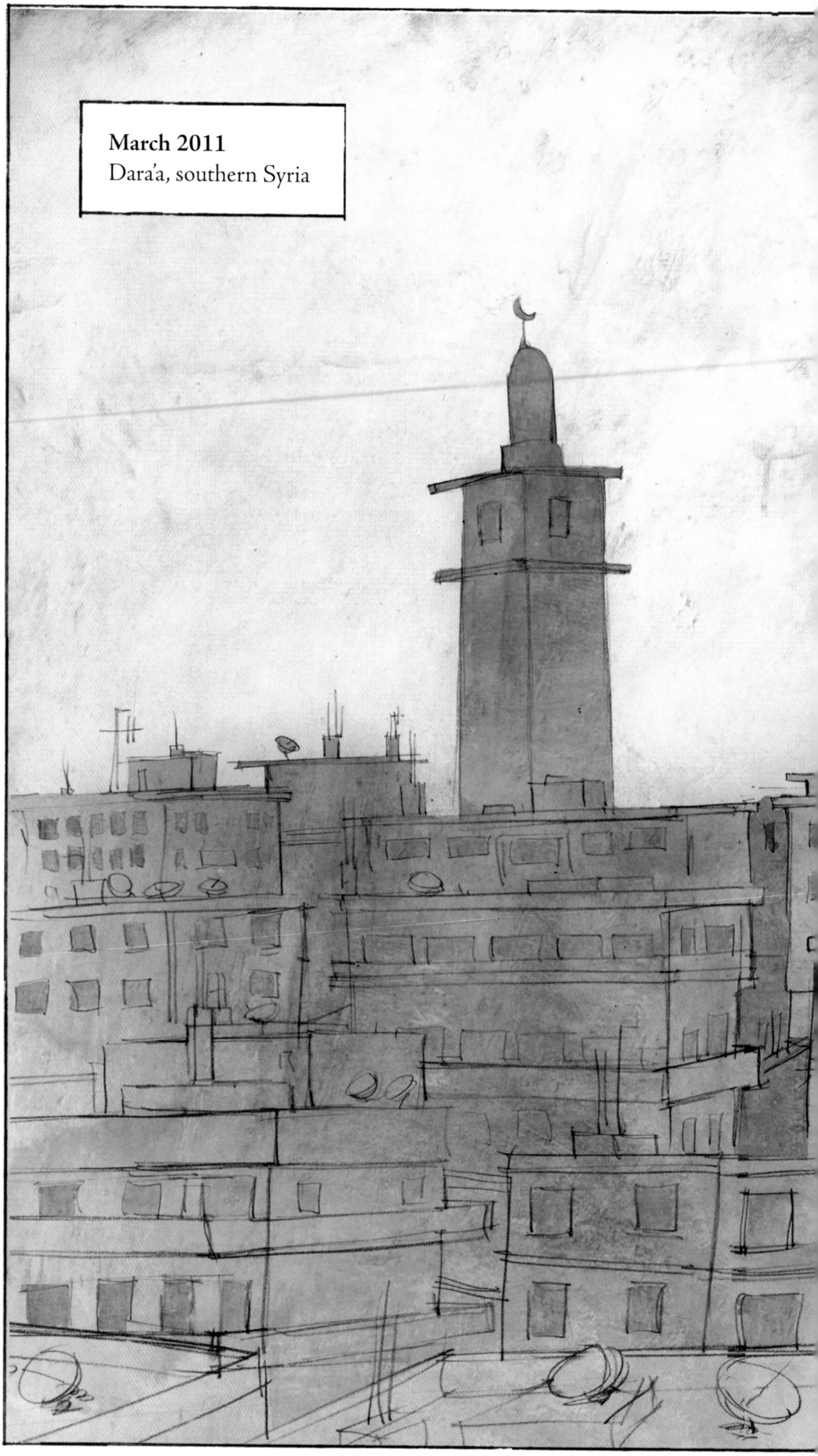
March 2011
Dara'a, southern Syria

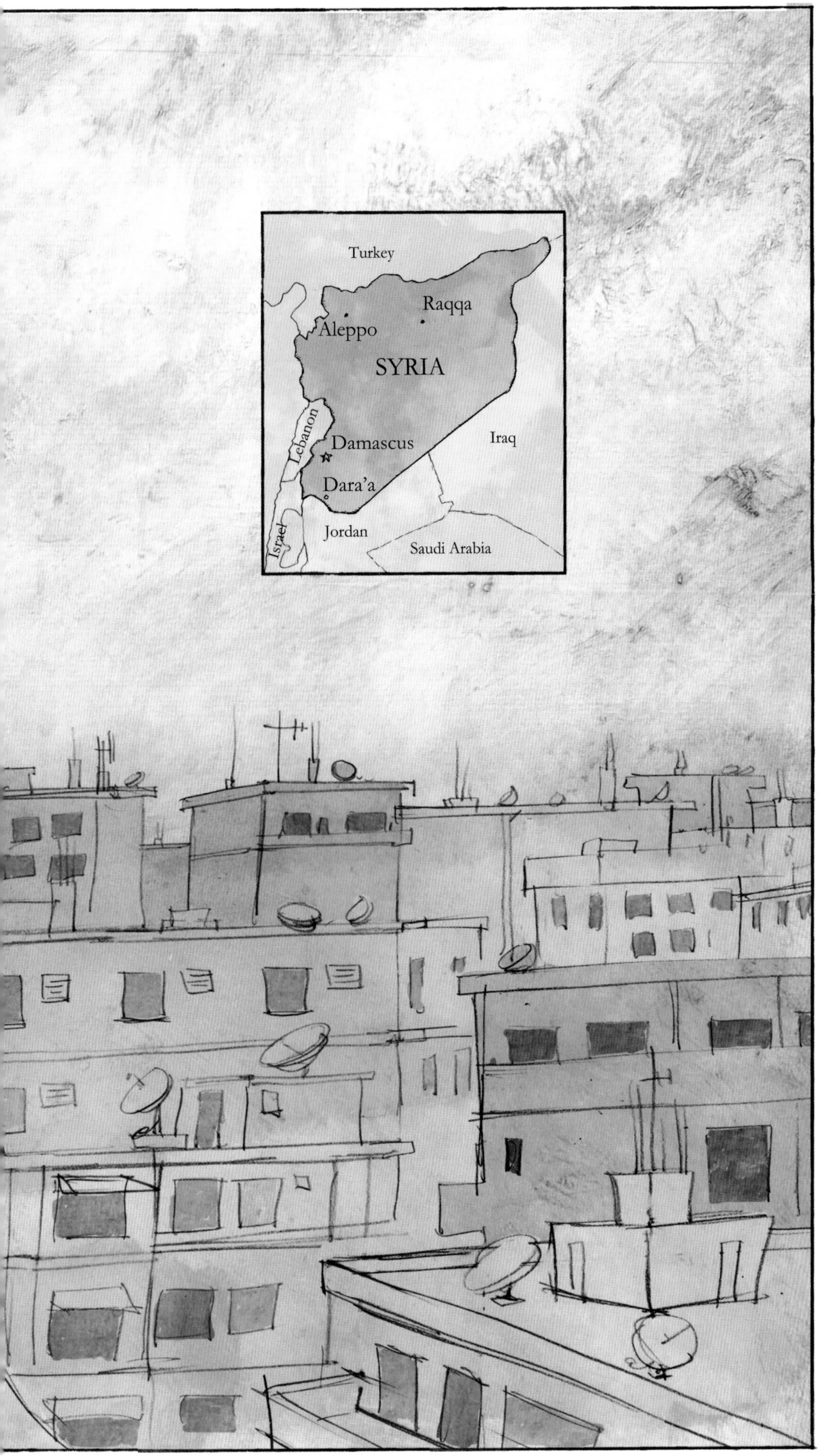
Turkey
Raqqa
Aleppo
SYRIA
Lebanon
Damascus
Iraq
Dara'a
Israel
Jordan
Saudi Arabia

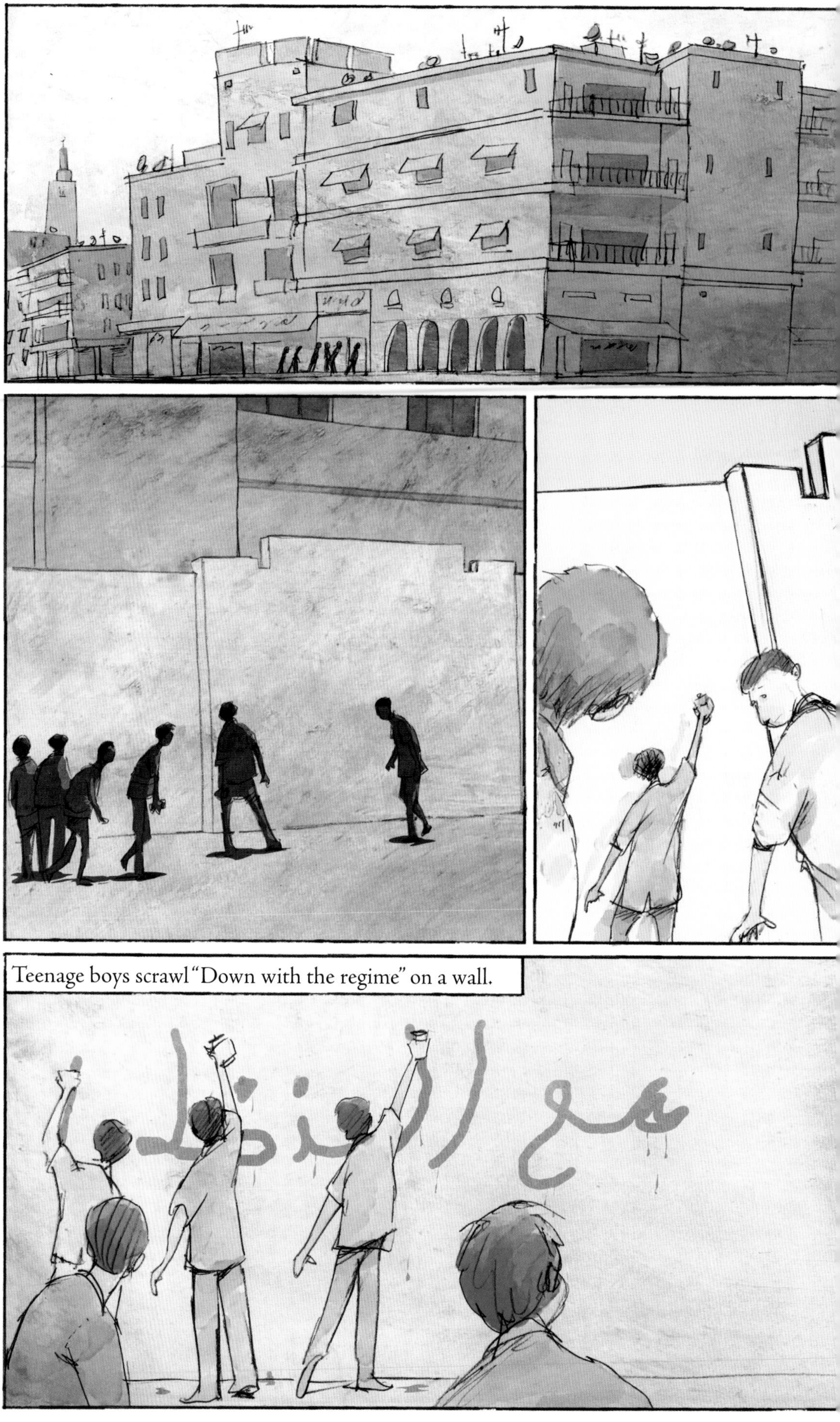
Teenage boys scrawl “Down with the regime” on a wall.

It was a demand for the end of the Syrian president Bashar al-Assad's one-man rule. Assad's father seized power in 1970, one of a string of dictators who had come and gone in Syria since its independence in 1947. The Assad family has ruled ever since, crushing anyone who challenged them.

Syria was not alone; similar tyrannies could be found across North Africa and the Middle East. In 2010, oppressed people in those countries protested, sparking uprisings nicknamed the Arab Spring. Tunisia and Egypt saw their governments upended.

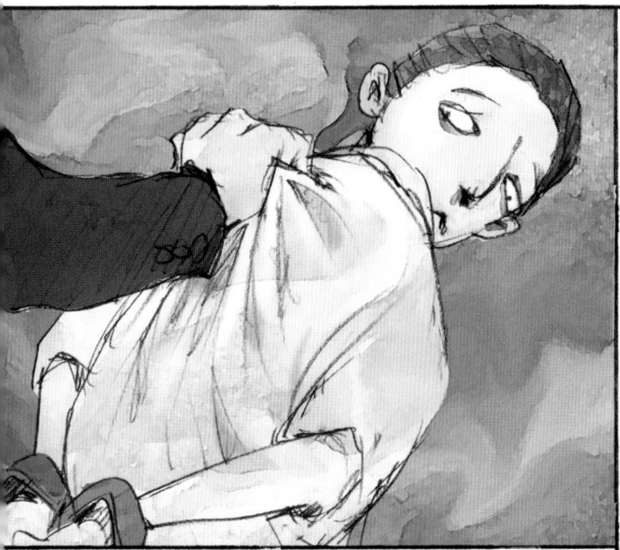

The Dara'a boys are arrested, imprisoned . . . and tortured.

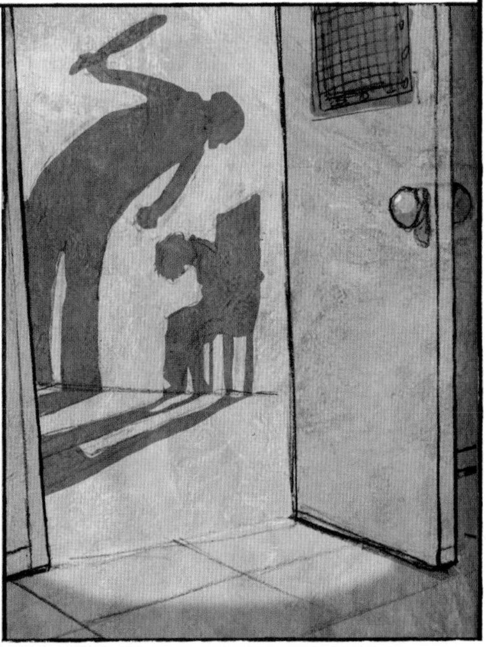

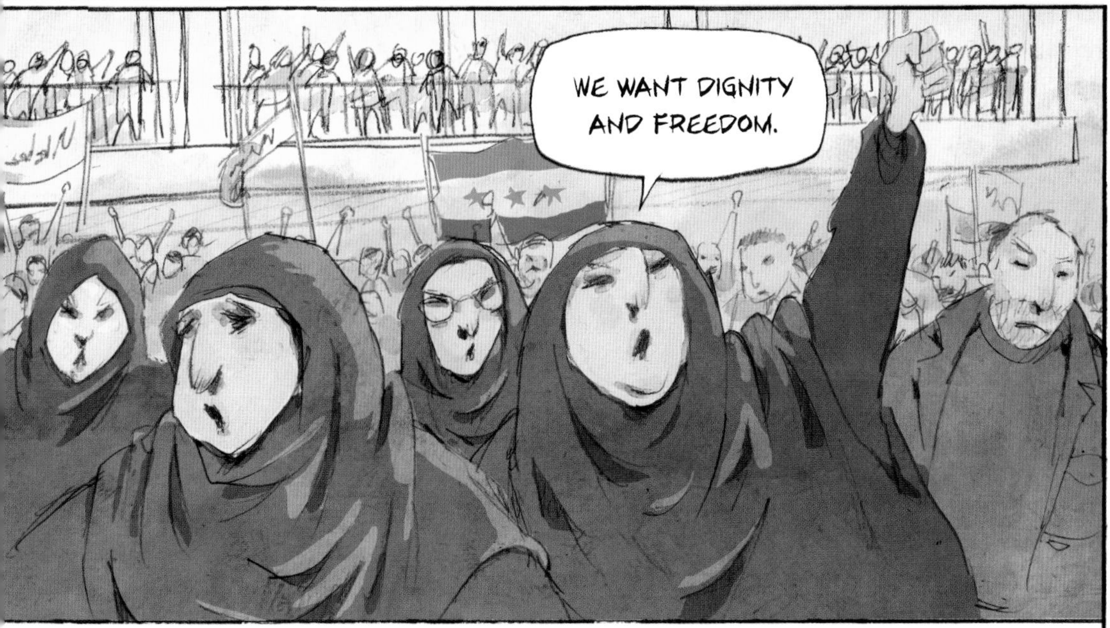
WE WANT DIGNITY AND FREEDOM.

At first, family and friends protest the boys' imprisonment, and then angry thousands join the demand for the boys' freedom. The boys are released weeks later, but people's fury doesn't end. They're angry at Assad's undemocratic rule, angry at his cruel security forces, angry about government corruption and no jobs.

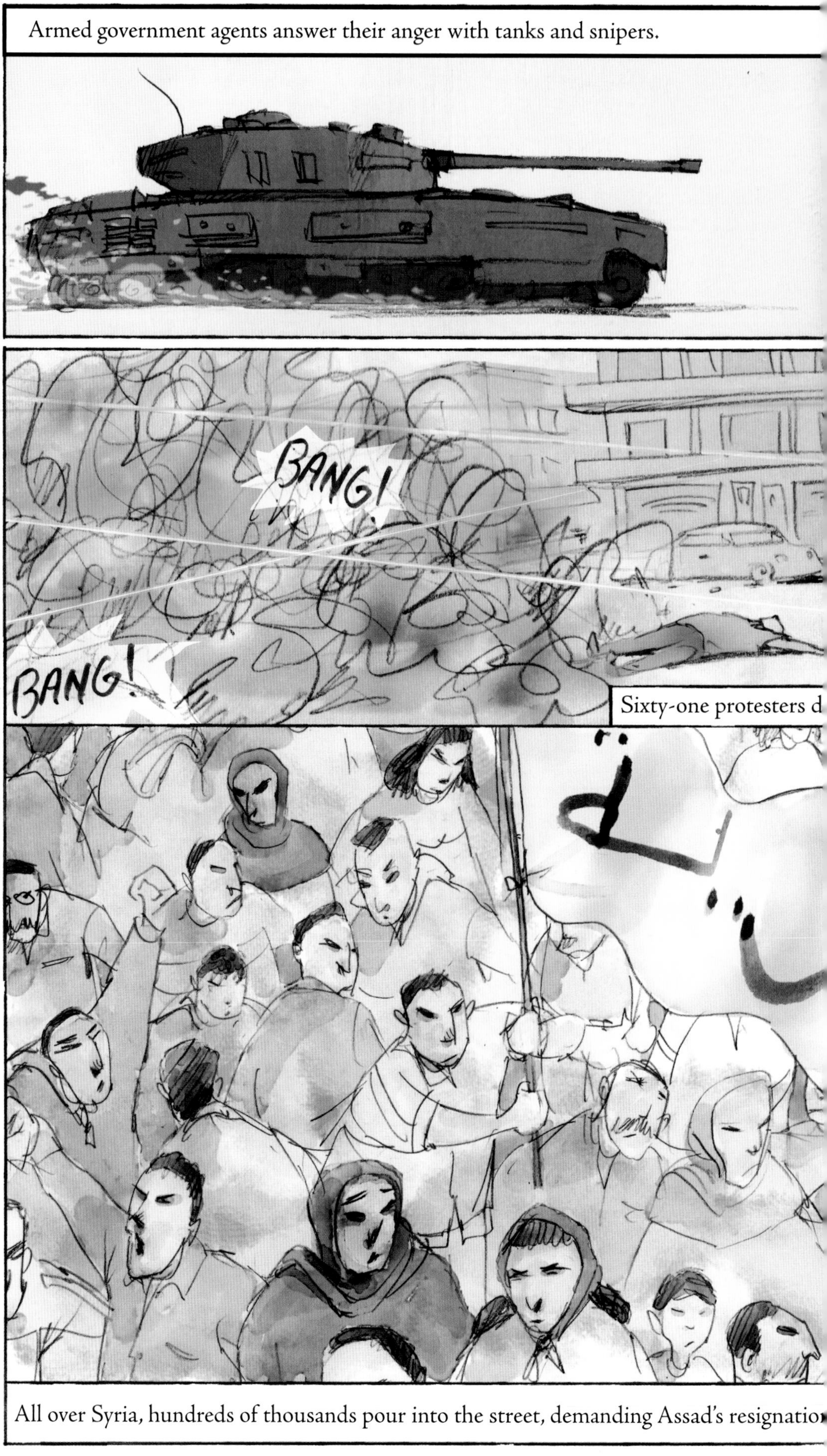
Armed government agents answer their anger with tanks and snipers.
BANG!
BANG!
Sixty-one protesters d
All over Syria, hundreds of thousands pour into the street, demanding Assad's resignatio

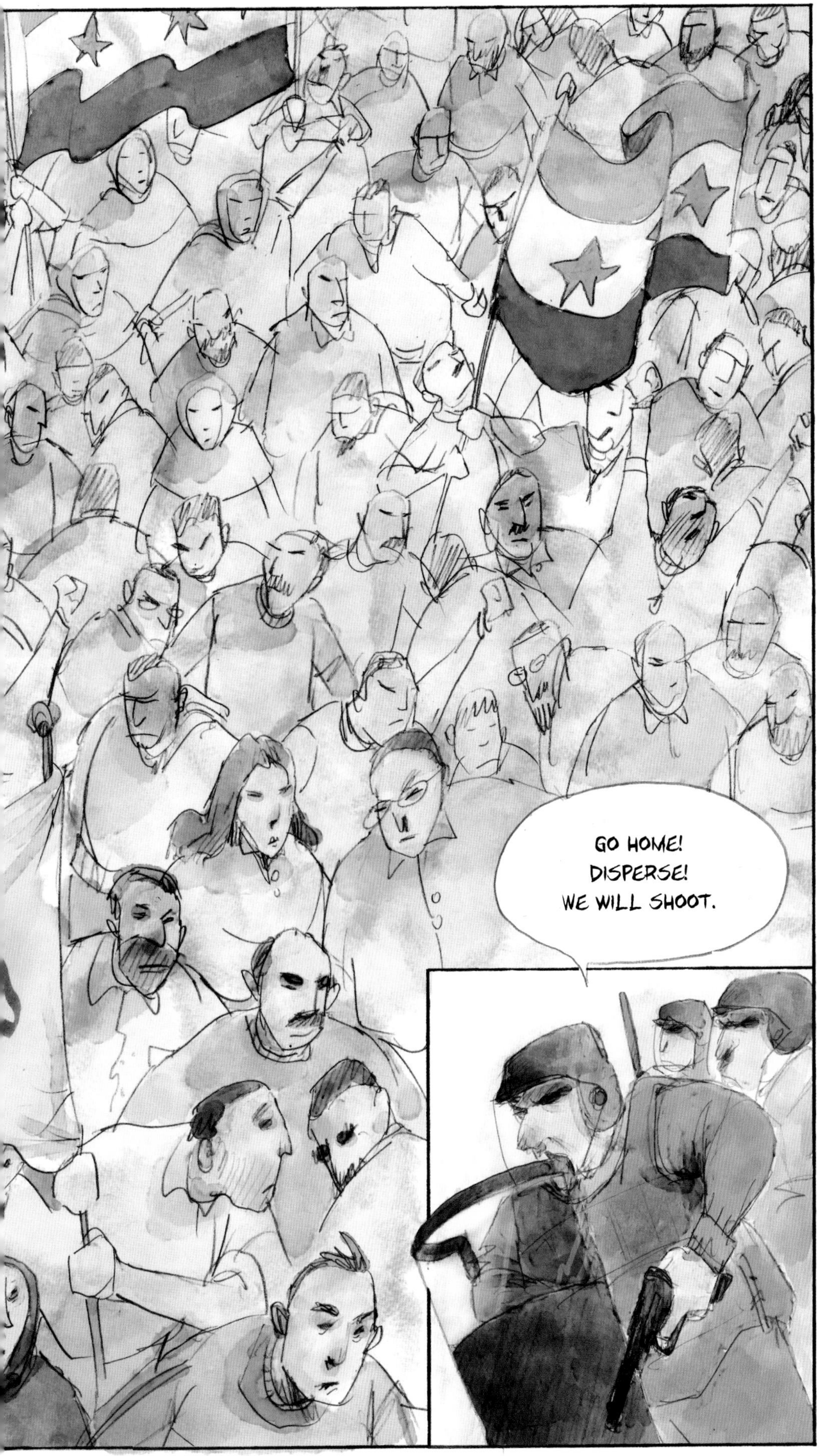
GO HOME!
DISPERSE!
WE WILL SHOOT.

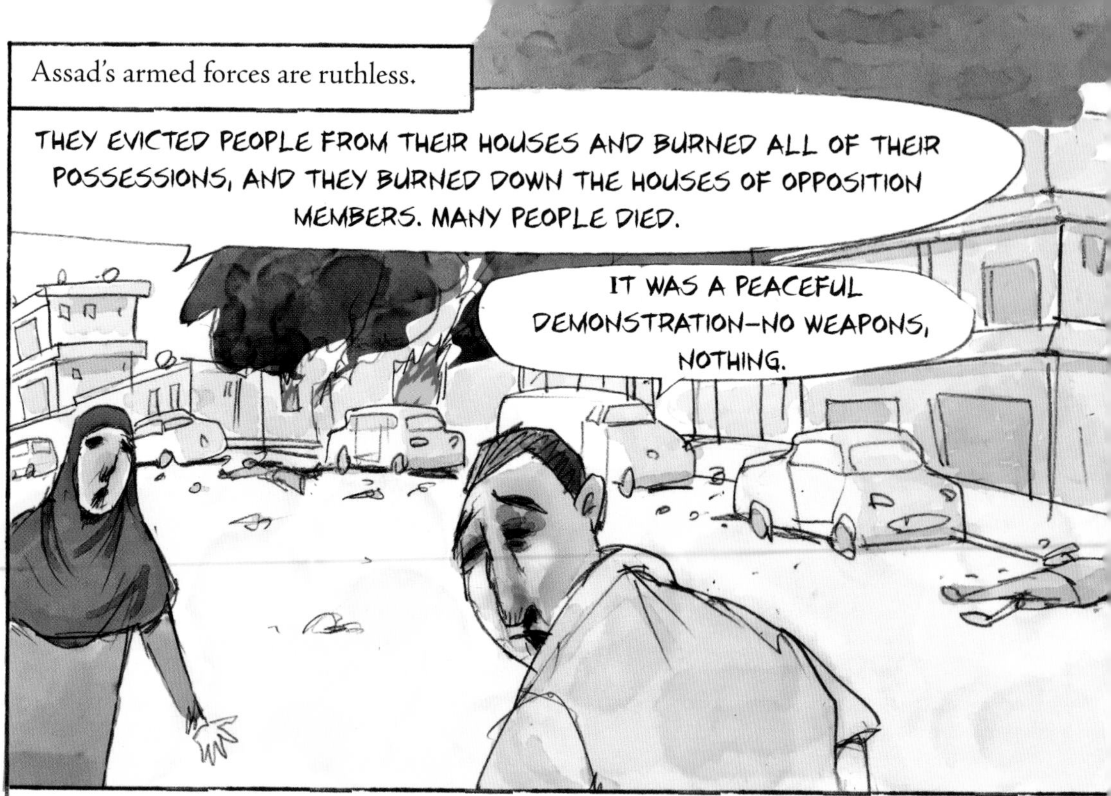
Assad's armed forces are ruthless.
THEY EVICTED PEOPLE FROM THEIR HOUSES AND BURNED ALL OF THEIR POSSESSIONS, AND THEY BURNED DOWN THE HOUSES OF OPPOSITION MEMBERS. MANY PEOPLE DIED.
IT WAS A PEACEFUL DEMONSTRATION—NO WEAPONS, NOTHING.

Within months, the protest grows, and so does the violence:

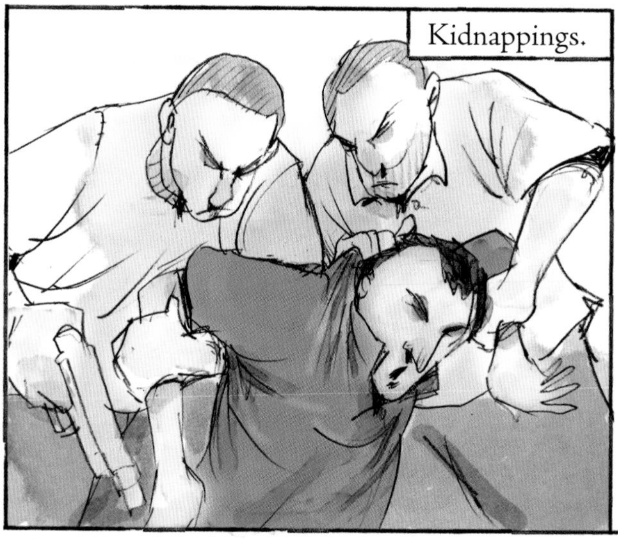
Kidnappings.

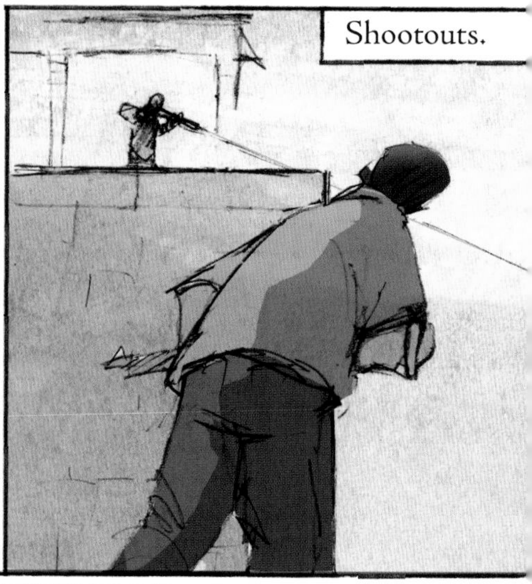
Shootouts.

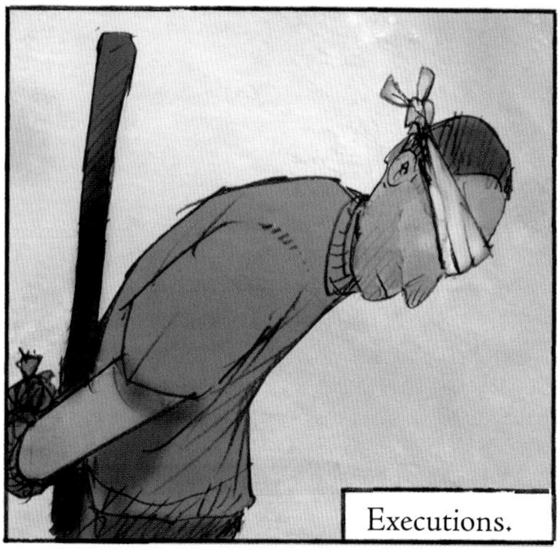
Executions.

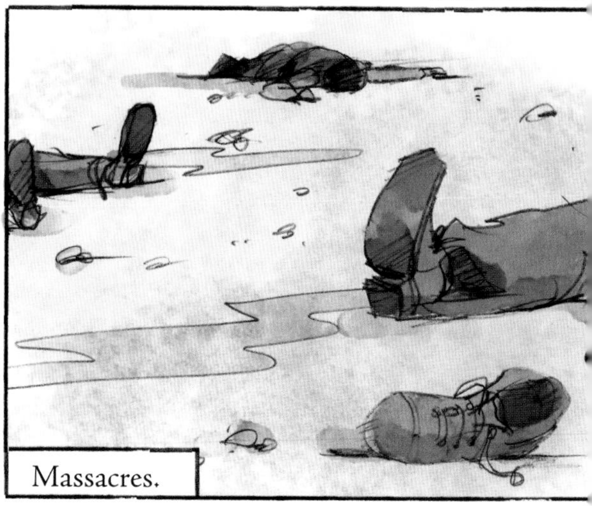
Massacres.

Across Syria, sides supporting and opposing Assad are drawn, mostly along religious lines.

Just as Christianity comprises Catholics, Episcopalians, Methodists, Baptists, and the like, Islam is roughly split into Shia and Sunni. President Assad mostly finds support with Shia Muslims and Alawites, a Shia sect of which he's a member. Some Christians favor him too, while others try to remain neutral. Sunni Muslims—about three-quarters of the population—mostly oppose him. The divisions explode into civil war.

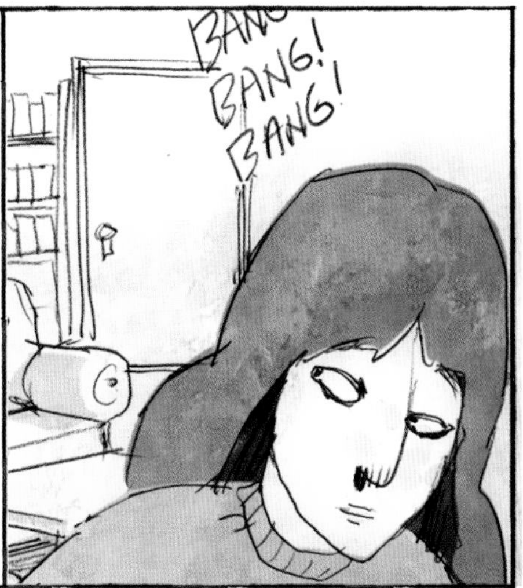
BANG!
BANG!

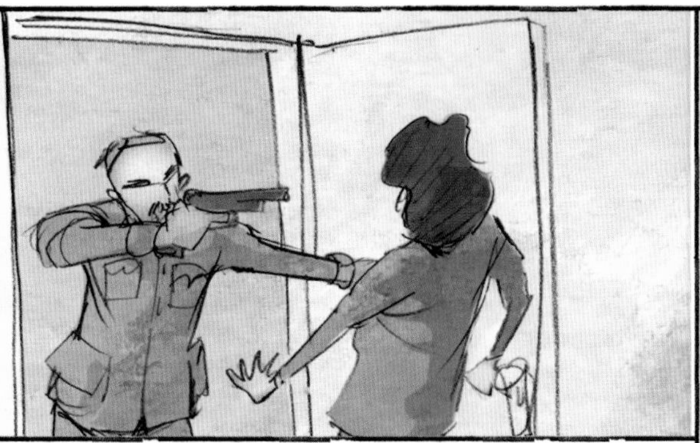

Assad uses arrests and violence to hang on to power.

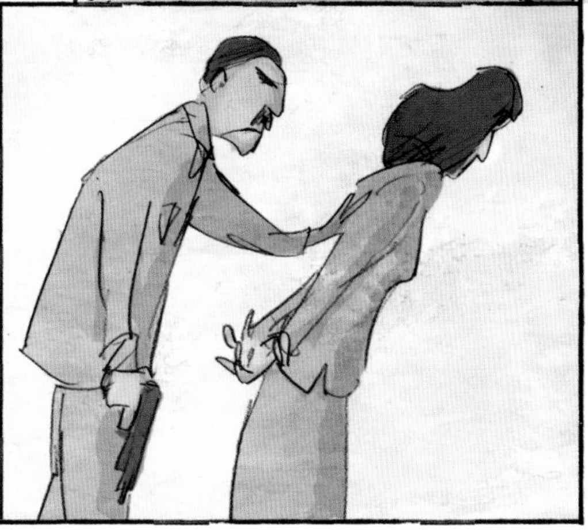

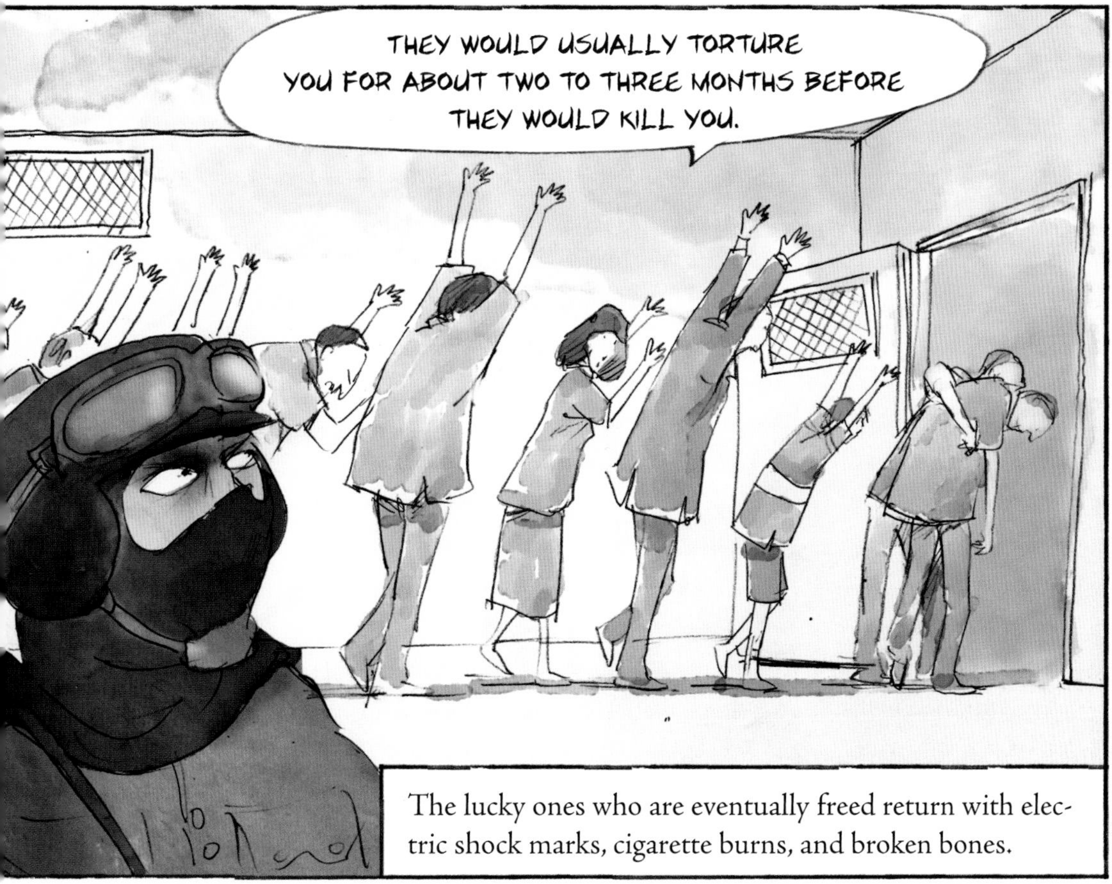
THEY WOULD USUALLY TORTURE YOU FOR ABOUT TWO TO THREE MONTHS BEFORE THEY WOULD KILL YOU.

The lucky ones who are eventually freed return with electric shock marks, cigarette burns, and broken bones.

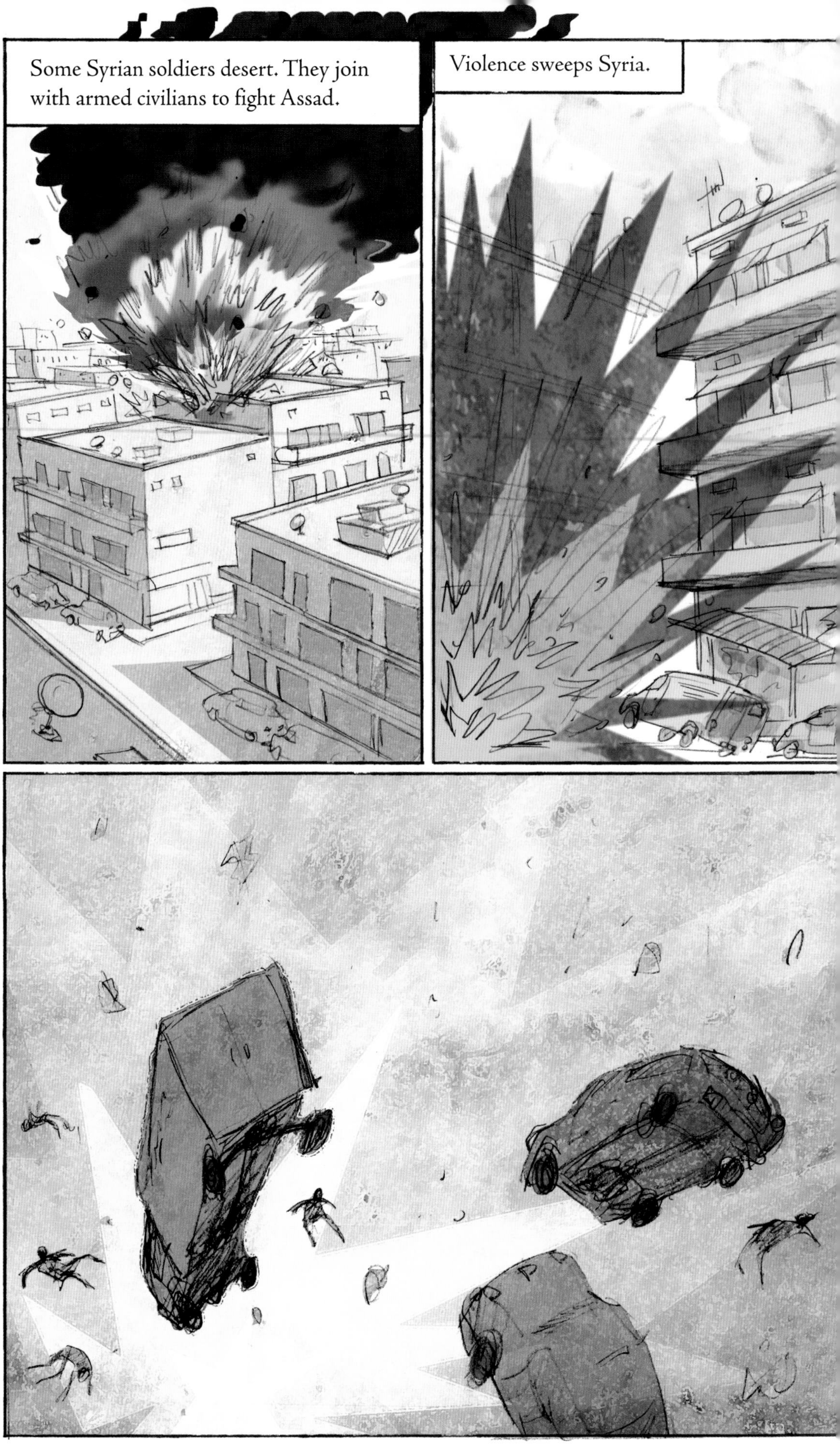
Some Syrian soldiers desert. They join with armed civilians to fight Assad.
Violence sweeps Syria.

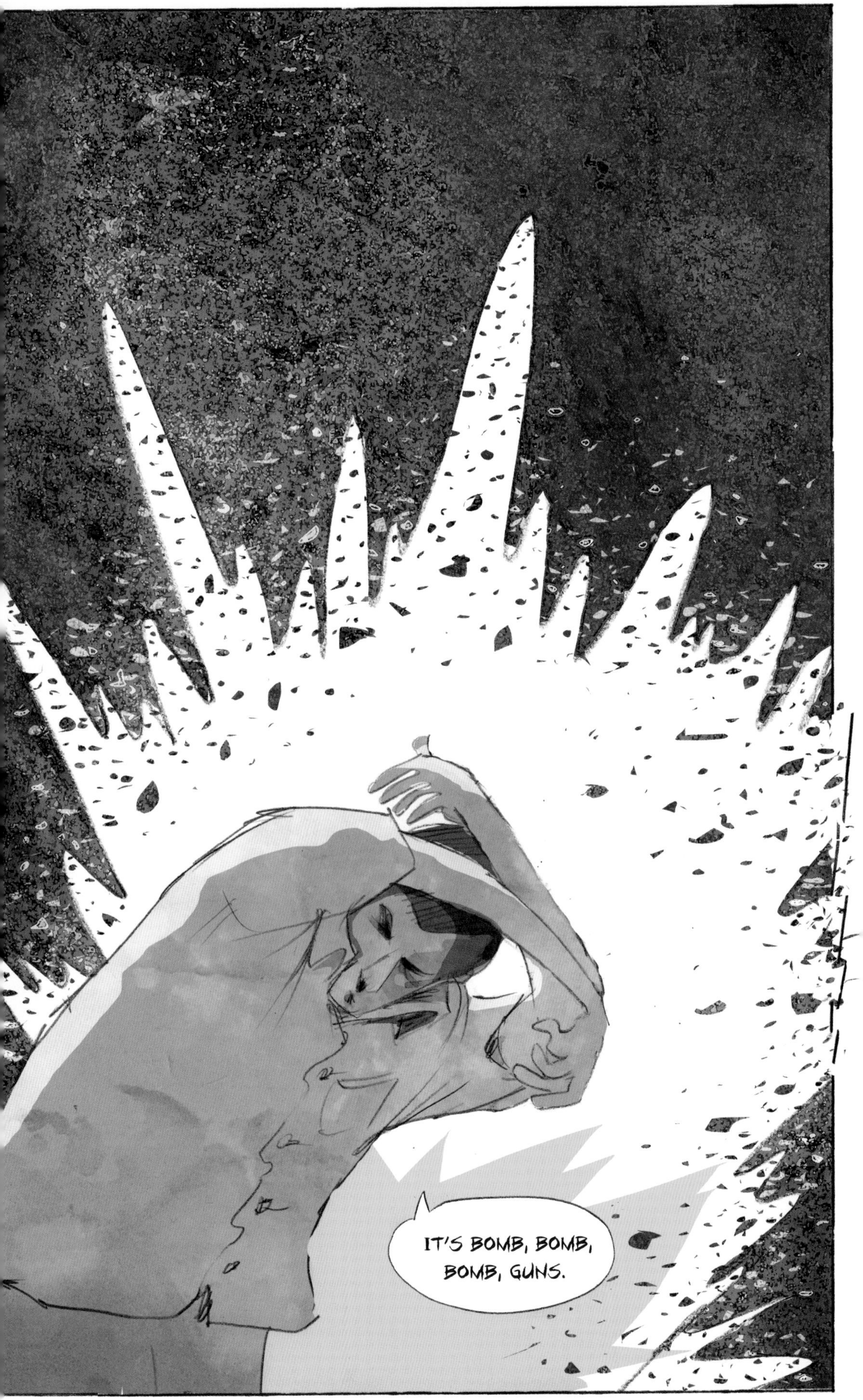
IT'S BOMB, BOMB,
BOMB, GUNS.

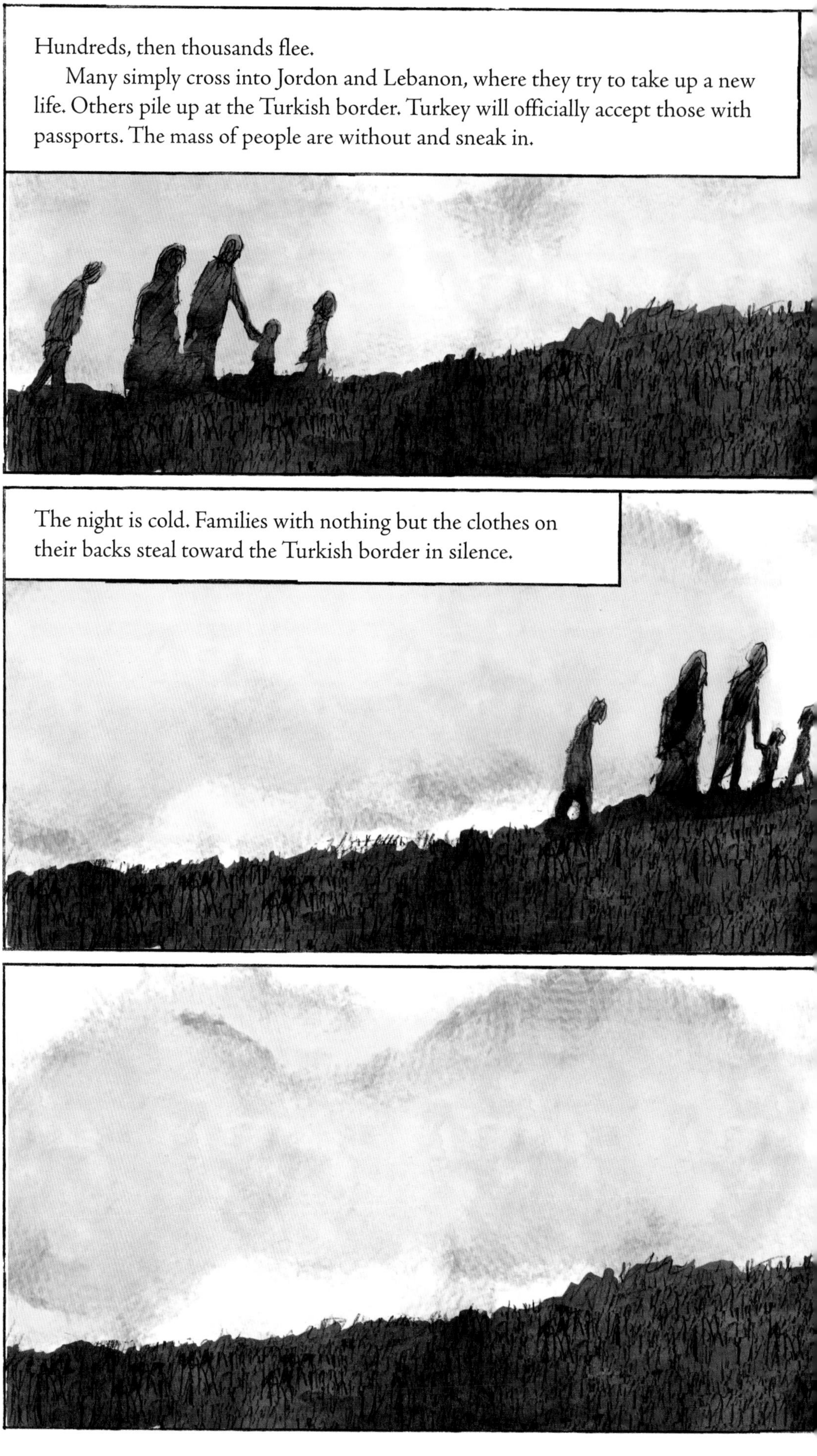
Hundreds, then thousands flee.
Many simply cross into Jordon and Lebanon, where they try to take up a new life. Others pile up at the Turkish border. Turkey will officially accept those with passports. The mass of people are without and sneak in.
The night is cold. Families with nothing but the clothes on their backs steal toward the Turkish border in silence.

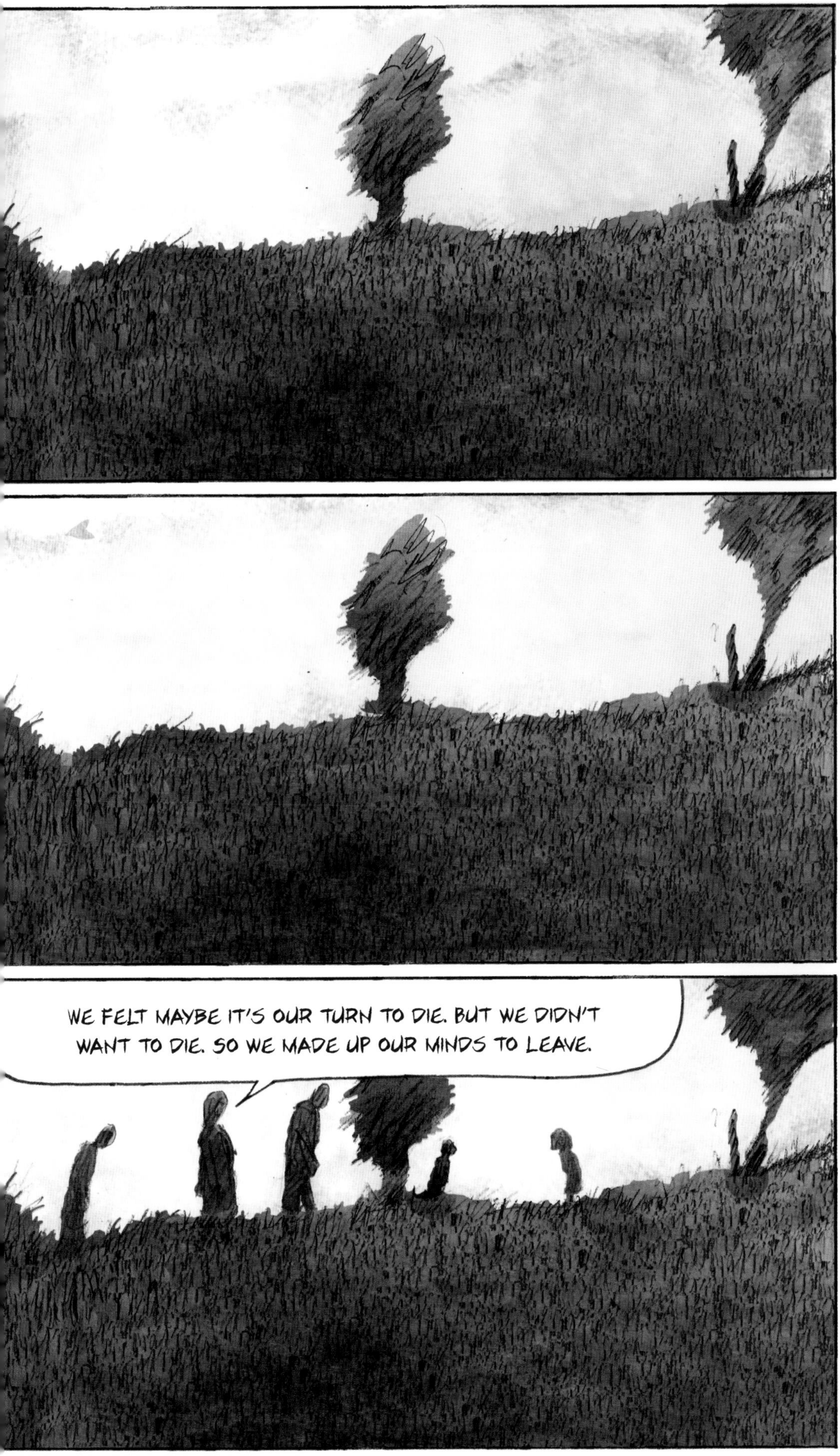
WE FELT MAYBE IT'S OUR TURN TO DIE. BUT WE DIDN'T WANT TO DIE. SO WE MADE UP OUR MINDS TO LEAVE.

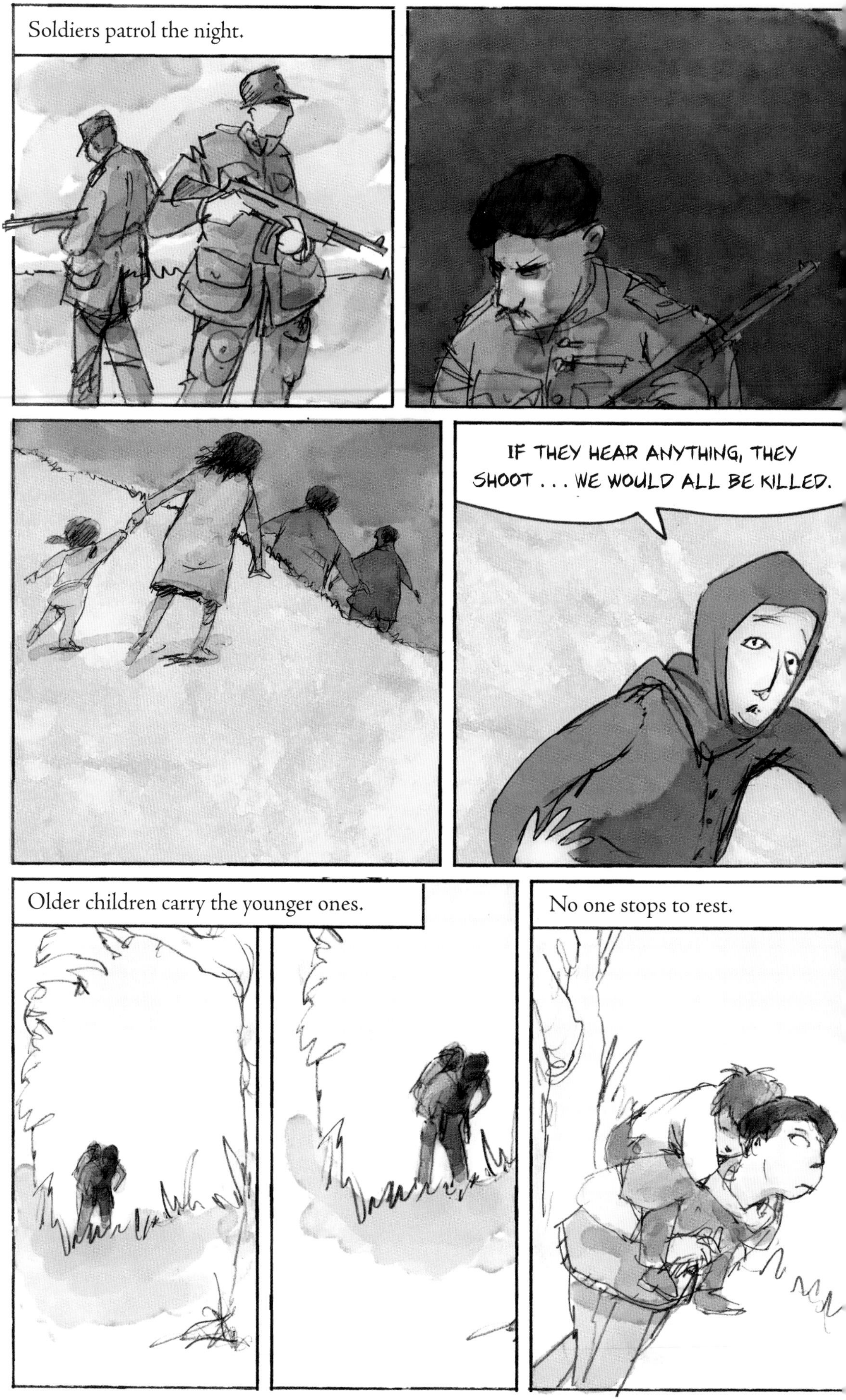
Soldiers patrol the night.
IF THEY HEAR ANYTHING, THEY SHOOT . . . WE WOULD ALL BE KILLED.
Older children carry the younger ones.
No one stops to rest.

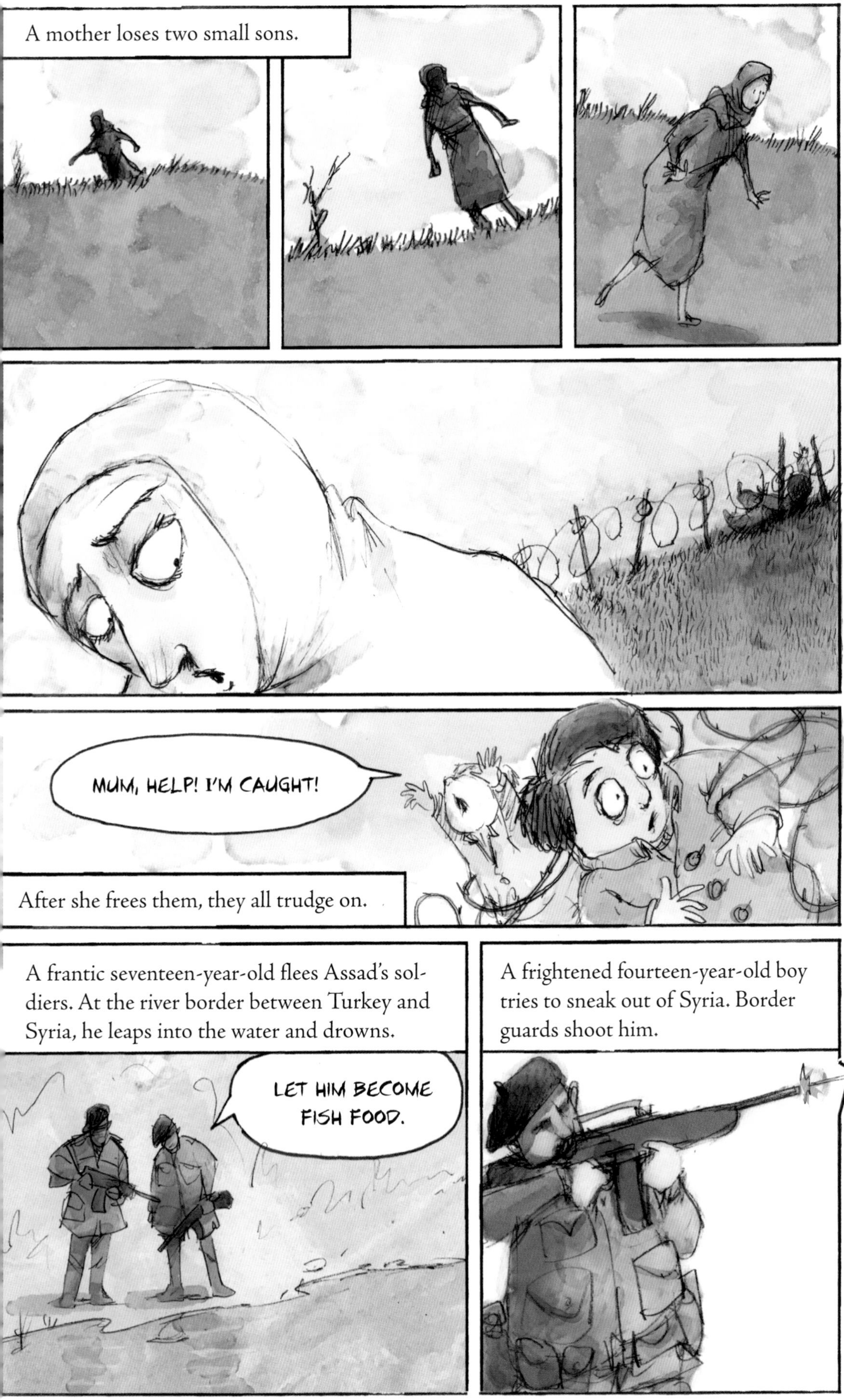
A mother loses two small sons.
MUM, HELP! I'M CAUGHT!
After she frees them, they all trudge on.
A frantic seventeen-year-old flees Assad's soldiers. At the river border between Turkey and Syria, he leaps into the water and drowns.
LET HIM BECOME FISH FOOD.
A frightened fourteen-year-old boy tries to sneak out of Syria. Border guards shoot him.

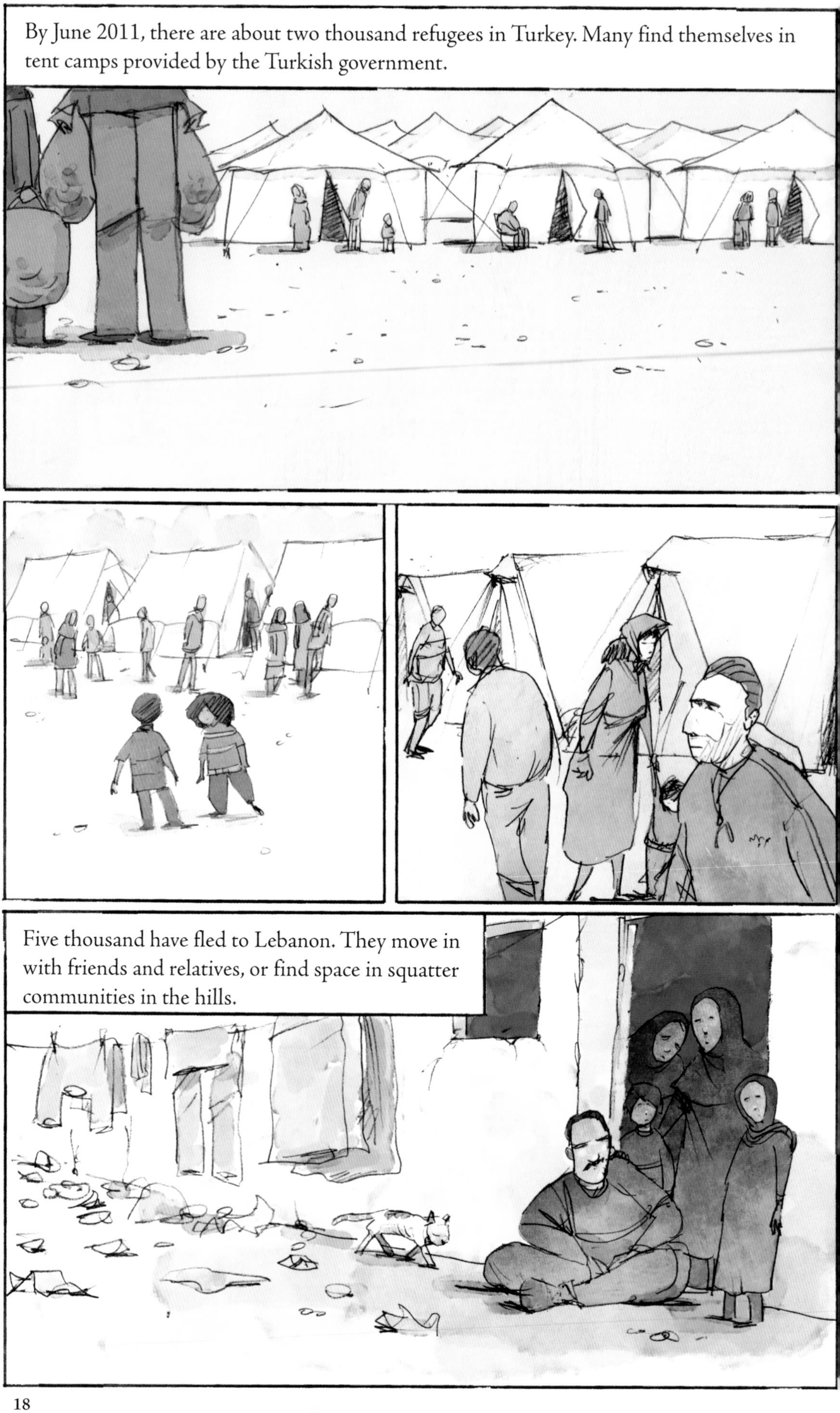
By June 2011, there are about two thousand refugees in Turkey. Many find themselves in tent camps provided by the Turkish government.
Five thousand have fled to Lebanon. They move in with friends and relatives, or find space in squatter communities in the hills.

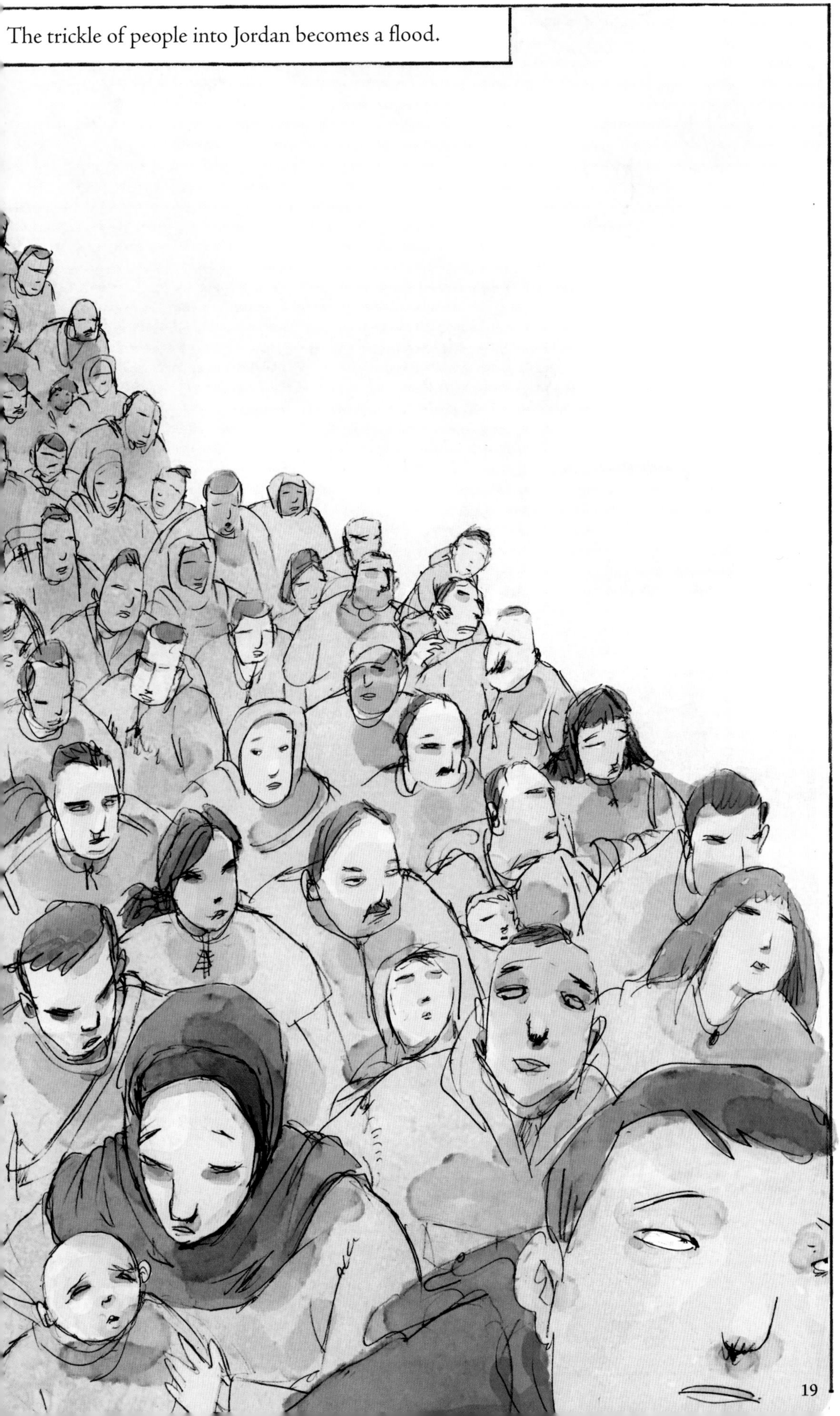
The trickle of people into Jordan becomes a flood.

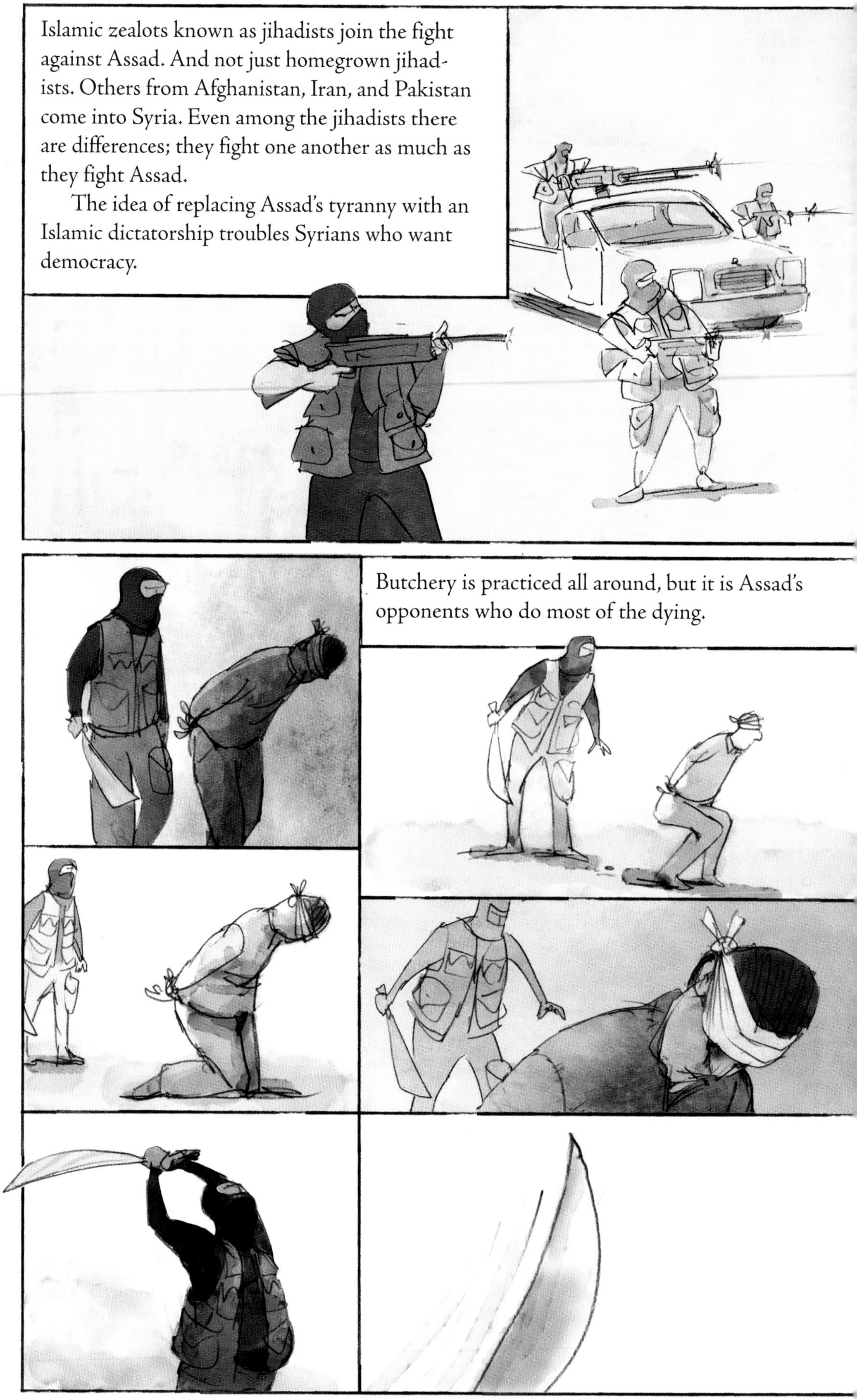
Islamic zealots known as jihadists join the fight against Assad. And not just homegrown jihadists. Others from Afghanistan, Iran, and Pakistan come into Syria. Even among the jihadists there are differences; they fight one another as much as they fight Assad.
The idea of replacing Assad's tyranny with an Islamic dictatorship troubles Syrians who want democracy.
Butchery is practiced all around, but it is Assad's opponents who do most of the dying.

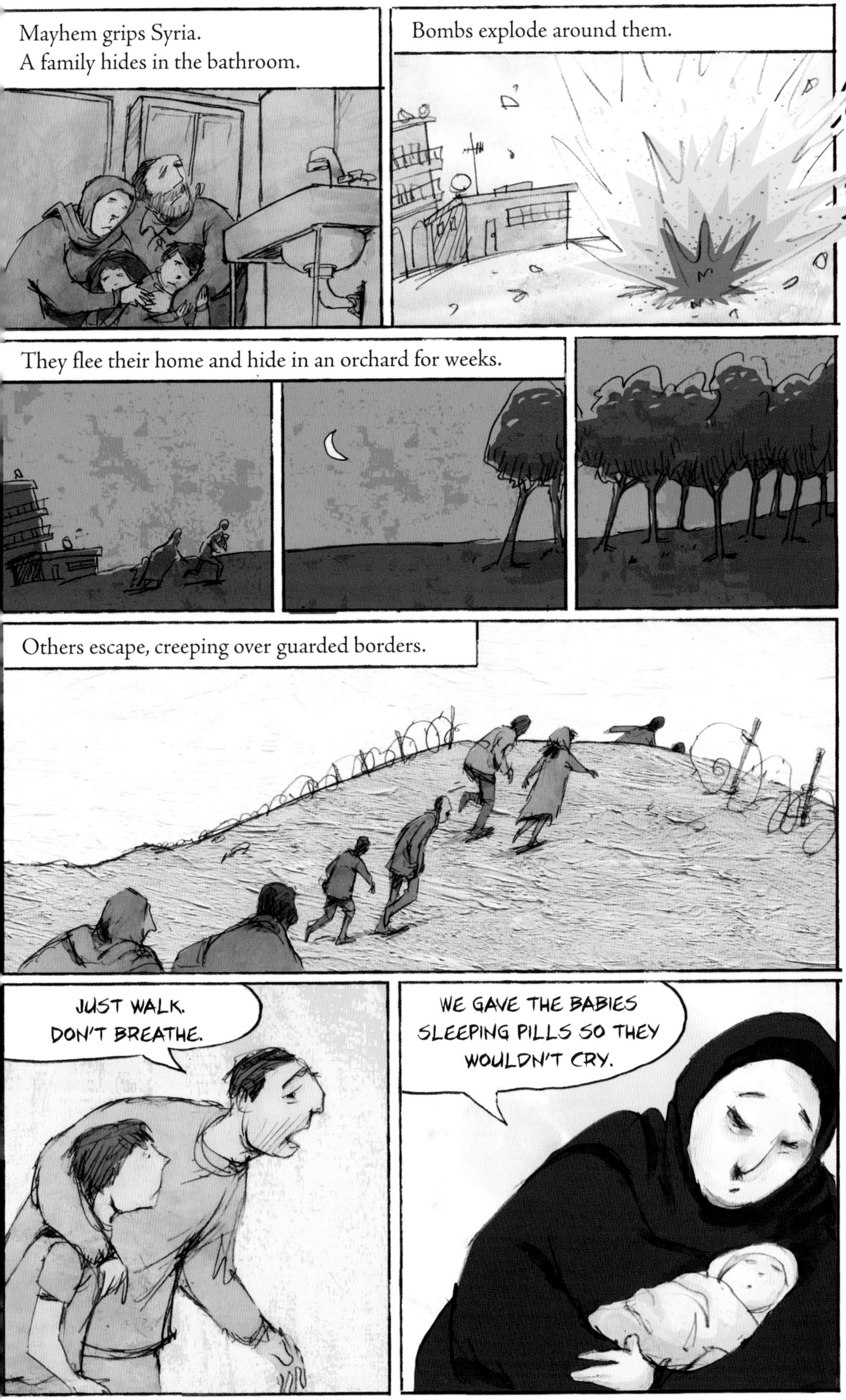
Mayhem grips Syria.
A family hides in the bathroom.
Bombs explode around them.
They flee their home and hide in an orchard for weeks.
Others escape, creeping over guarded borders.
JUST WALK. DON'T BREATHE.
WE GAVE THE BABIES SLEEPING PILLS SO THEY WOULDN'T CRY.

Roads everywhere are controlled by both government and opposition forces.

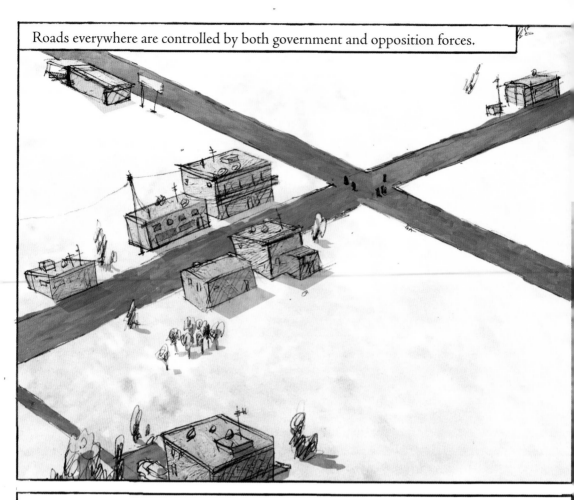

A pickup truck carrying a piano is stopped at a checkpoint manned by ISIS fighters, a notable band of ruthless jihadists who invoke God to defend their breathtaking brutality.

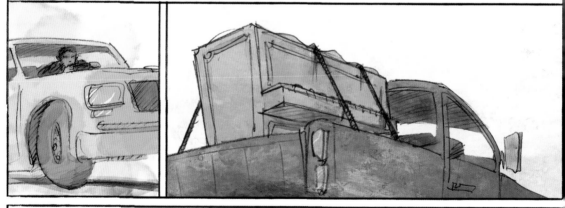

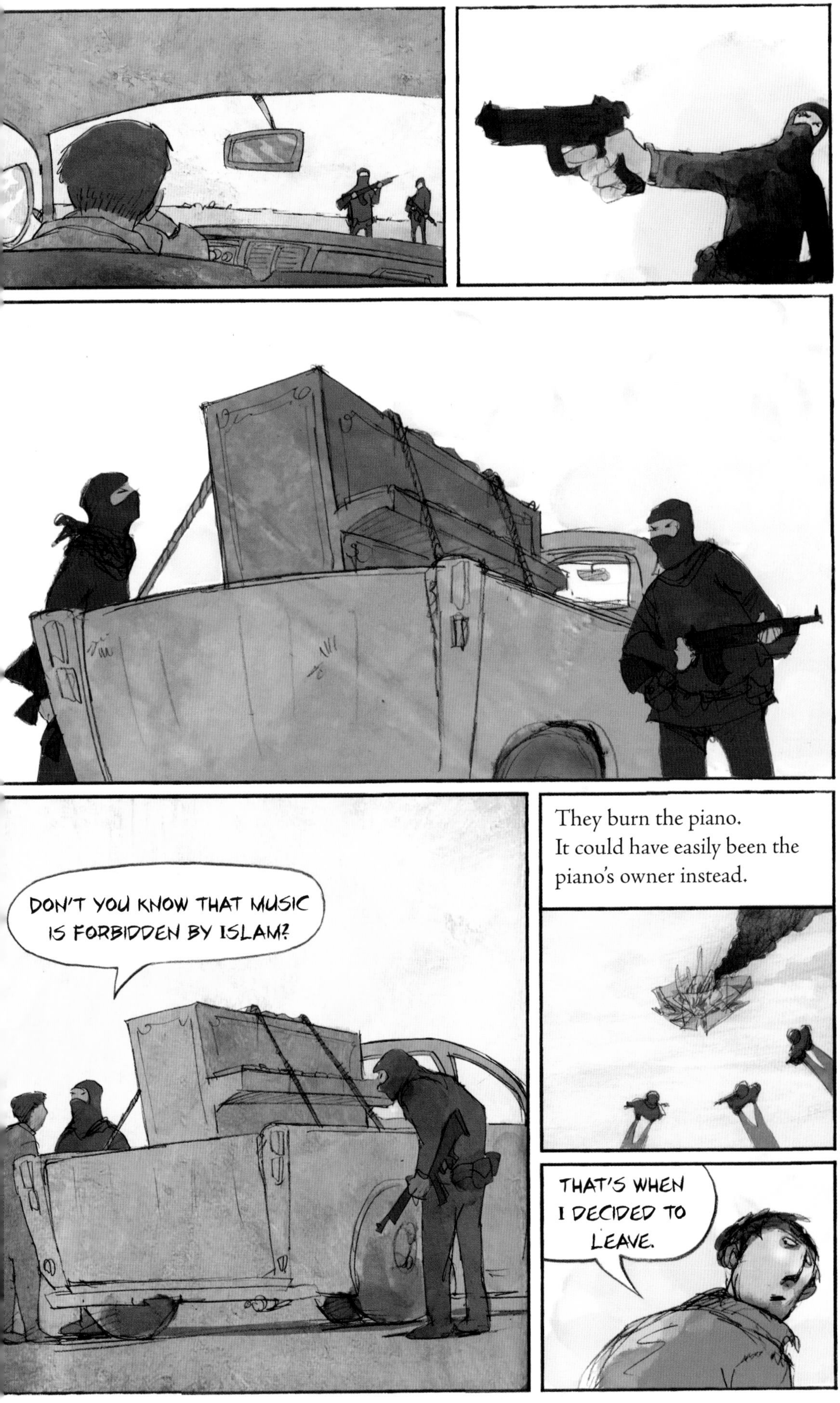
DON'T YOU KNOW THAT MUSIC IS FORBIDDEN BY ISLAM?
They burn the piano.
It could have easily been the piano's owner instead.
THAT'S WHEN I DECIDED TO LEAVE.

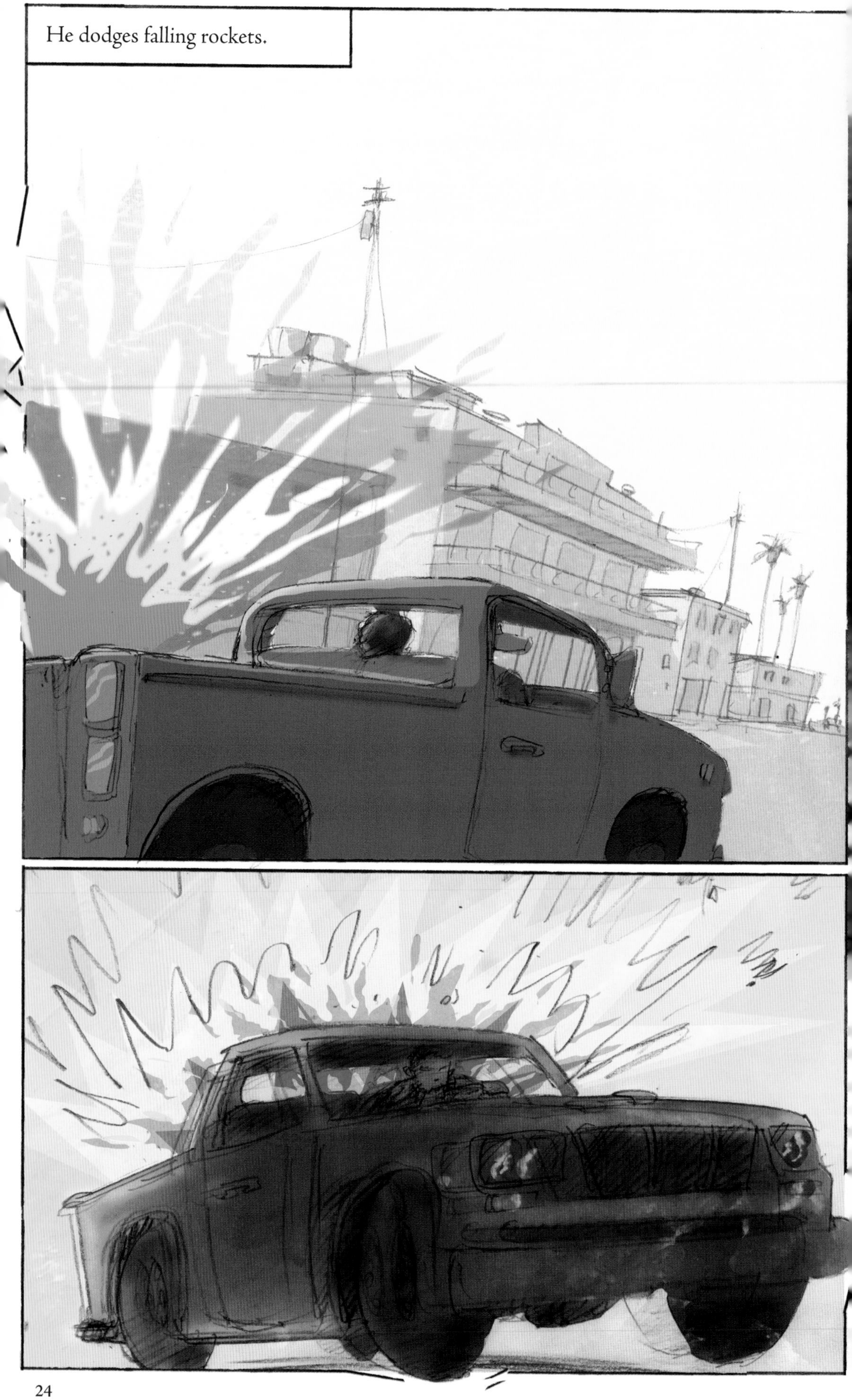
He dodges falling rockets.

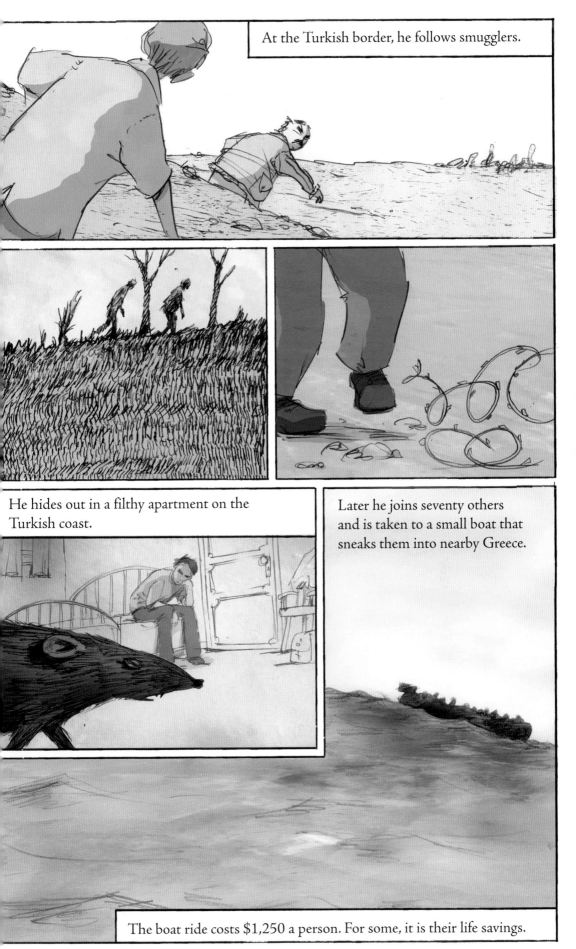

At the Turkish border, he follows smugglers.

He hides out in a filthy apartment on the Turkish coast.

Later he joins seventy others and is taken to a small boat that sneaks them into nearby Greece.

The boat ride costs $1,250 a person. For some, it is their life savings.

All kinds of people jump at the chance to fatten their wallets at the expense of the refugees. Smugglers provide outboard-powered inflated boats to the refugees, who pilot themselves to Greece and afterward discard them.

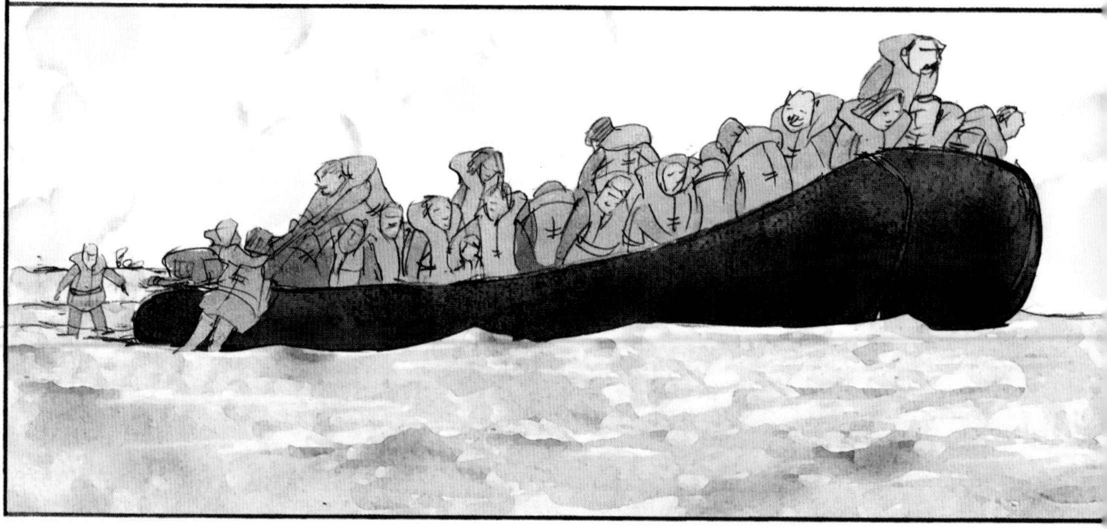

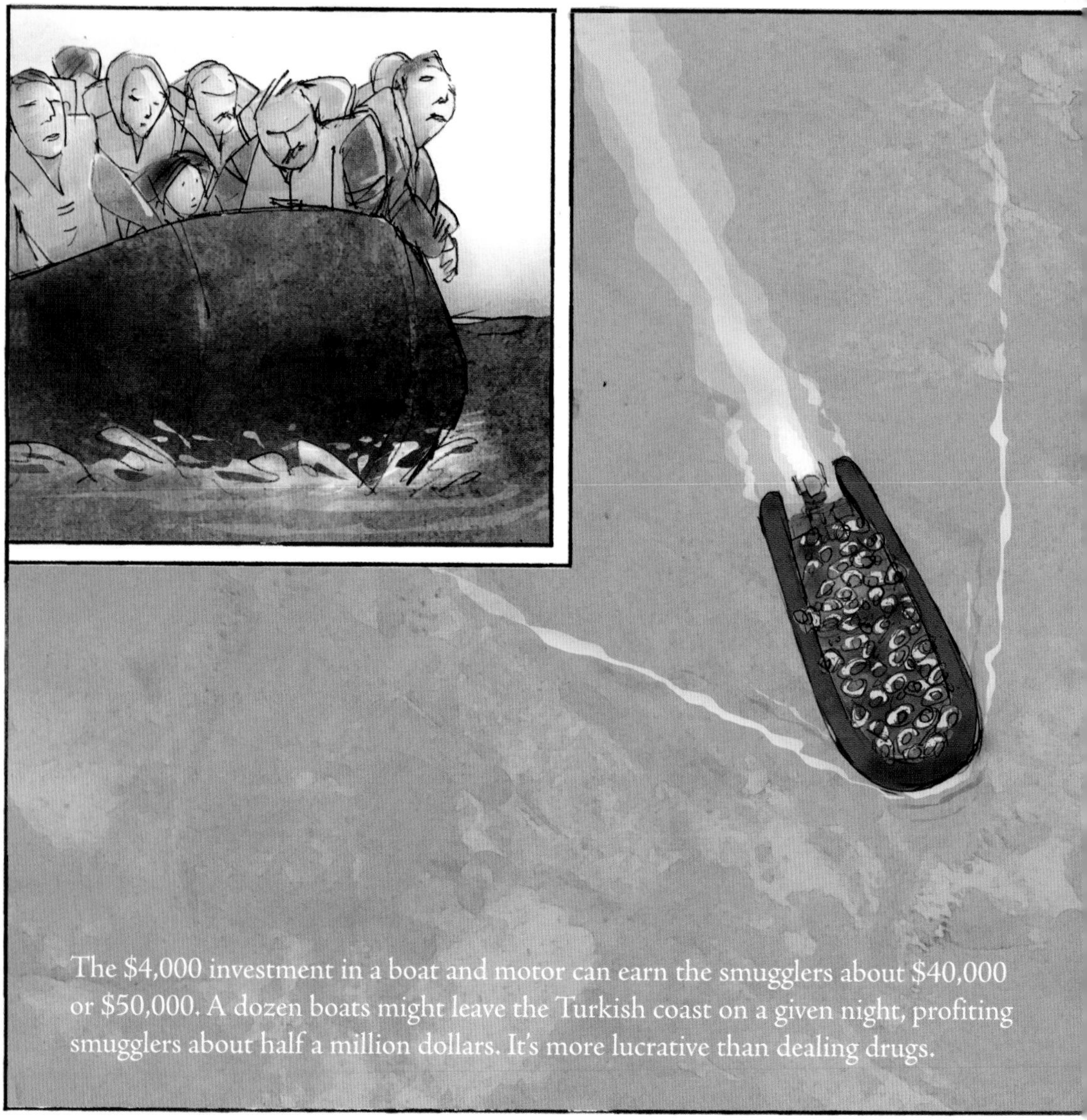
The $4,000 investment in a boat and motor can earn the smugglers about $40,000 or $50,000. A dozen boats might leave the Turkish coast on a given night, profiting smugglers about half a million dollars. It's more lucrative than dealing drugs.

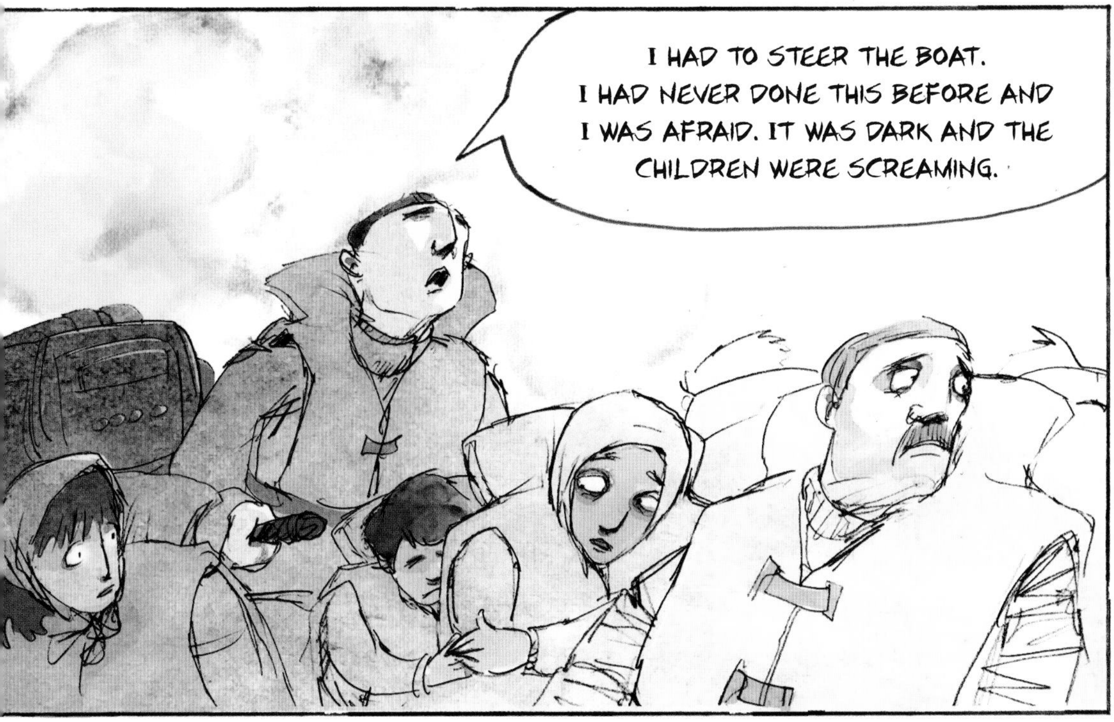
I HAD TO STEER THE BOAT.
I HAD NEVER DONE THIS BEFORE AND I WAS AFRAID. IT WAS DARK AND THE CHILDREN WERE SCREAMING.

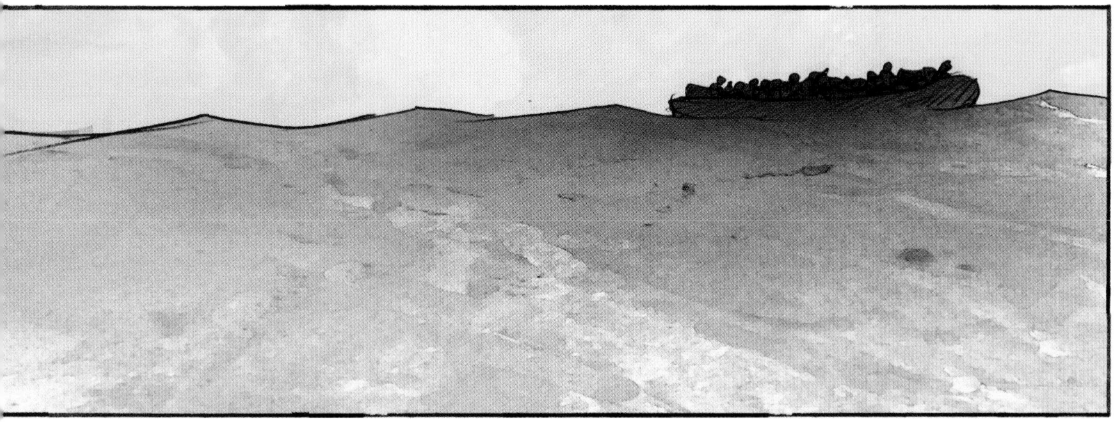

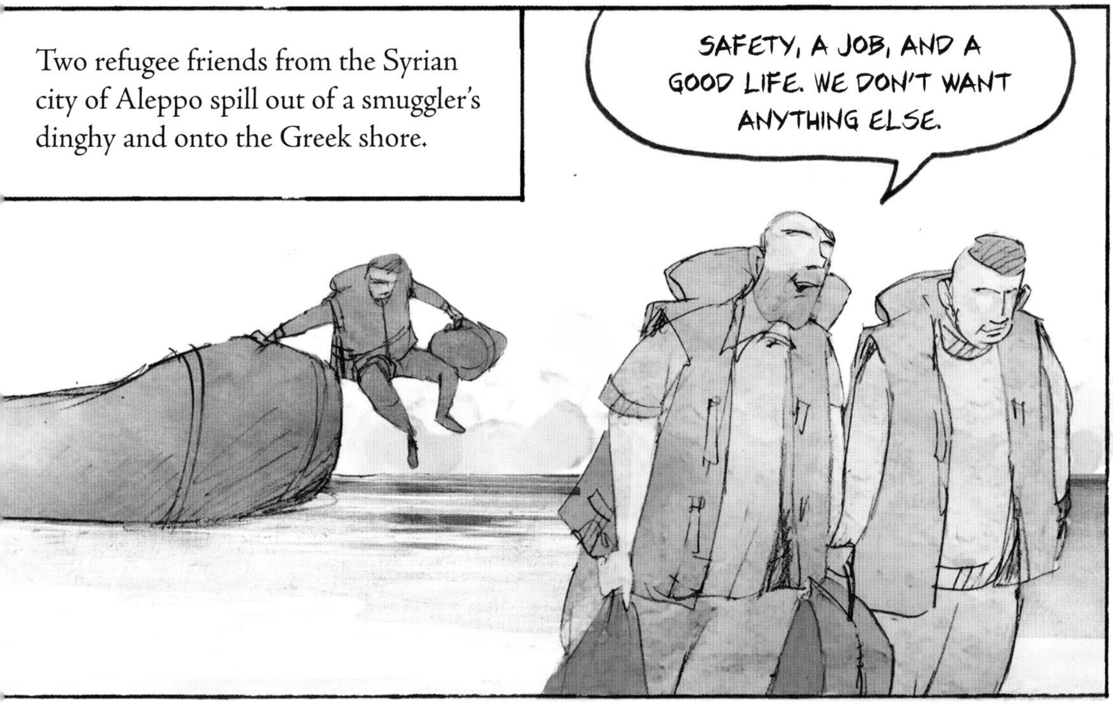
Two refugee friends from the Syrian city of Aleppo spill out of a smuggler's dinghy and onto the Greek shore.
SAFETY, A JOB, AND A GOOD LIFE. WE DON'T WANT ANYTHING ELSE.

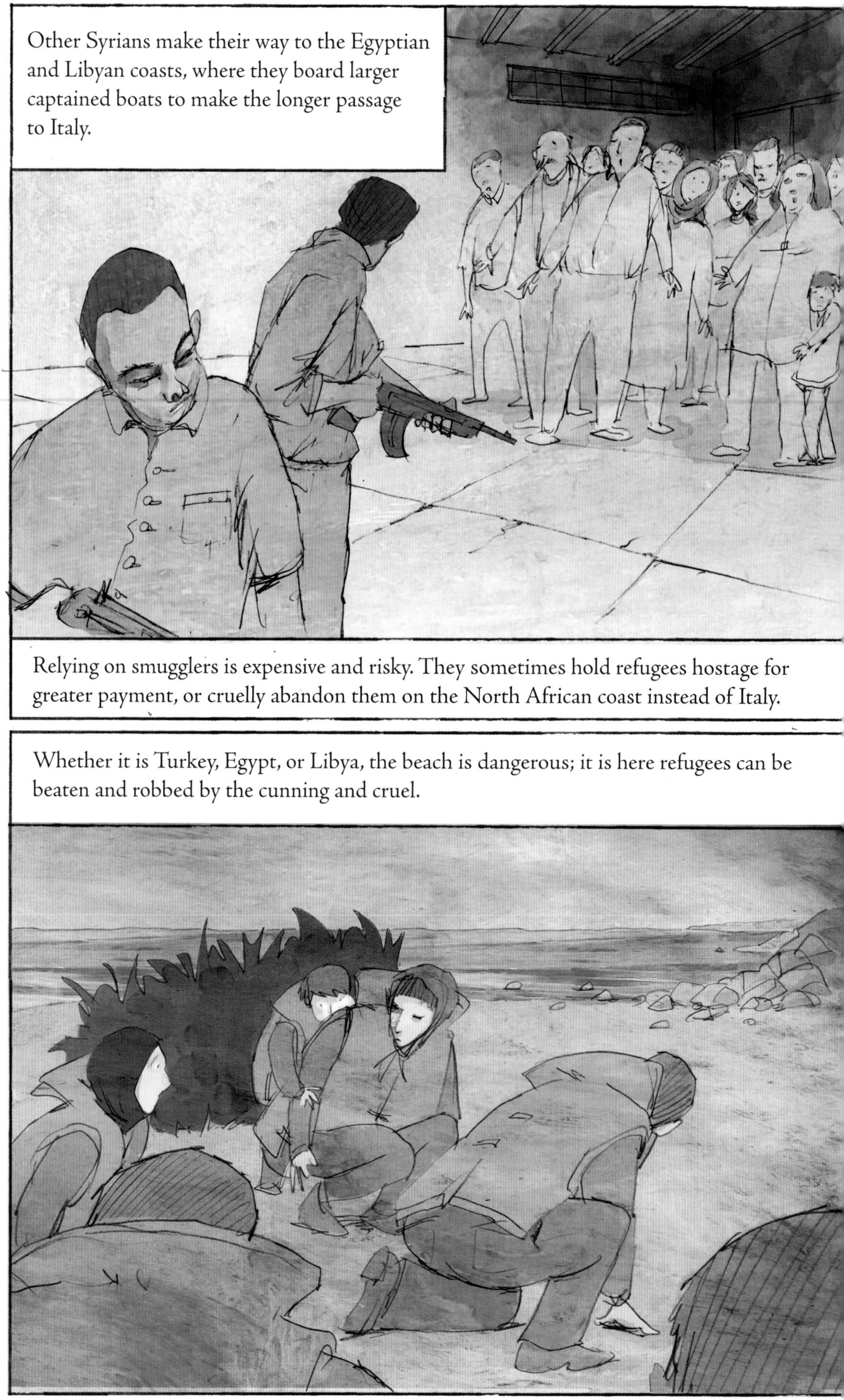
Other Syrians make their way to the Egyptian and Libyan coasts, where they board larger captained boats to make the longer passage to Italy.
Relying on smugglers is expensive and risky. They sometimes hold refugees hostage for greater payment, or cruelly abandon them on the North African coast instead of Italy.
Whether it is Turkey, Egypt, or Libya, the beach is dangerous; it is here refugees can be beaten and robbed by the cunning and cruel.

A young smuggler spies two small motorboats approaching and whips the refugees out of hiding.

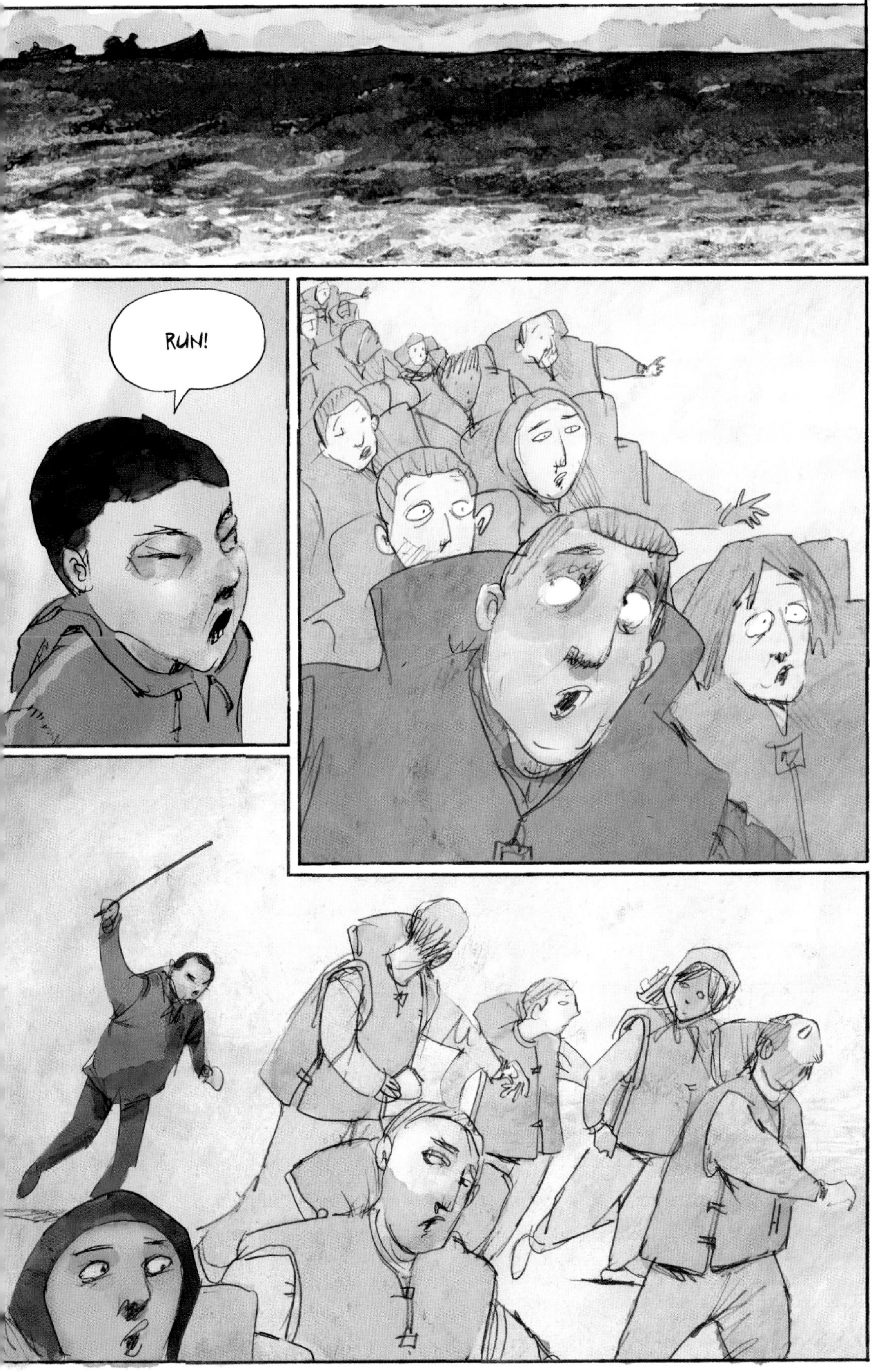
RUN!

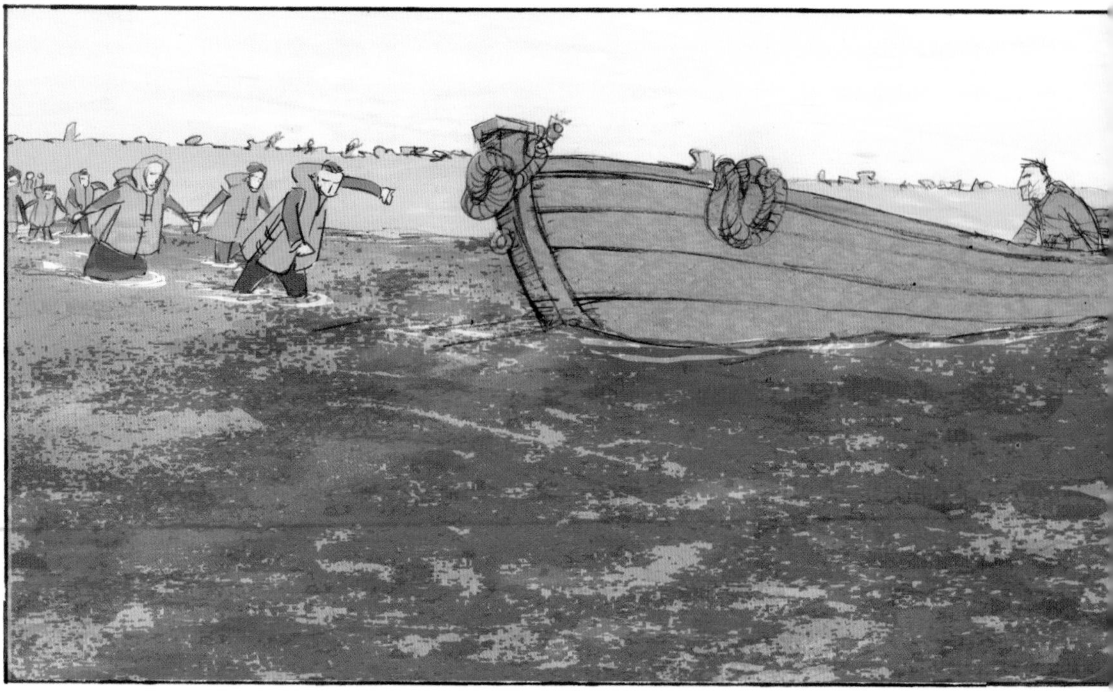

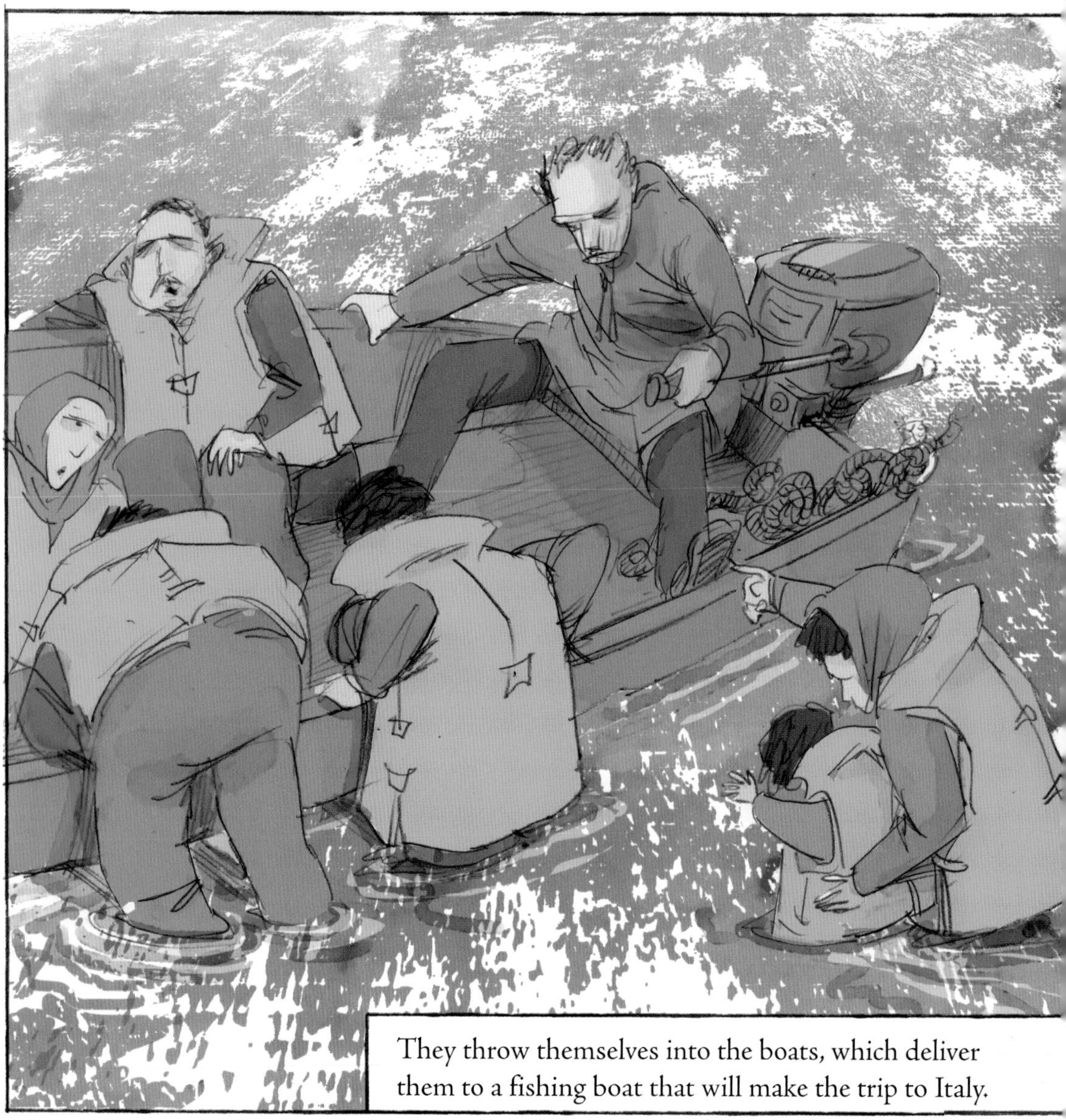
They throw themselves into the boats, which deliver them to a fishing boat that will make the trip to Italy.

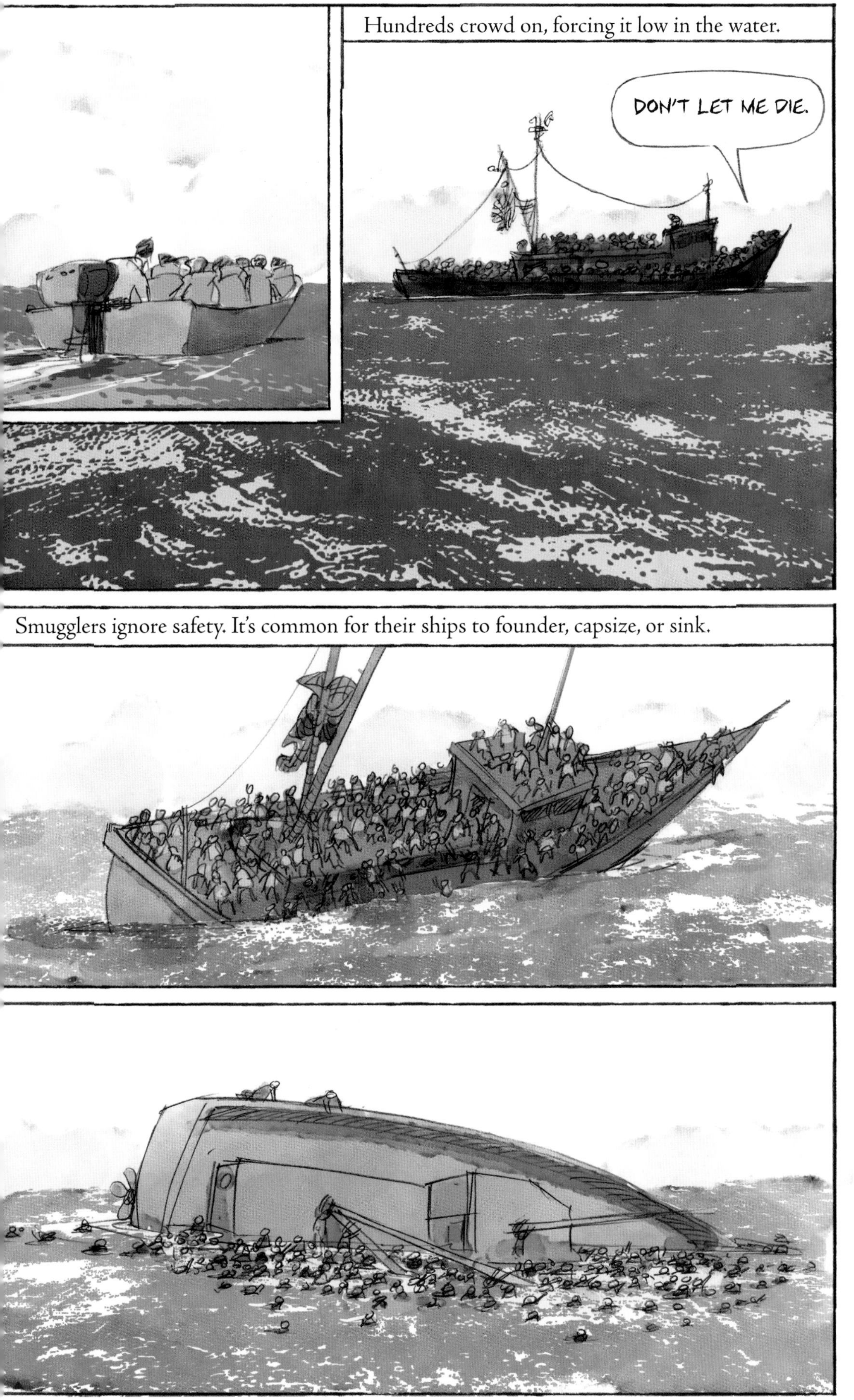
Hundreds crowd on, forcing it low in the water.
DON'T LET ME DIE.
Smugglers ignore safety. It's common for their ships to founder, capsize, or sink.

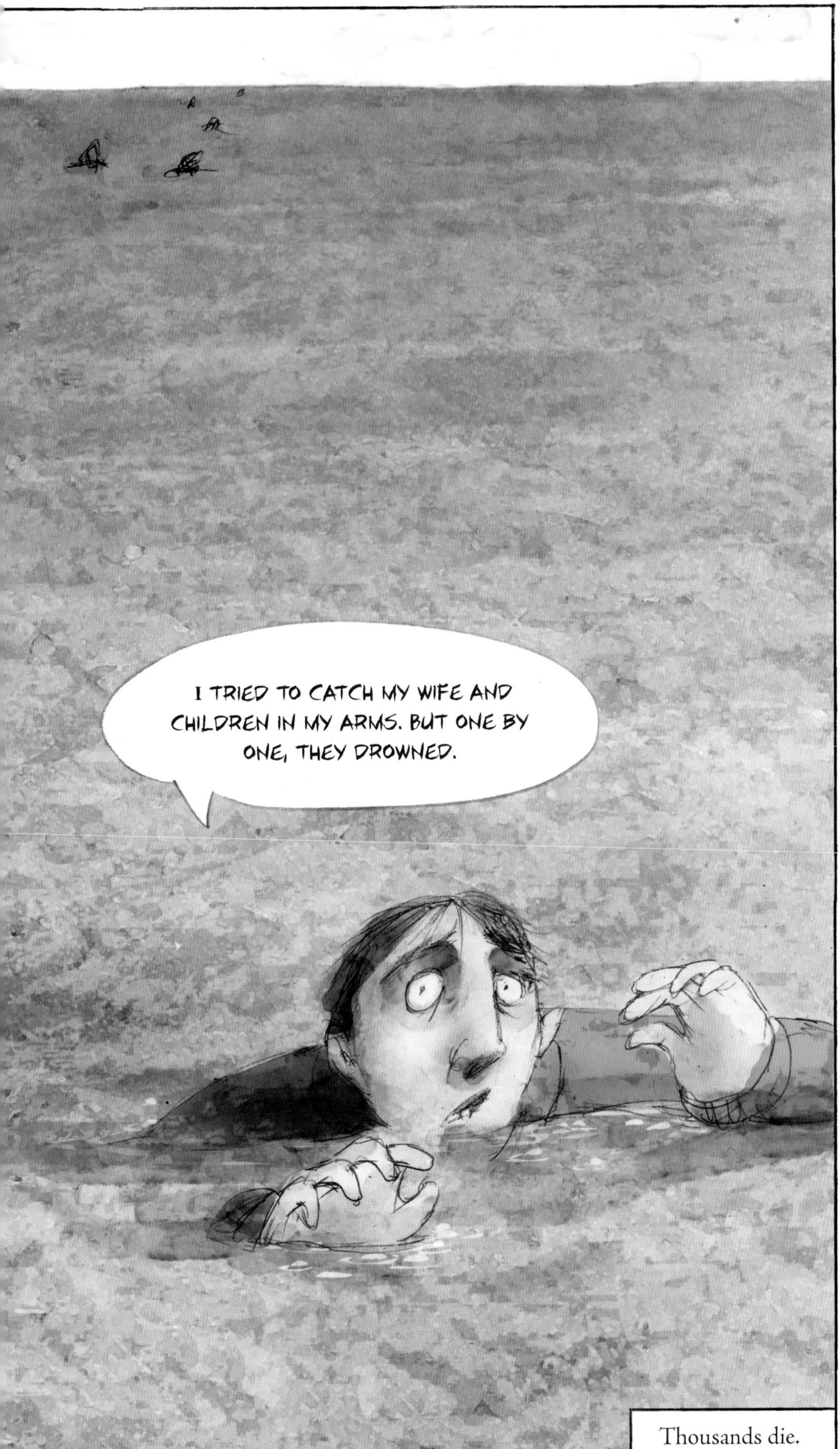
I TRIED TO CATCH MY WIFE AND CHILDREN IN MY ARMS. BUT ONE BY ONE, THEY DROWNED.
Thousands die.

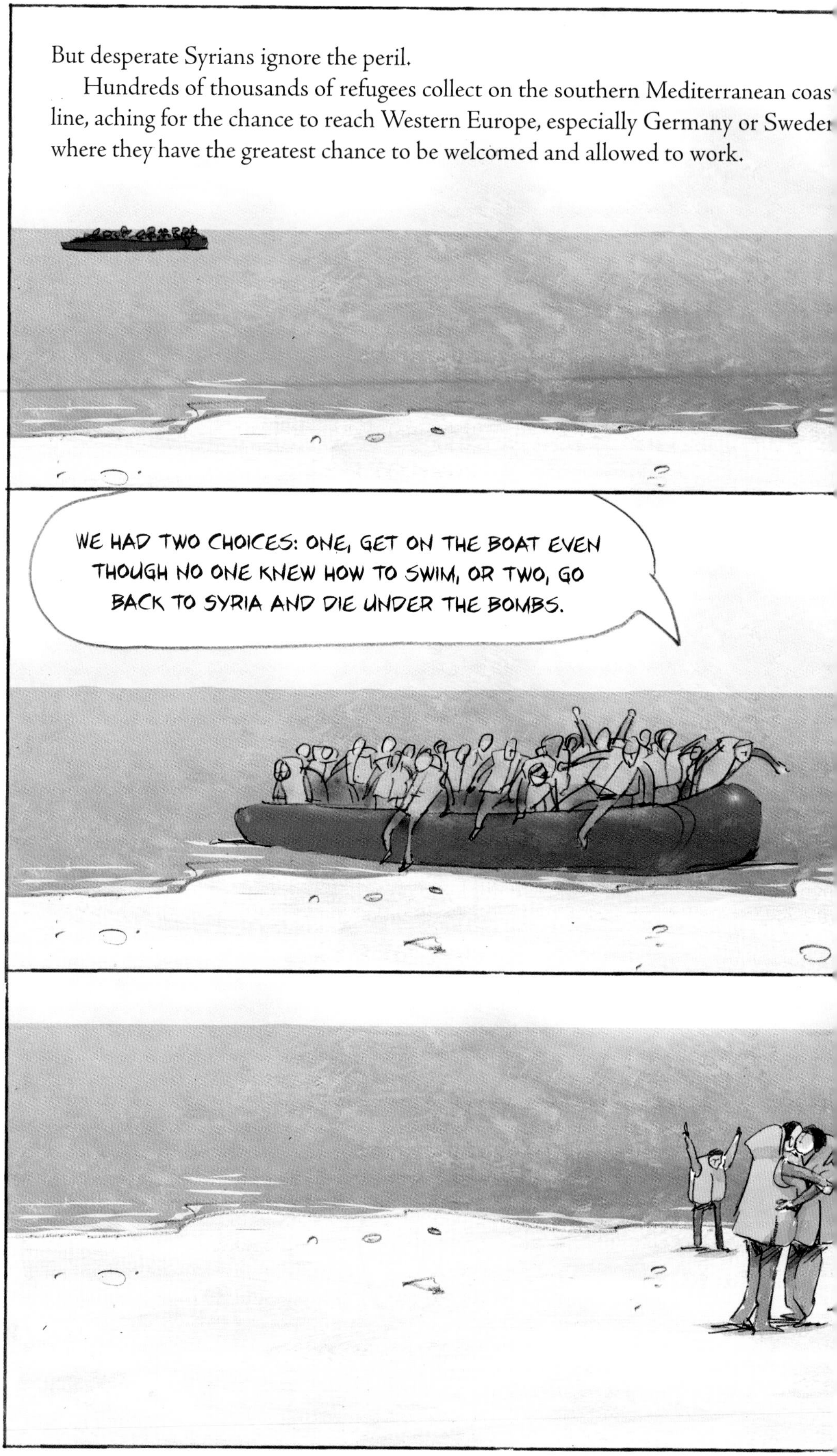
But desperate Syrians ignore the peril.
Hundreds of thousands of refugees collect on the southern Mediterranean coas
line, aching for the chance to reach Western Europe, especially Germany or Sweder
where they have the greatest chance to be welcomed and allowed to work.
WE HAD TWO CHOICES: ONE, GET ON THE BOAT EVEN THOUGH NO ONE KNEW HOW TO SWIM, OR TWO, GO BACK TO SYRIA AND DIE UNDER THE BOMBS.

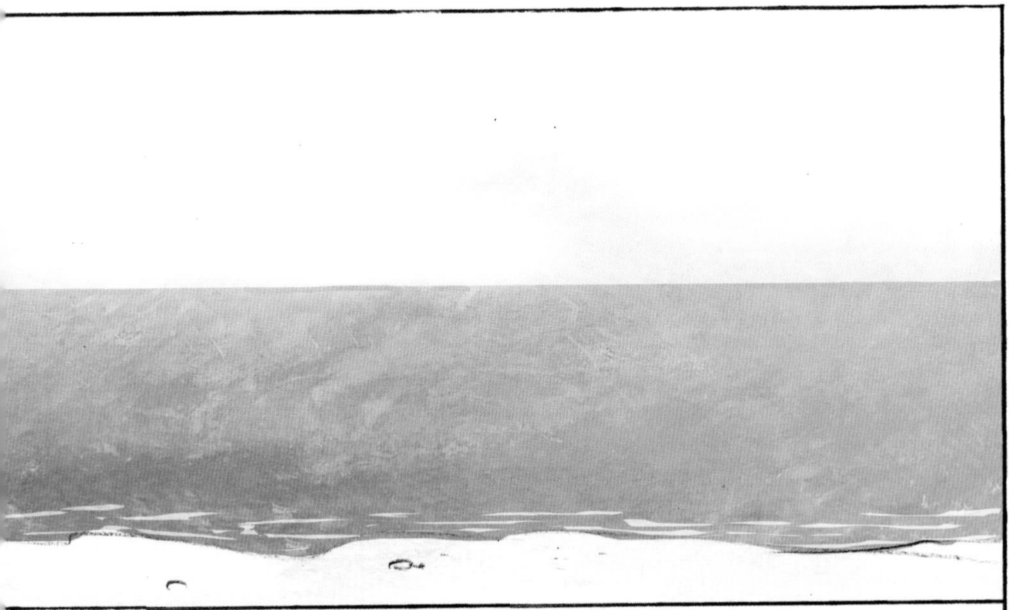

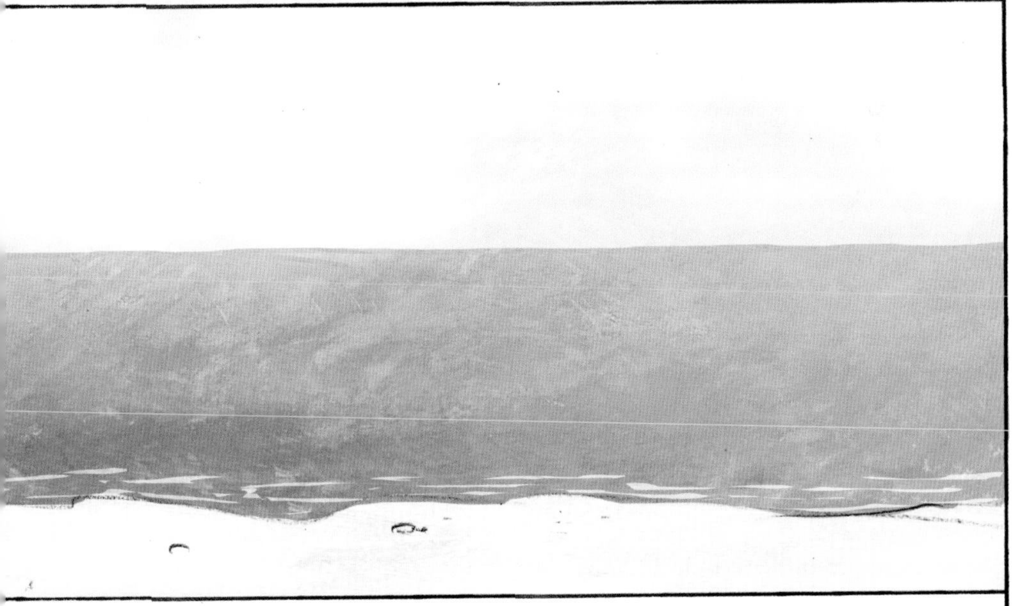

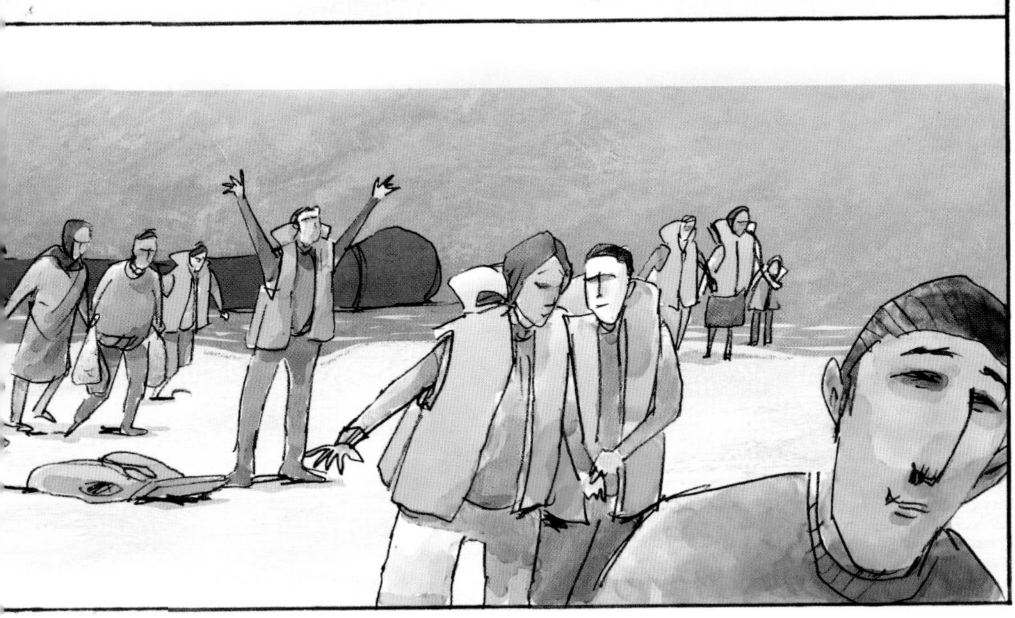

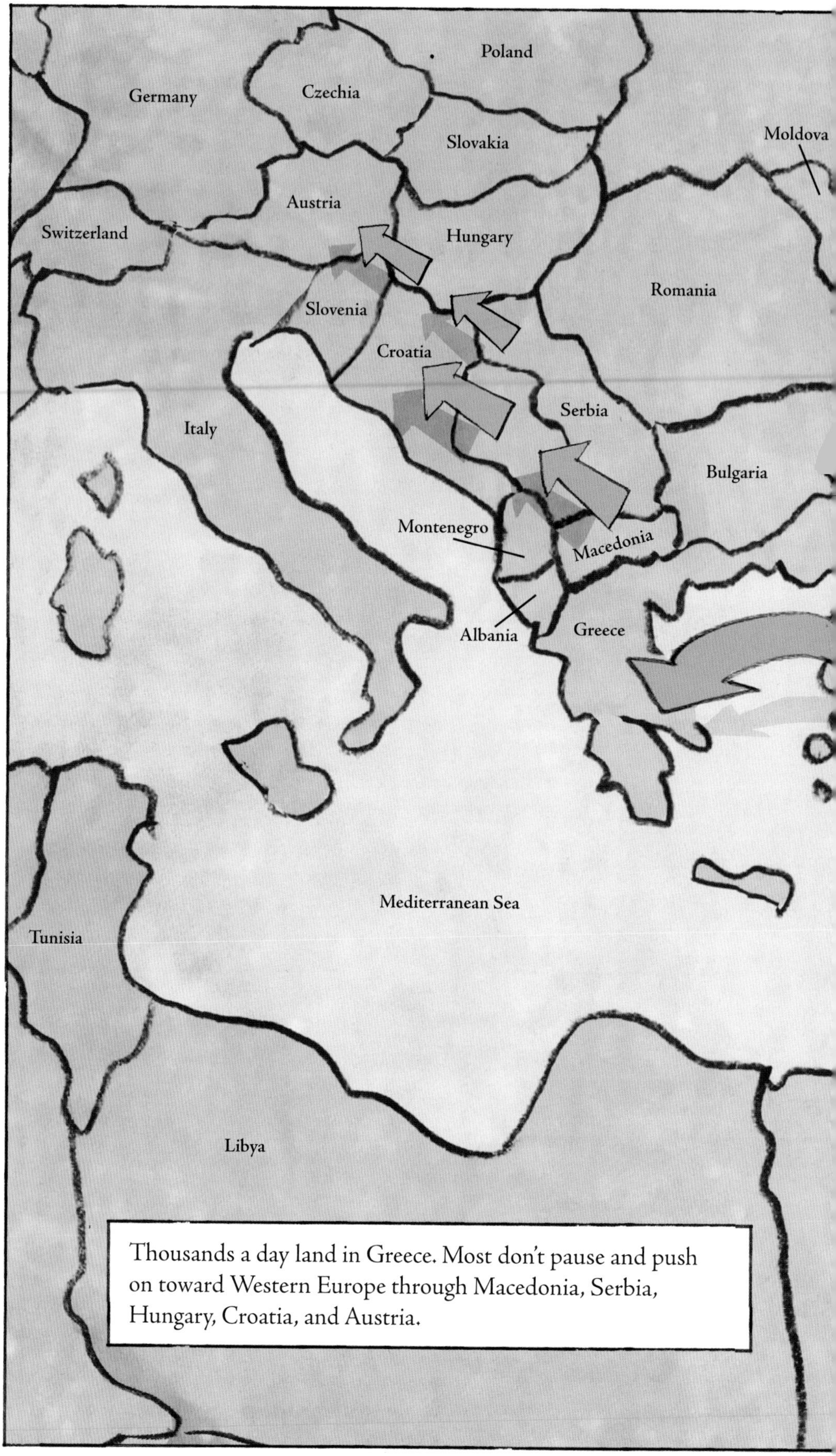
Poland
Germany
Czechia
Slovakia
Moldova
Austria
Switzerland
Hungary
Romania
Slovenia
Croatia
Serbia
Italy
Bulgaria
Montenegro
Macedonia
Albania
Greece
Mediterranean Sea
Tunisia
Libya

Thousands a day land in Greece. Most don't pause and push on toward Western Europe through Macedonia, Serbia, Hungary, Croatia, and Austria.

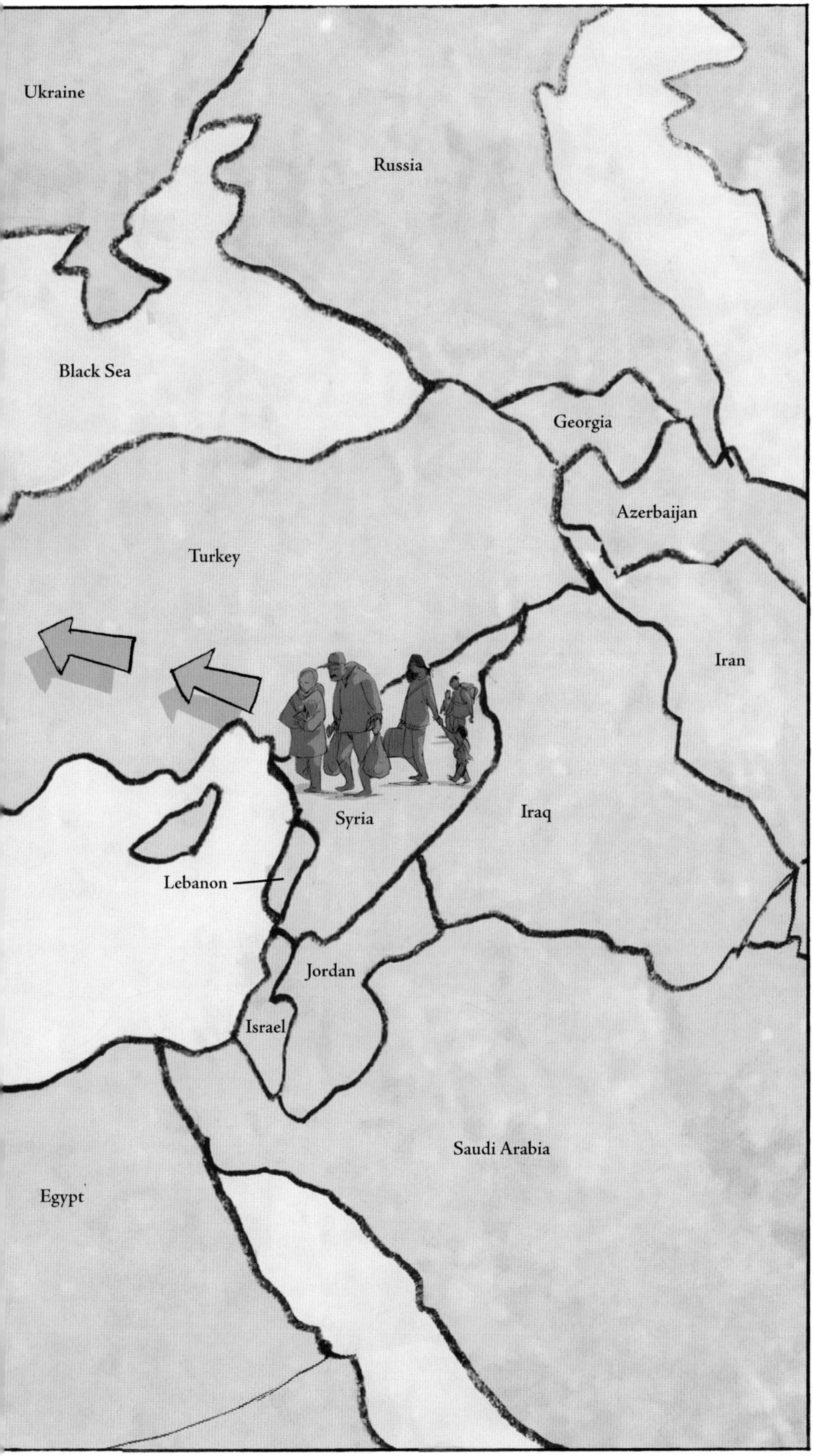
Ukraine
Russia
Black Sea
Georgia
Azerbaijan
Turkey
Iran
Syria
Iraq
Lebanon
Jordan
Israel
Saudi Arabia
Egypt

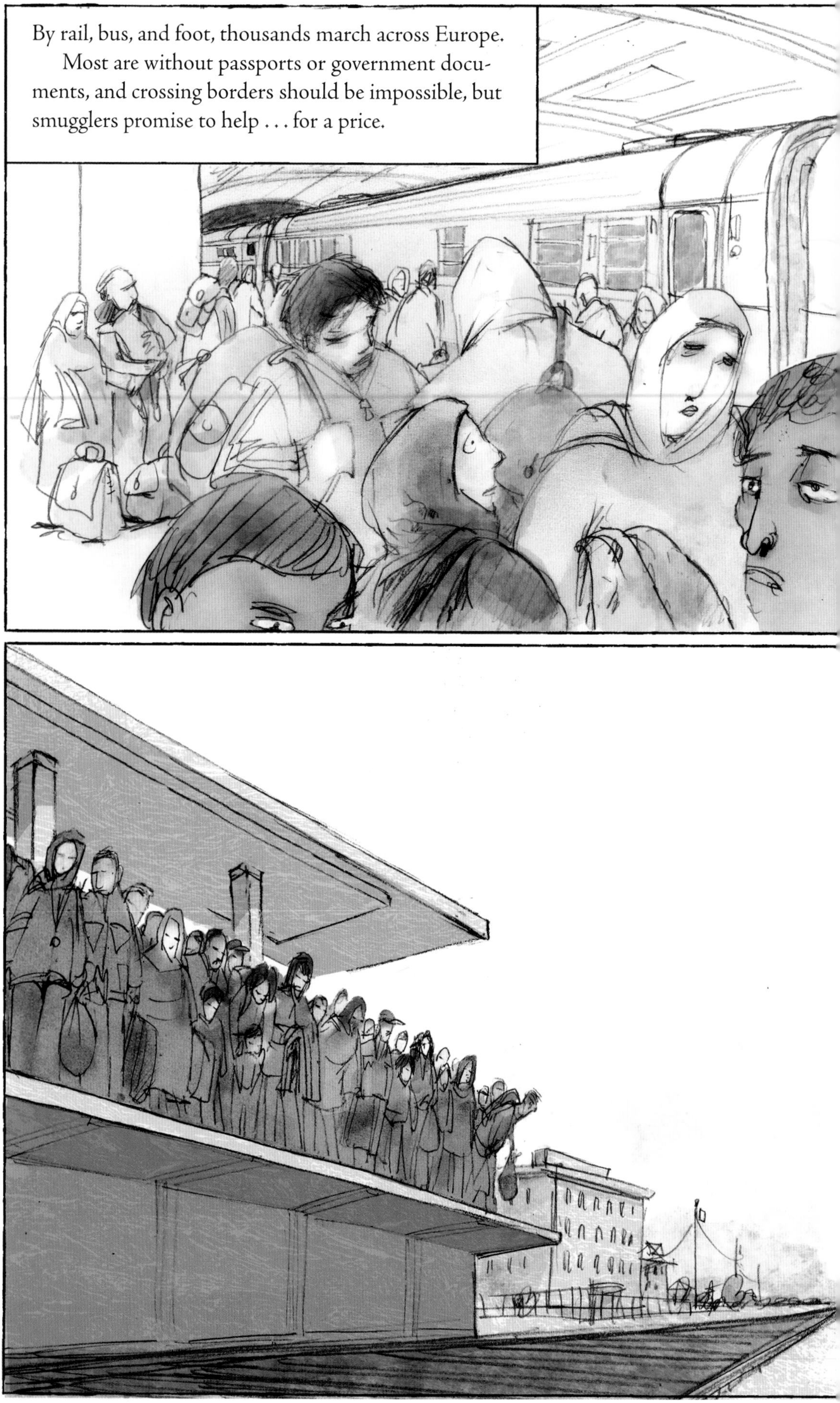
By rail, bus, and foot, thousands march across Europe.
Most are without passports or government documents, and crossing borders should be impossible, but smugglers promise to help . . . for a price.

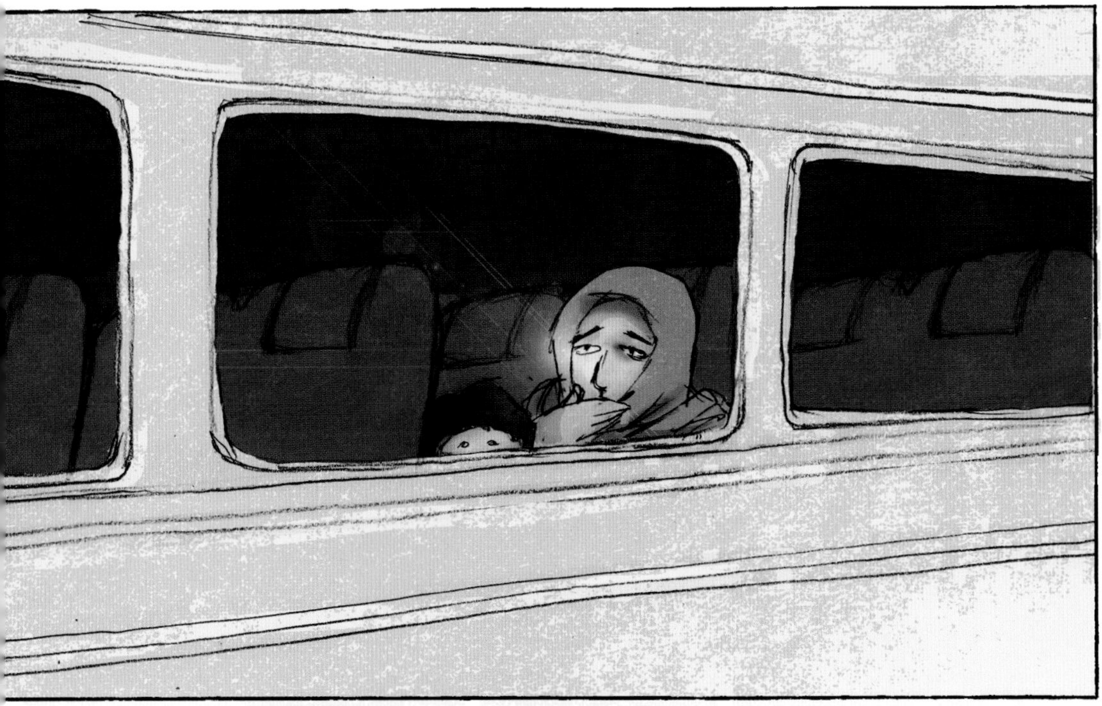

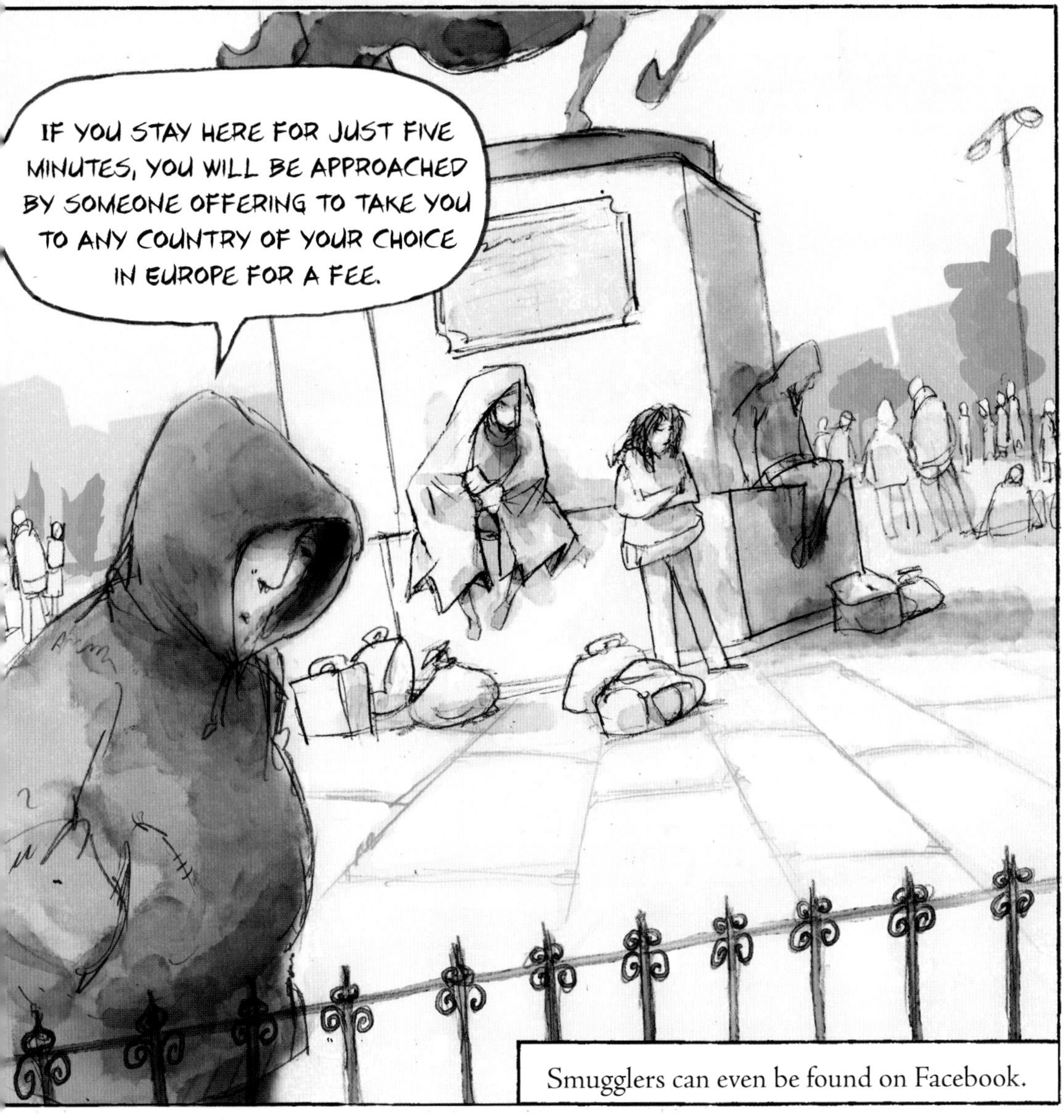
IF YOU STAY HERE FOR JUST FIVE MINUTES, YOU WILL BE APPROACHED BY SOMEONE OFFERING TO TAKE YOU TO ANY COUNTRY OF YOUR CHOICE IN EUROPE FOR A FEE.
Smugglers can even be found on Facebook.

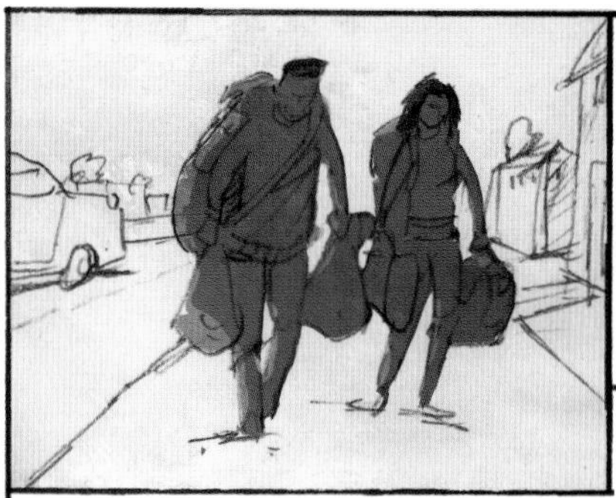

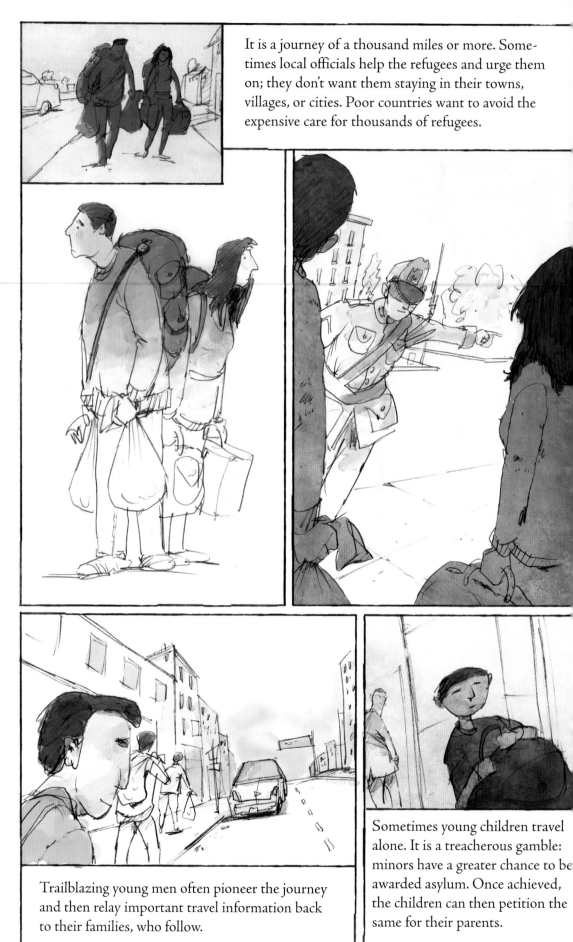

It is a journey of a thousand miles or more. Sometimes local officials help the refugees and urge them on; they don't want them staying in their towns, villages, or cities. Poor countries want to avoid the expensive care for thousands of refugees.

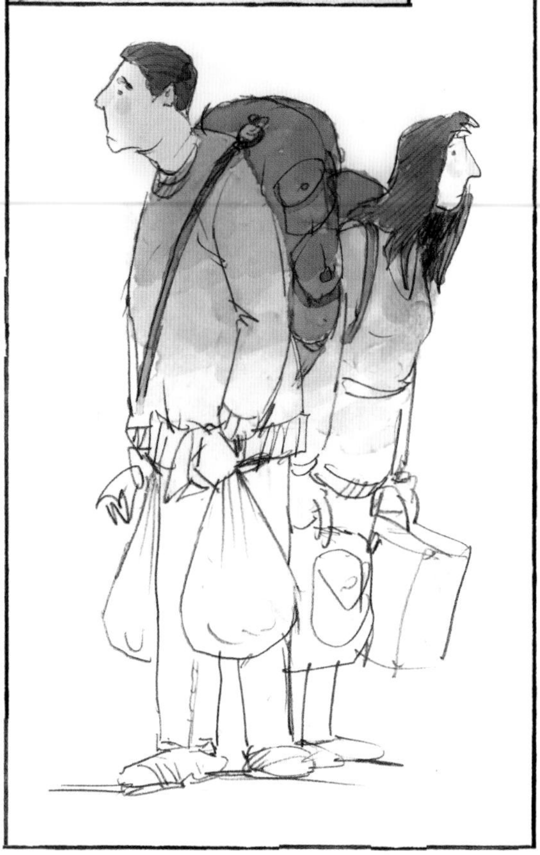

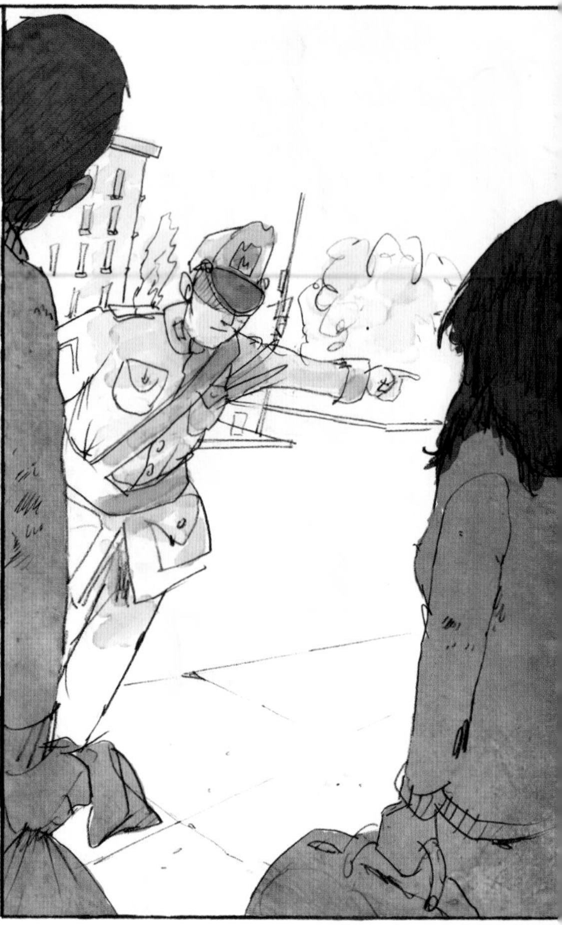

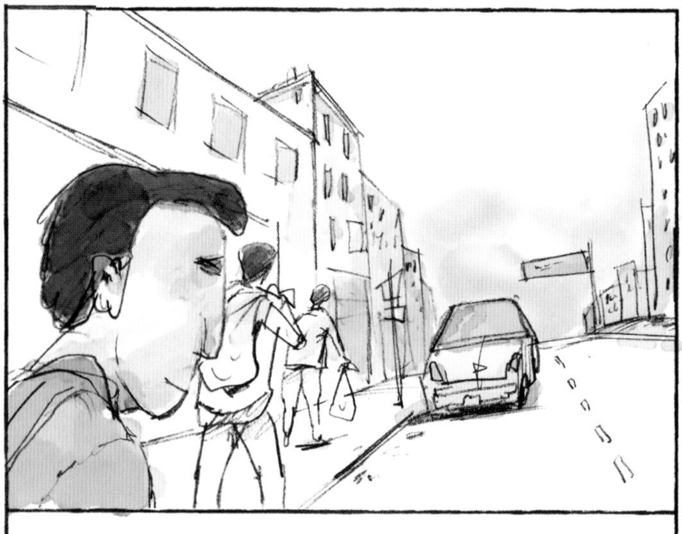

Trailblazing young men often pioneer the journey and then relay important travel information back to their families, who follow.

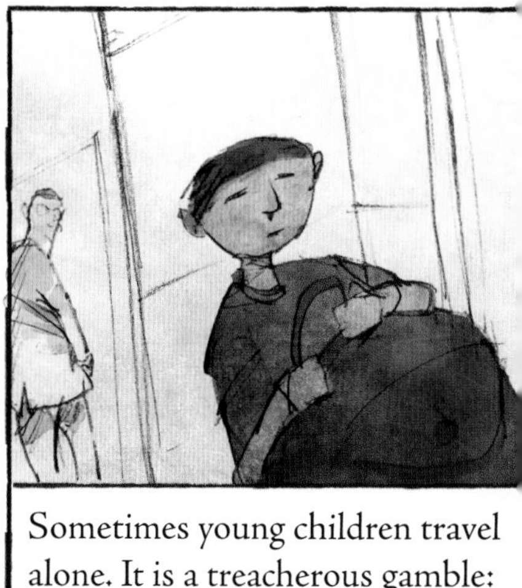

Sometimes young children travel alone. It is a treacherous gamble: minors have a greater chance to be awarded asylum. Once achieved, the children can then petition the same for their parents.

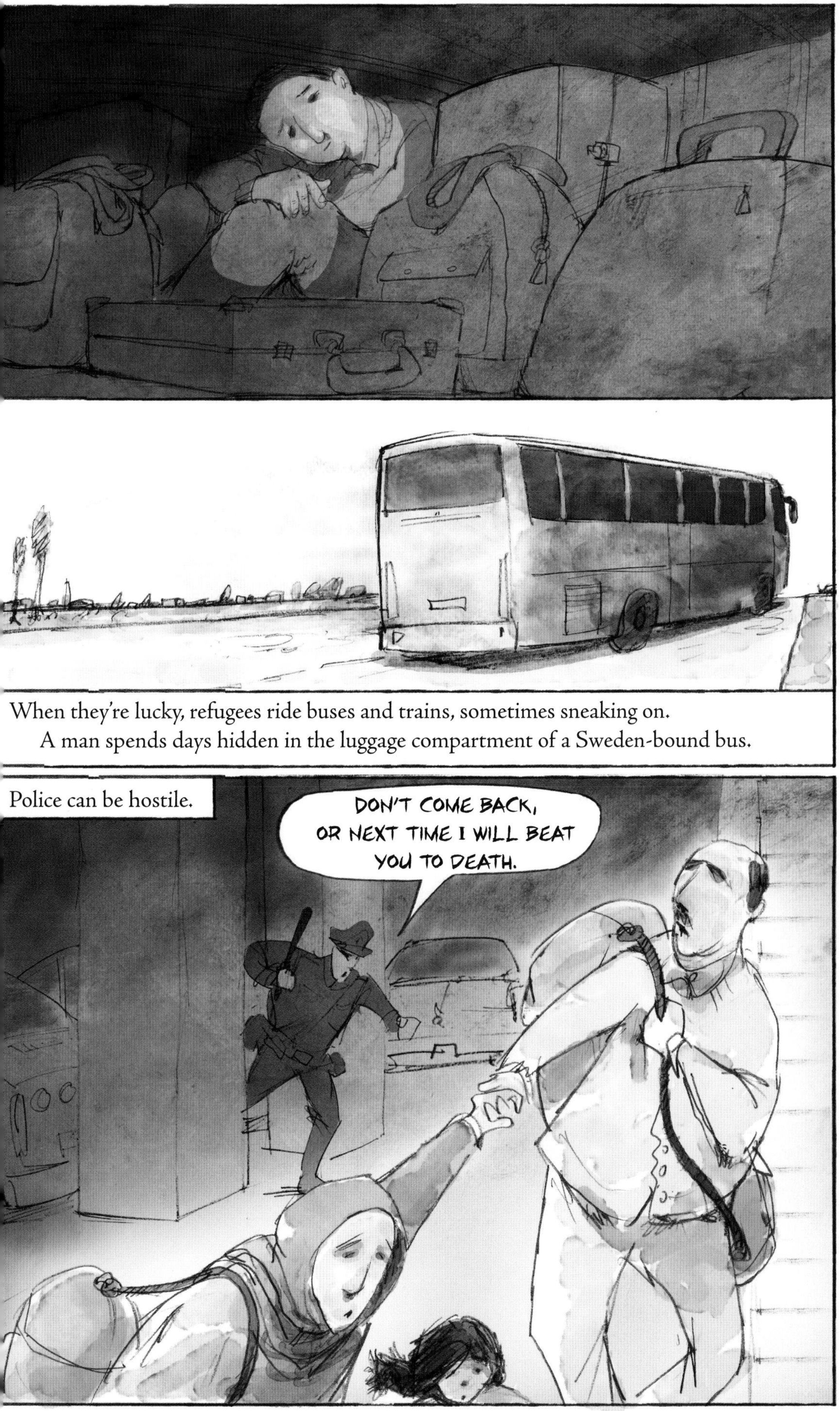
When they're lucky, refugees ride buses and trains, sometimes sneaking on.
A man spends days hidden in the luggage compartment of a Sweden-bound bus.
Police can be hostile.
DON'T COME BACK, OR NEXT TIME I WILL BEAT YOU TO DEATH.

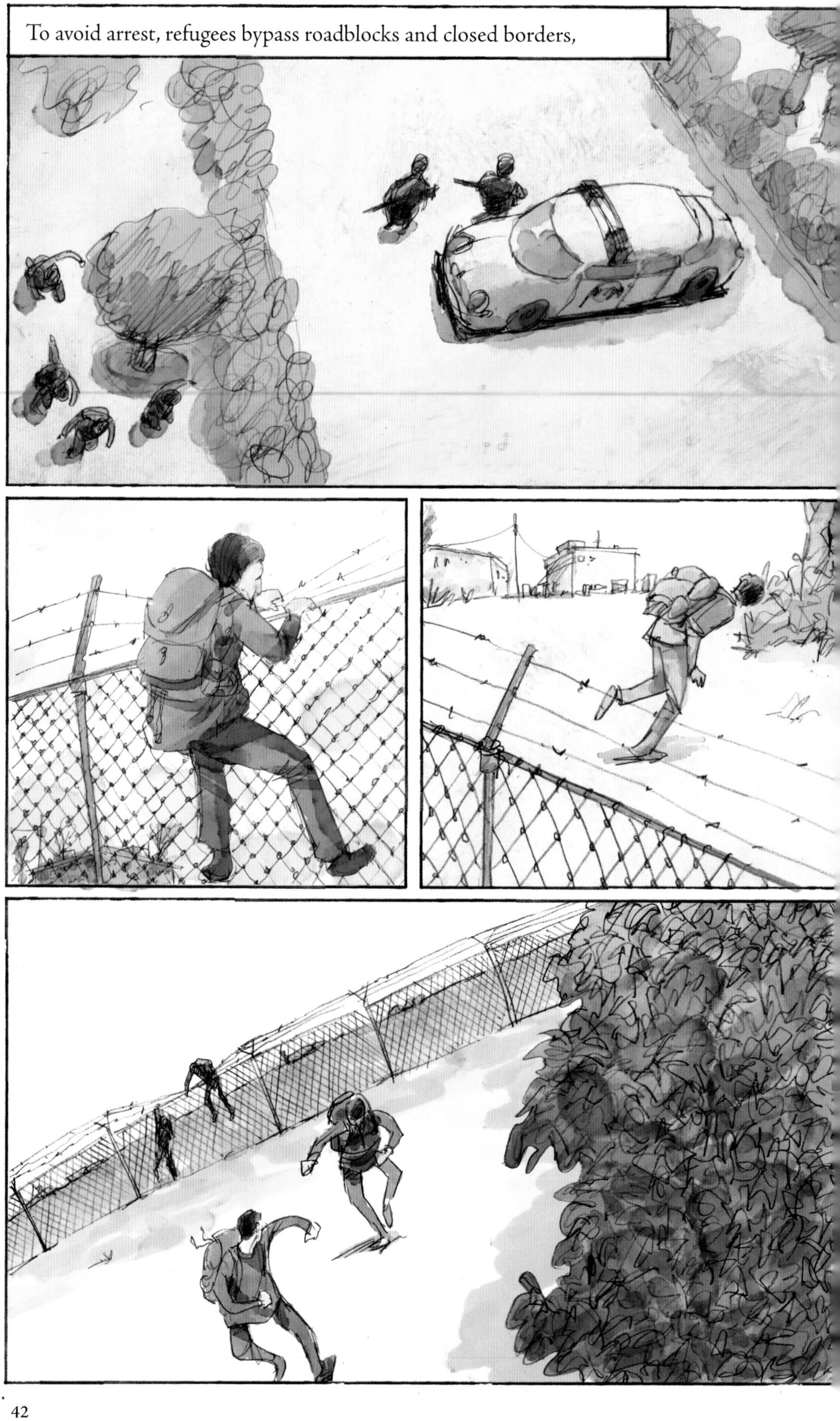
To avoid arrest, refugees bypass roadblocks and closed borders,

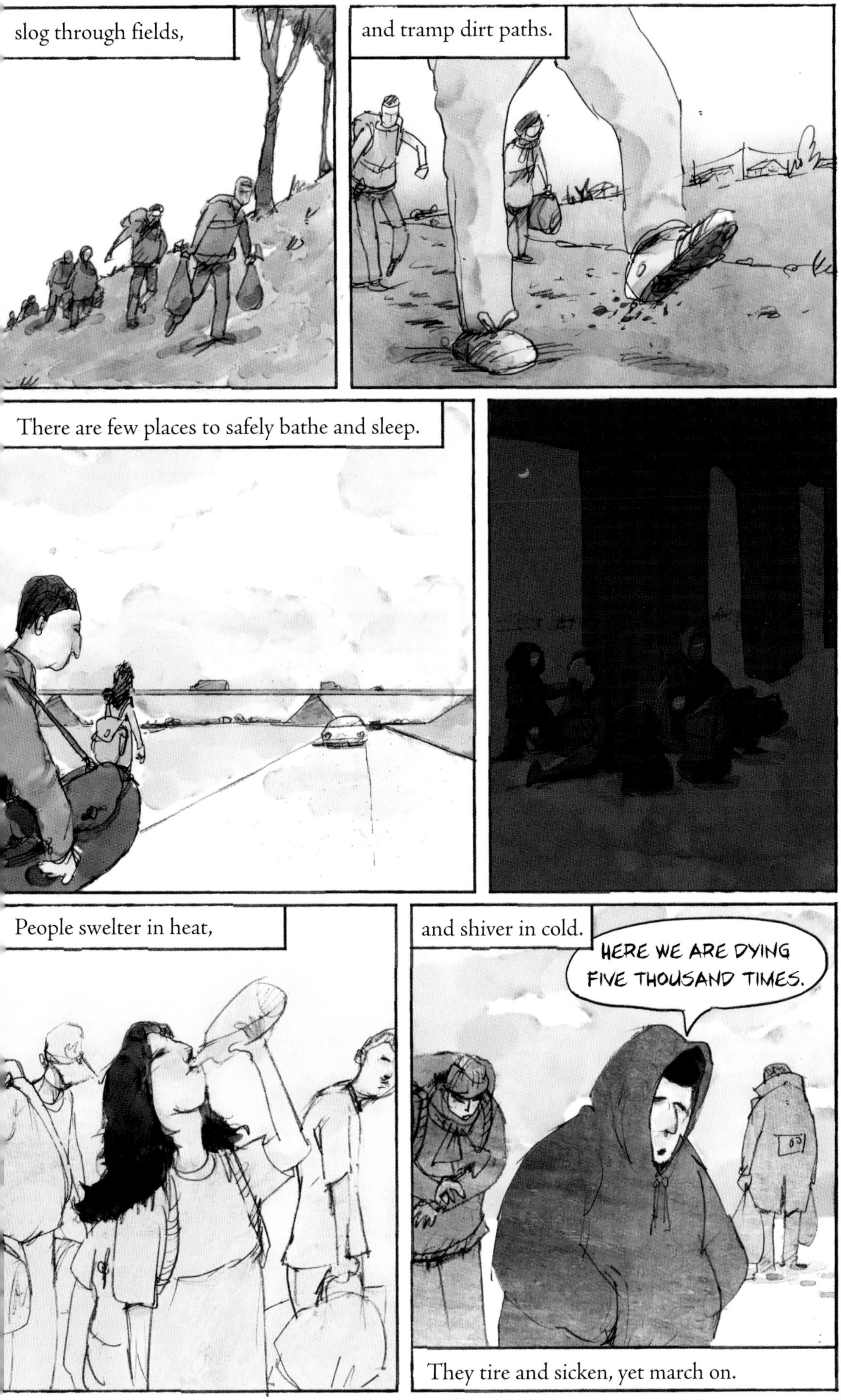
slog through fields,
and tramp dirt paths.
There are few places to safely bathe and sleep.
People swelter in heat,
and shiver in cold.
HERE WE ARE DYING FIVE THOUSAND TIMES.
They tire and sicken, yet march on.

The two Aleppo friends hide themselves in shrubs beside train tracks.

They eat candy and water, their only food.

They follow the rails across another guarded border and hope they won't be arrested . . . or beaten and robbed by bandits who roam the dark.

Refugees use cell phones' GPS to help them navigate strange lands. The phone is also a lifeline to friends and relatives in Syria or those already resettled in Europe who can provide help, such as additional money.

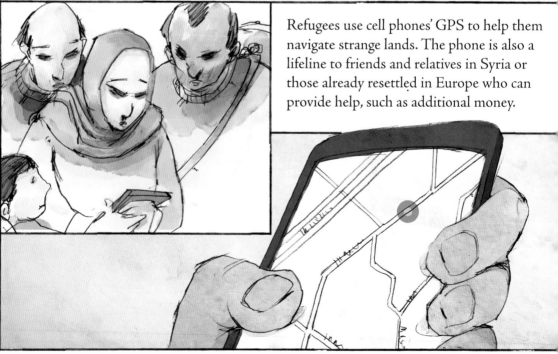

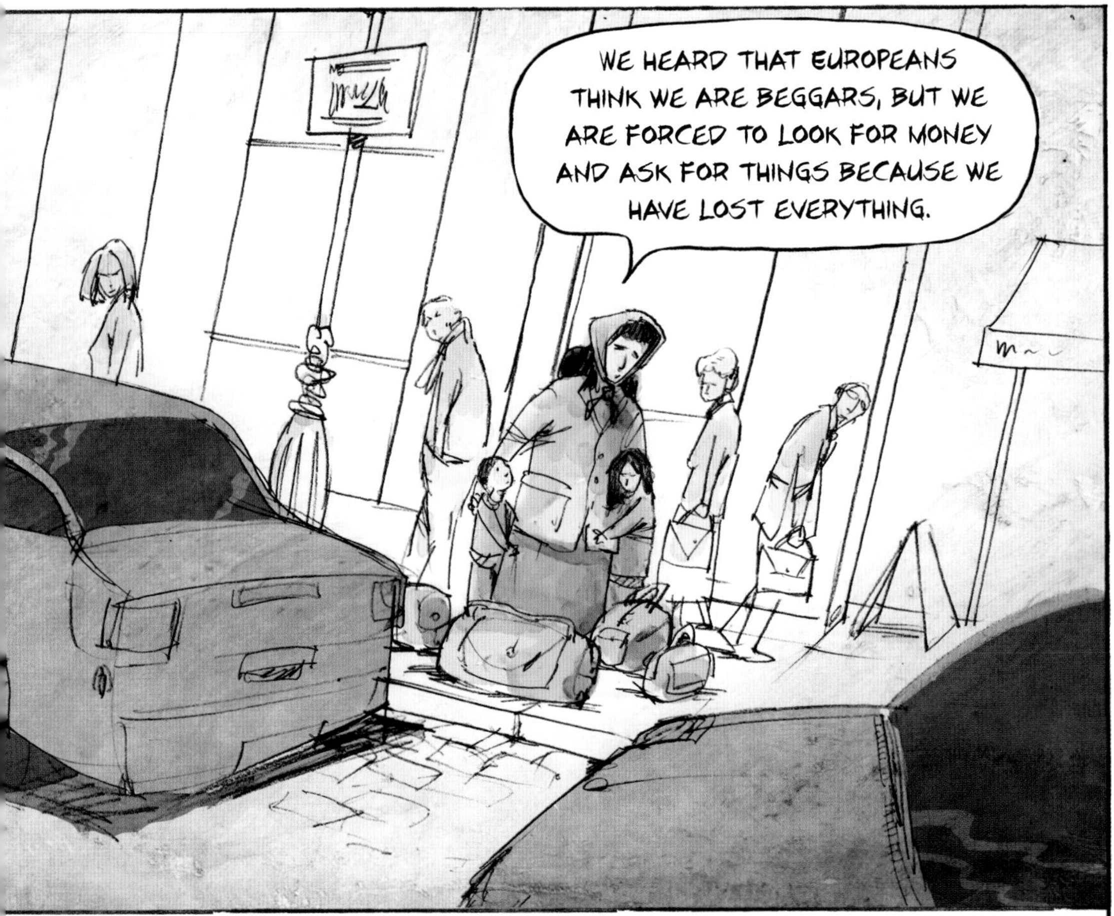
WE HEARD THAT EUROPEANS THINK WE ARE BEGGARS, BUT WE ARE FORCED TO LOOK FOR MONEY AND ASK FOR THINGS BECAUSE WE HAVE LOST EVERYTHING.

The refugees are often cheated and swindled, but sometimes kindhearted volunteers hand out clothes, food, coloring books, soap, and baby wipes.

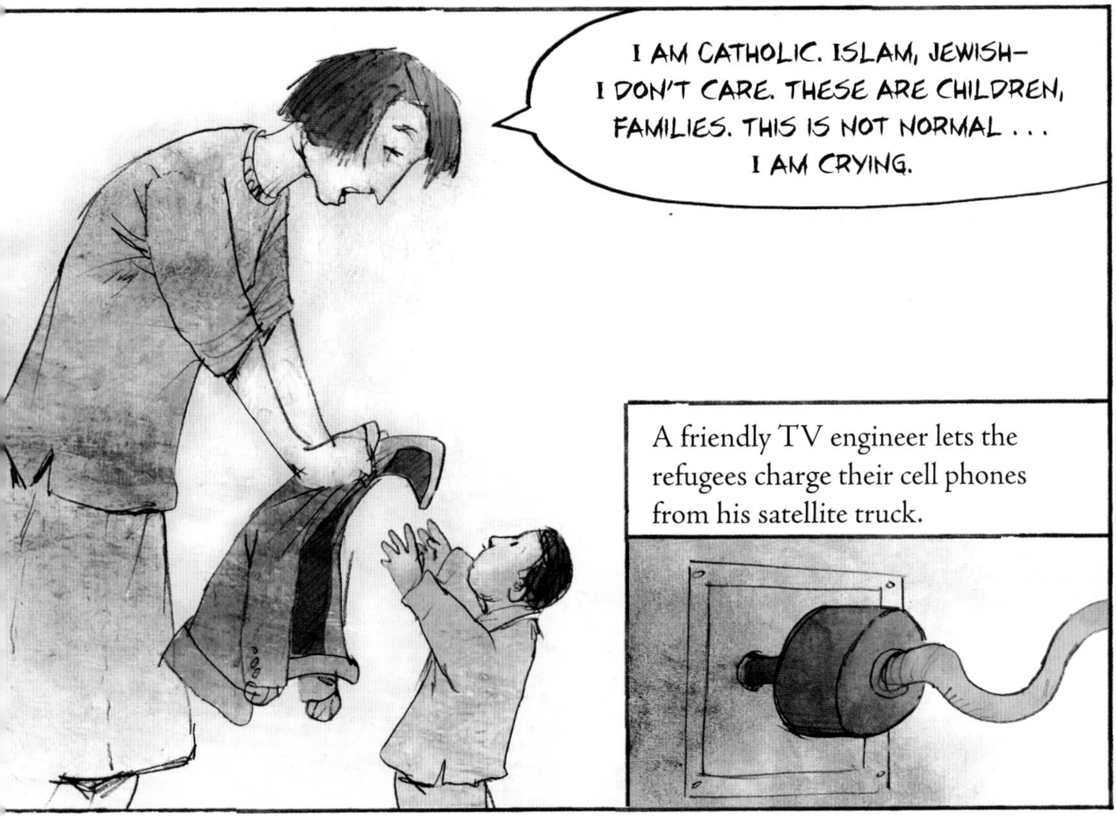
I AM CATHOLIC. ISLAM, JEWISH— I DON'T CARE. THESE ARE CHILDREN, FAMILIES. THIS IS NOT NORMAL . . . I AM CRYING.
A friendly TV engineer lets the refugees charge their cell phones from his satellite truck.

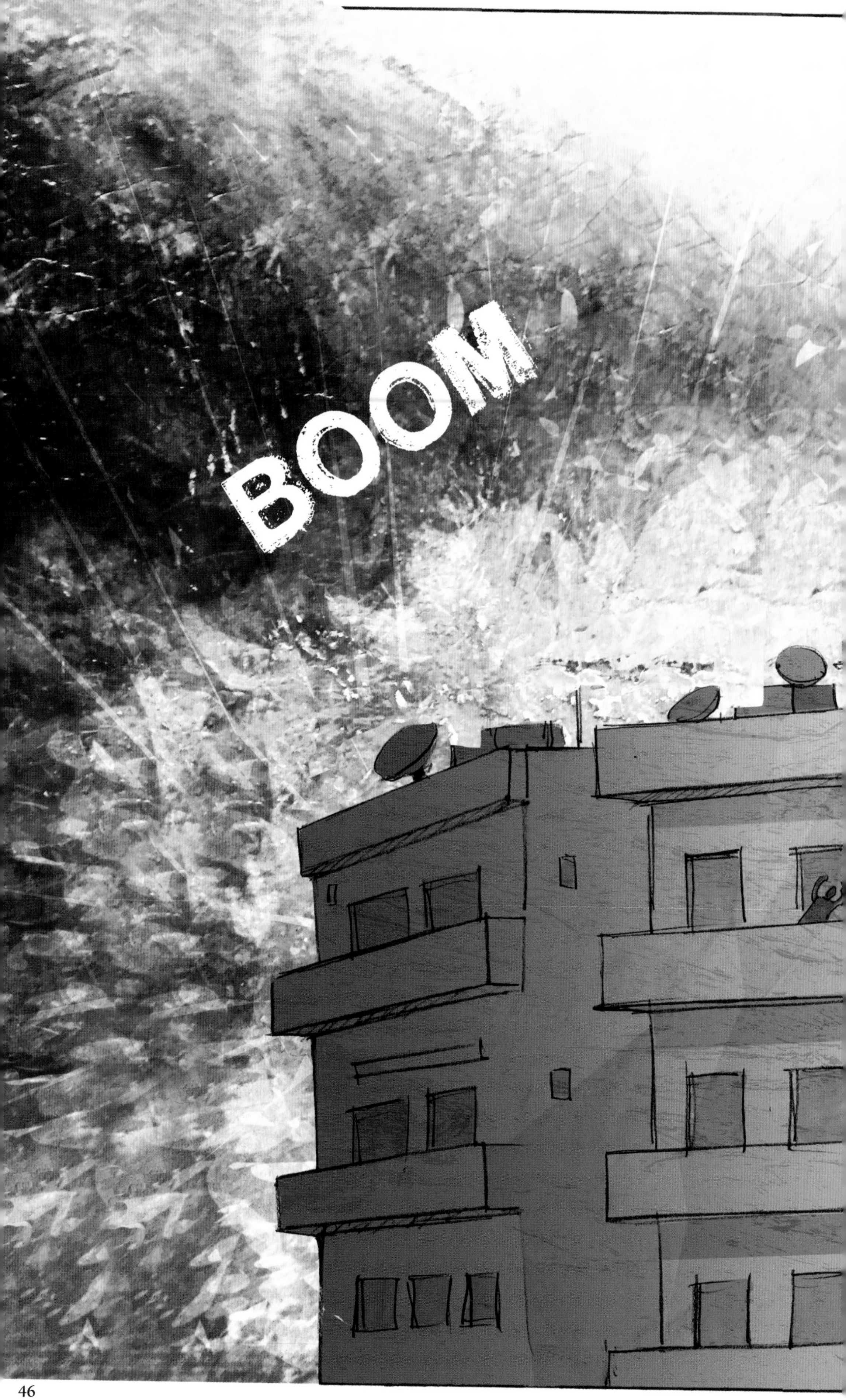
BOOM

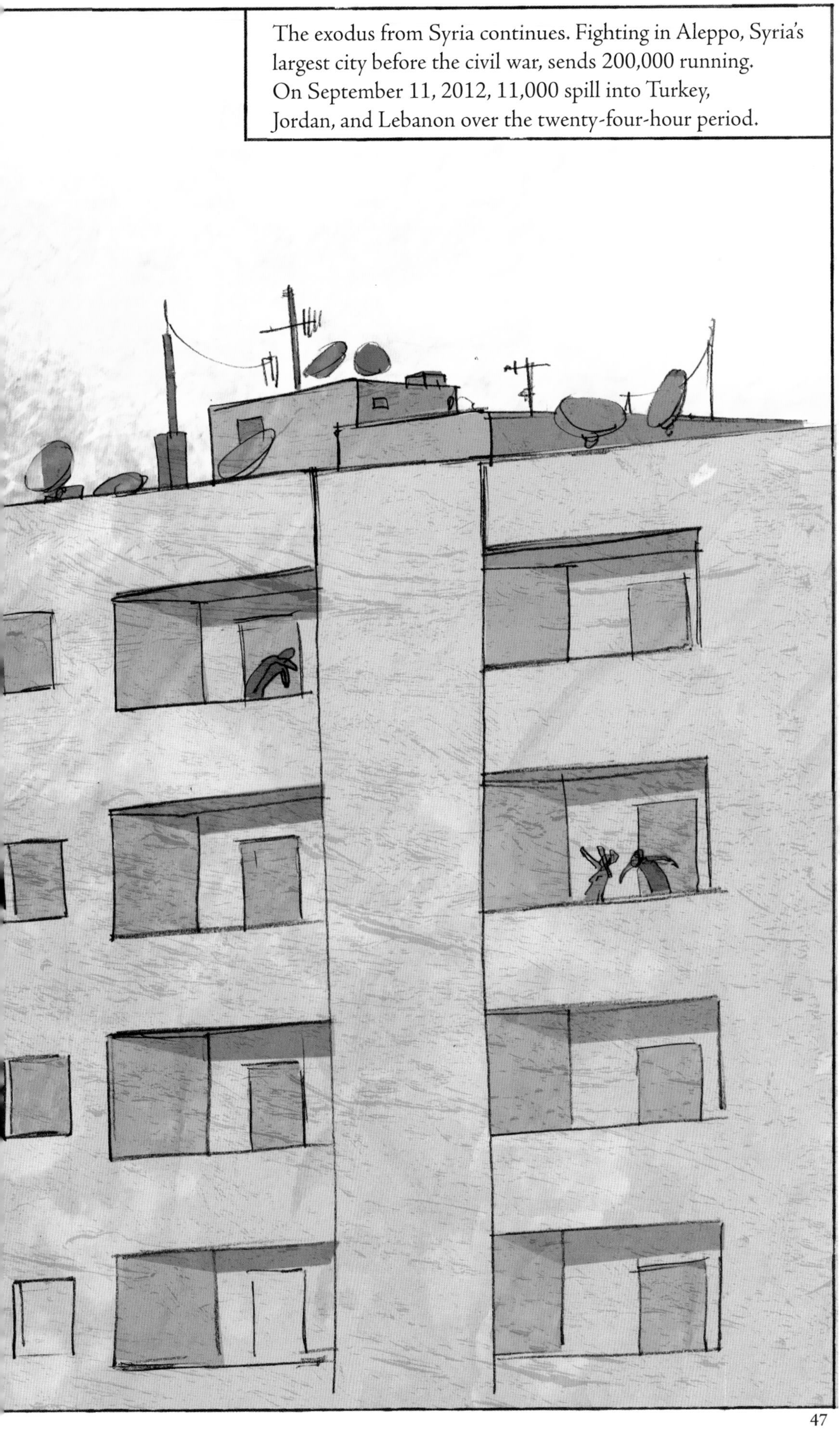
The exodus from Syria continues. Fighting in Aleppo, Syria's largest city before the civil war, sends 200,000 running. On September 11, 2012, 11,000 spill into Turkey, Jordan, and Lebanon over the twenty-four-hour period.

Soon, nearly a third of all people in Lebanon are Syrian refugees. It is the same as if all of Mexico suddenly moved to the United States. There are no government-sanctioned camps. With little official assistance, refugees find themselves sharing cramped apartments, sometimes fifteen to a room.

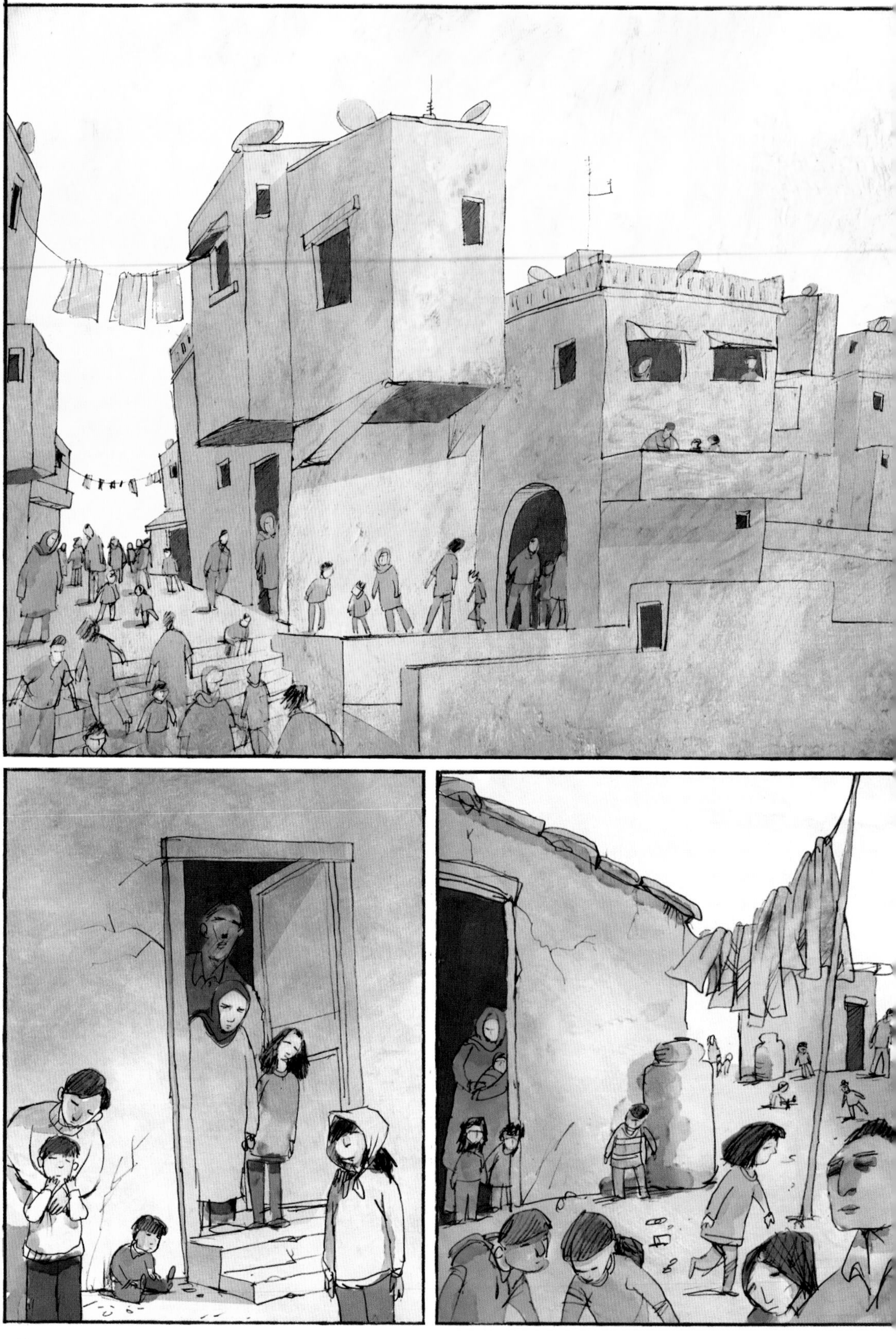

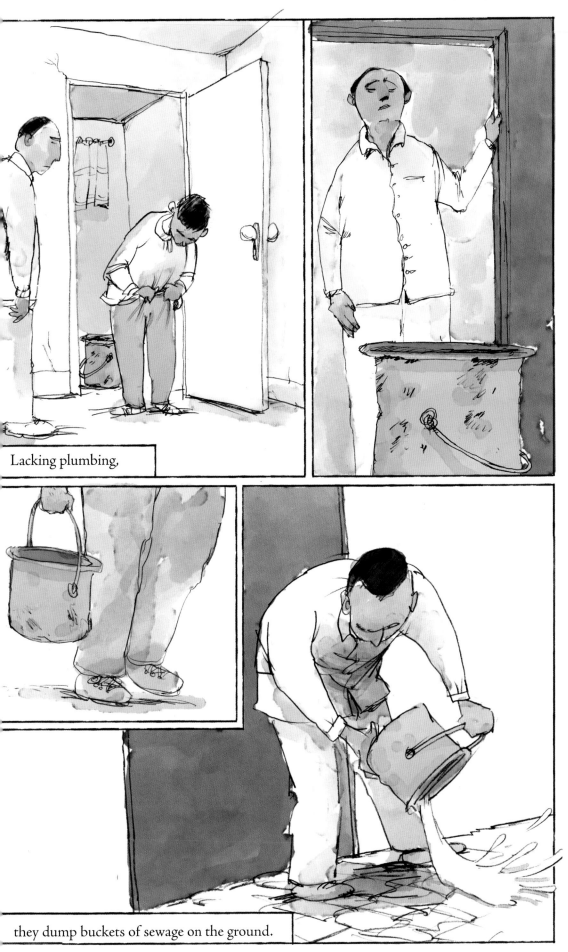

Lacking plumbing,

they dump buckets of sewage on the ground.

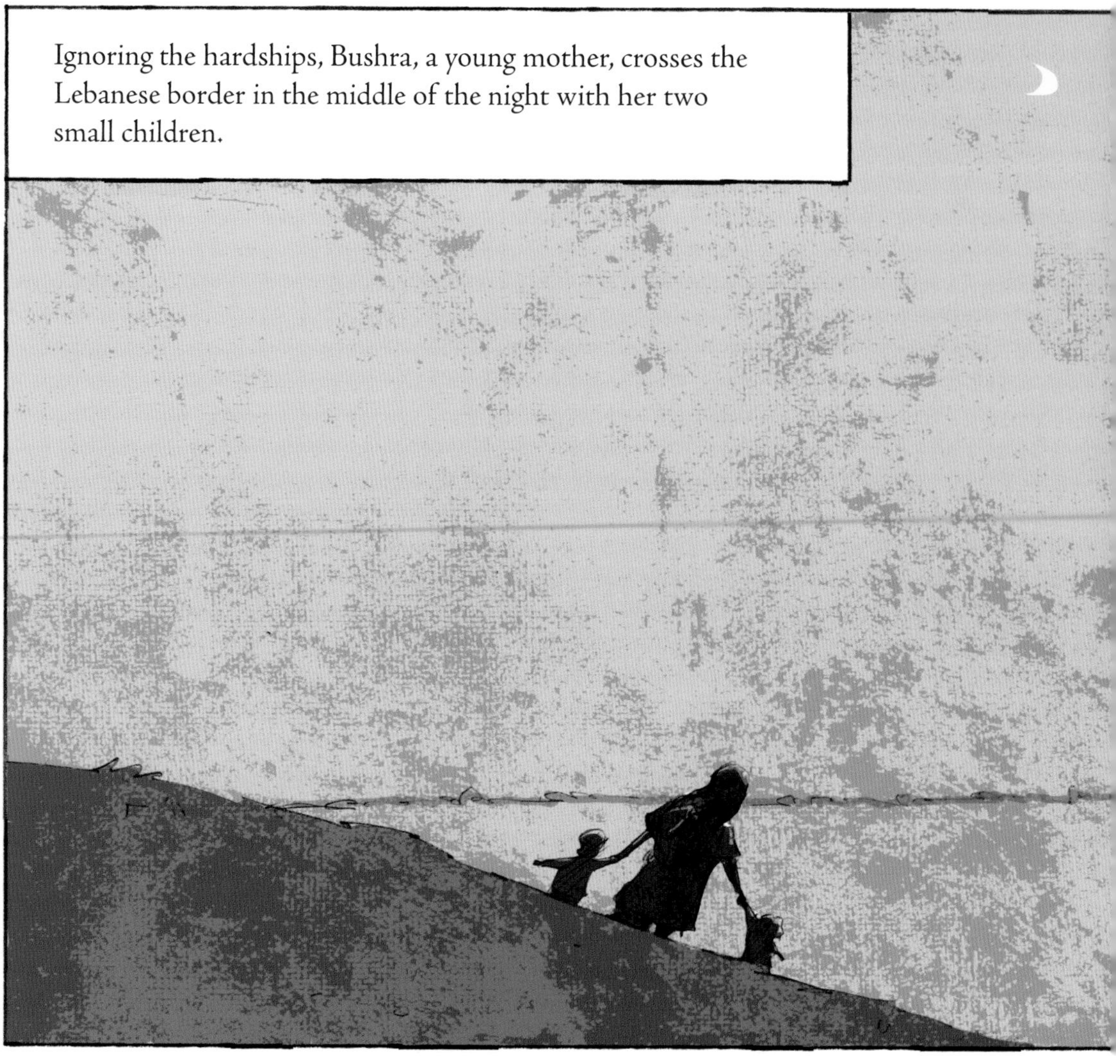
Ignoring the hardships, Bushra, a young mother, crosses the Lebanese border in the middle of the night with her two small children.

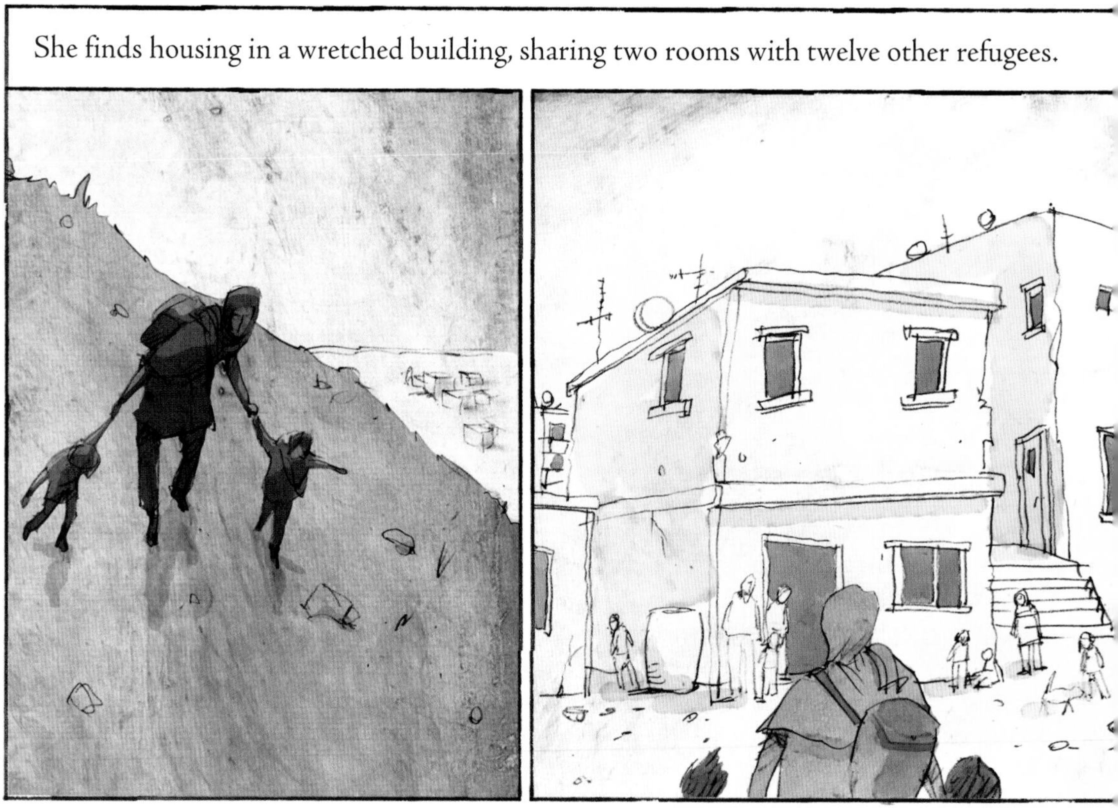
She finds housing in a wretched building, sharing two rooms with twelve other refugees.

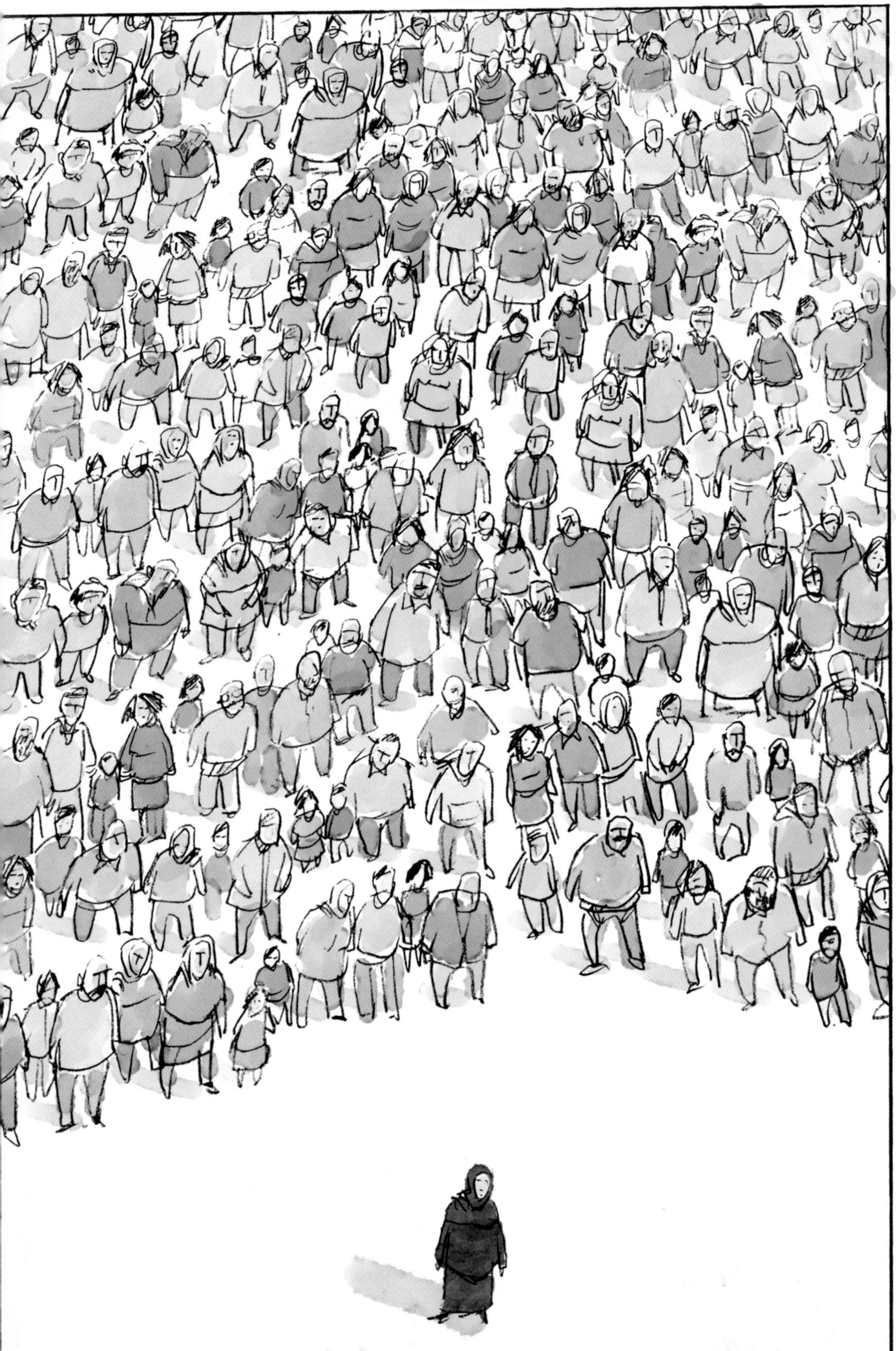

In 2013, Bushra becomes the millionth Syrian refugee *registered* by the United Nations. The number of actual refugees is higher when unregistered ones are included.

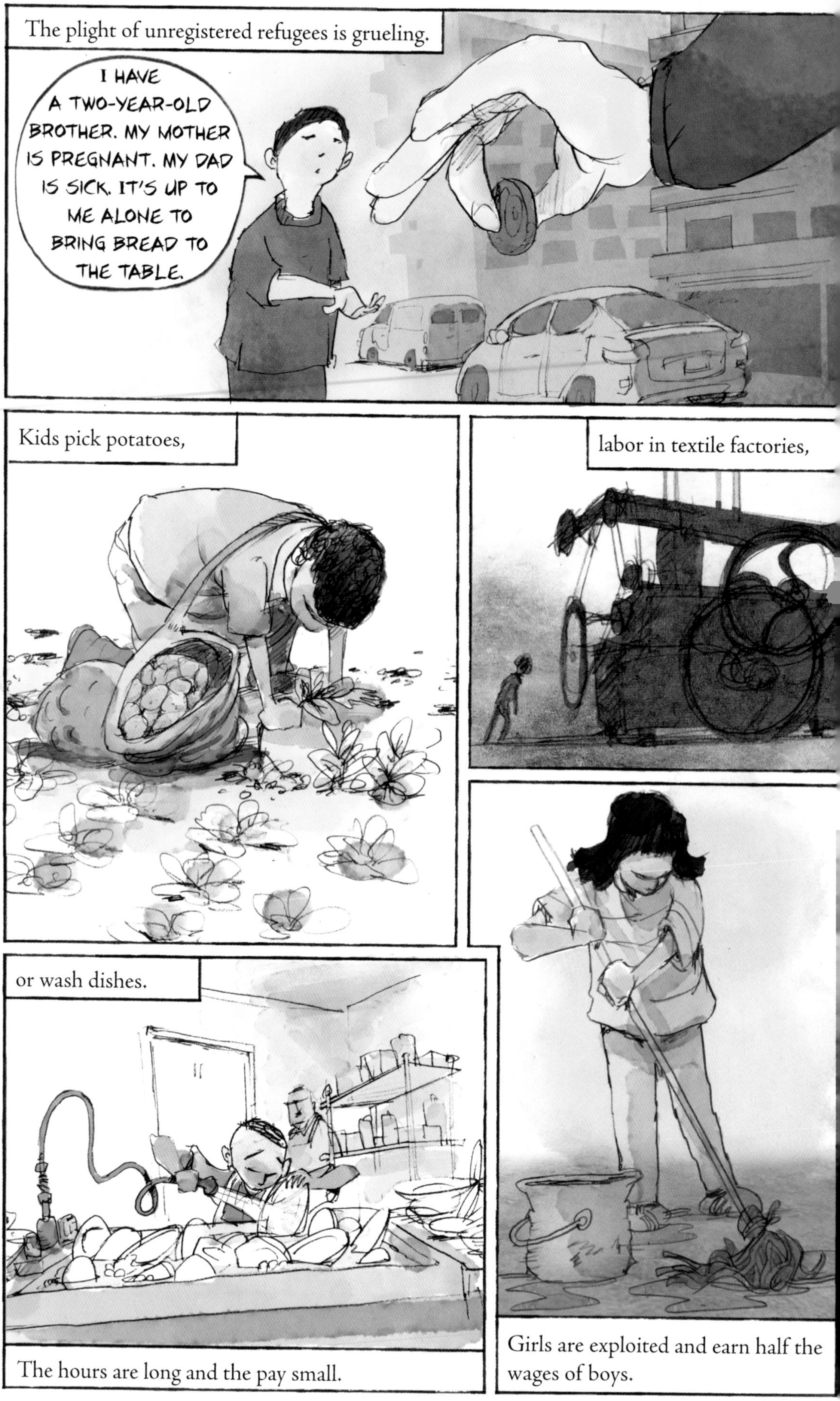
The plight of unregistered refugees is grueling.
I HAVE A TWO-YEAR-OLD BROTHER. MY MOTHER IS PREGNANT. MY DAD IS SICK. IT'S UP TO ME ALONE TO BRING BREAD TO THE TABLE.
Kids pick potatoes,
labor in textile factories,
or wash dishes.
The hours are long and the pay small.
Girls are exploited and earn half the wages of boys.

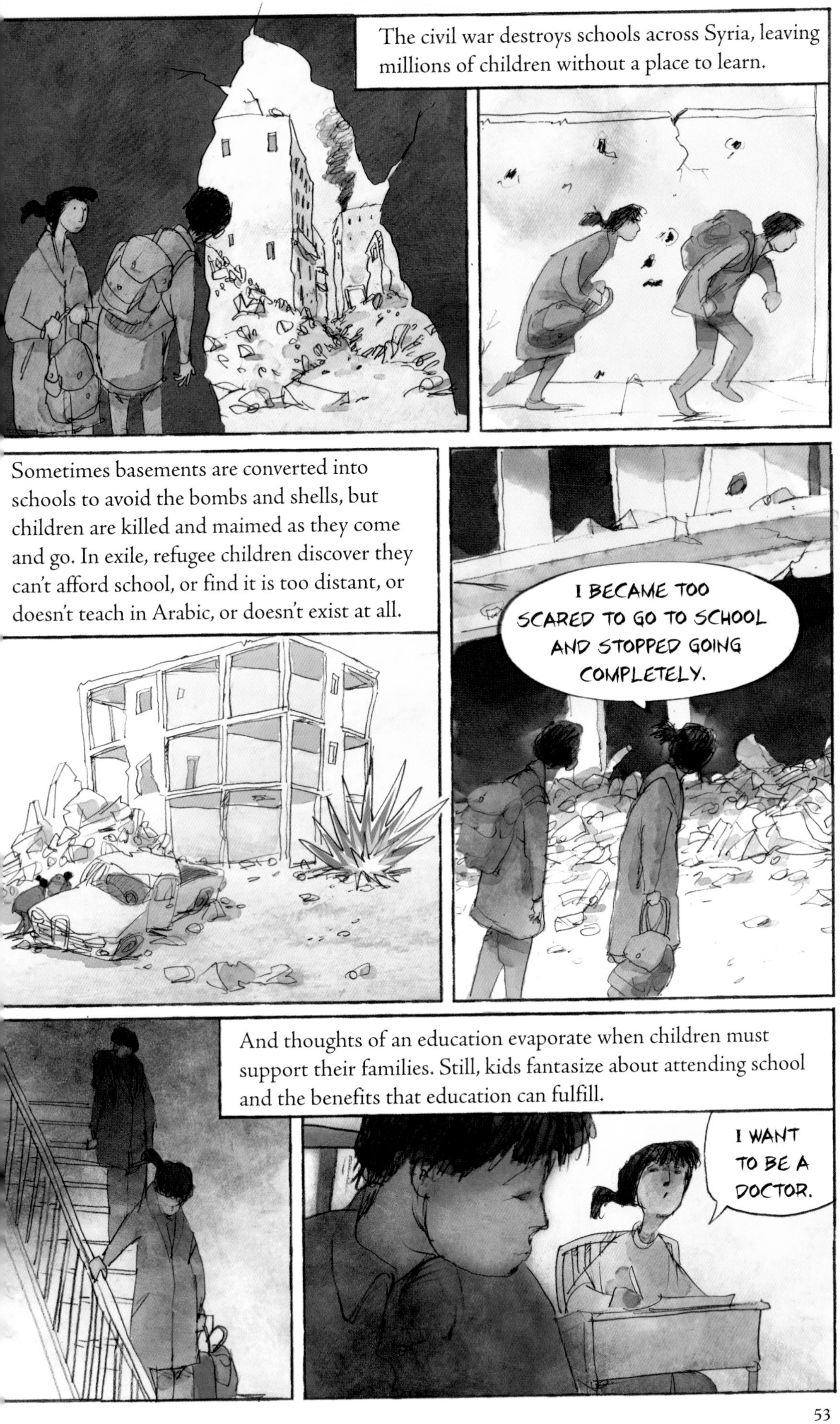
The civil war destroys schools across Syria, leaving millions of children without a place to learn.
Sometimes basements are converted into schools to avoid the bombs and shells, but children are killed and maimed as they come and go. In exile, refugee children discover they can't afford school, or find it is too distant, or doesn't teach in Arabic, or doesn't exist at all.
I BECAME TOO SCARED TO GO TO SCHOOL AND STOPPED GOING COMPLETELY.
And thoughts of an education evaporate when children must support their families. Still, kids fantasize about attending school and the benefits that education can fulfill.
I WANT TO BE A DOCTOR.

At the start of 2014, Jordan is bursting with refugees.
A widow and her three children live in a park and forage for food.

About 125,000 endure a government camp in the middle of the desert at Zaatari. Two thousand new refugees arrive each day.

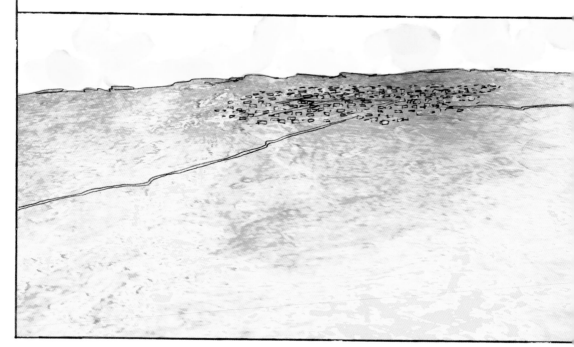

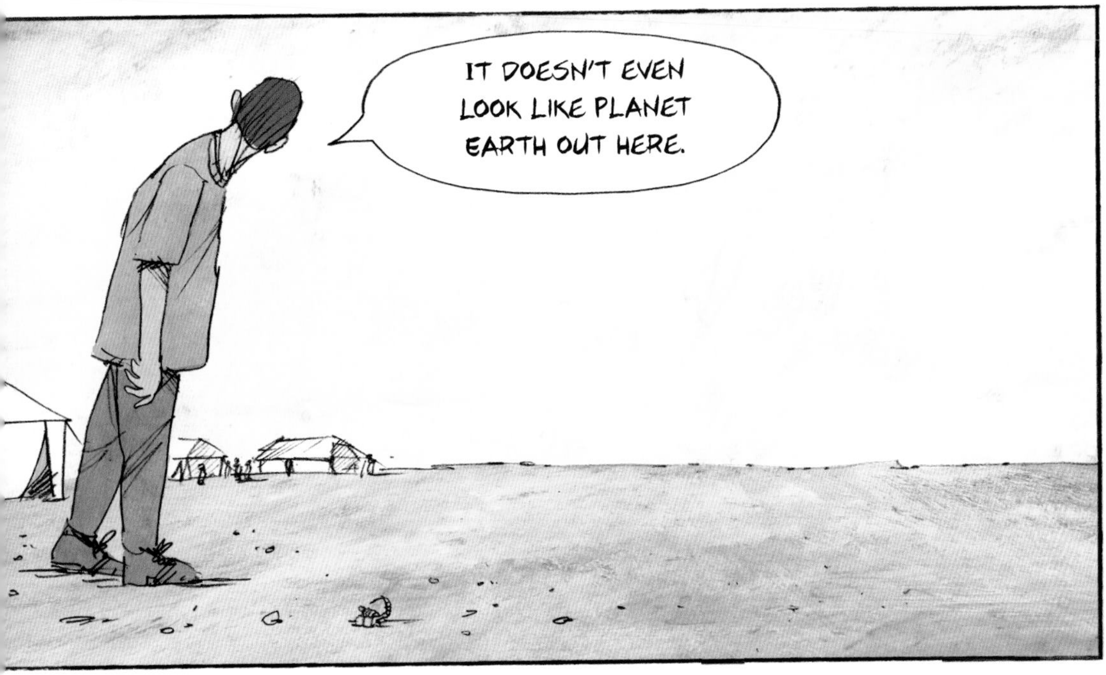
IT DOESN'T EVEN LOOK LIKE PLANET EARTH OUT HERE.

Still, thousands of businesses spring up in the camp and sell groceries, dresses, and mobile phones. The refugees build a local economy worth millions of dollars.

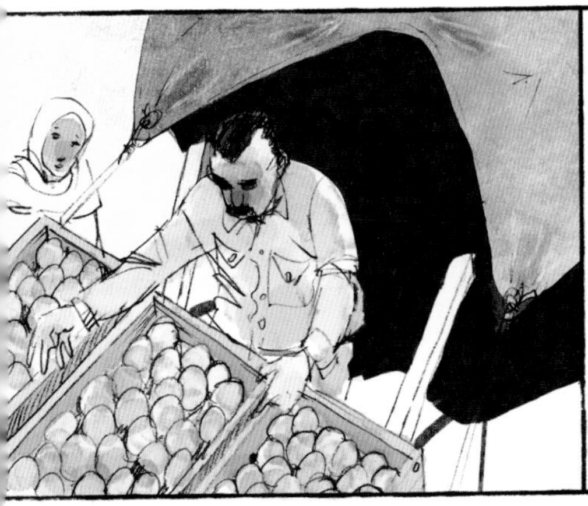

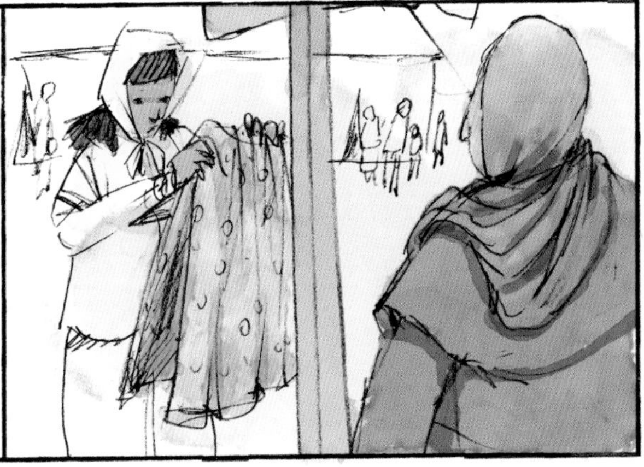

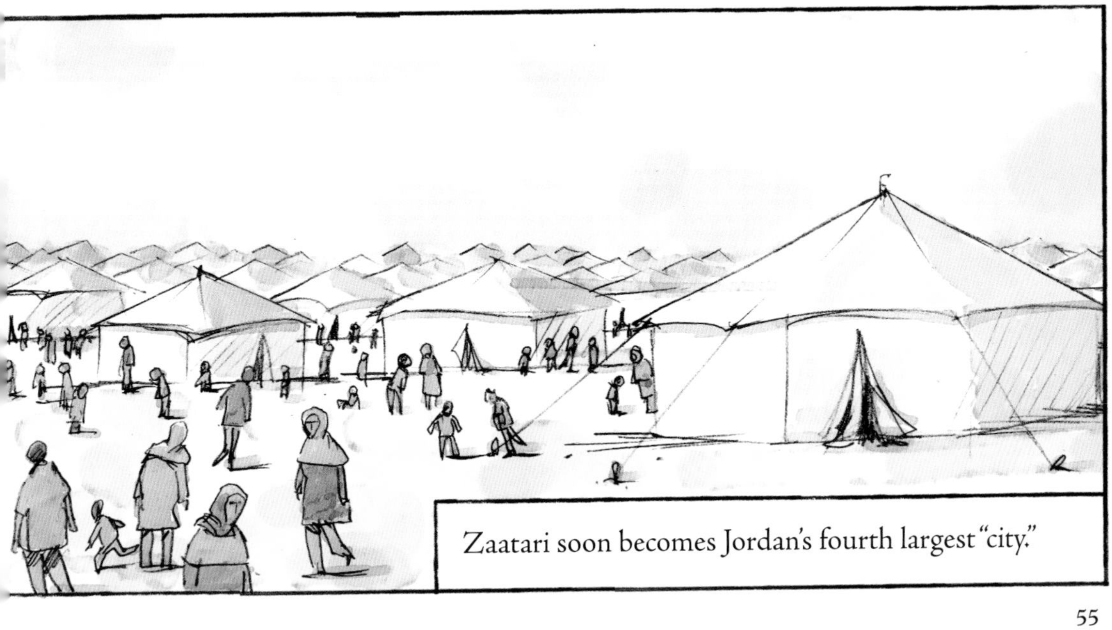
Zaatari soon becomes Jordan's fourth largest "city."

Turkey, too, is flooded with refugees. The Turks open camps and spend billions housing, feeding, educating, and nursing refugees, whose numbers grow to more than 700,000 by the middle of 2014.

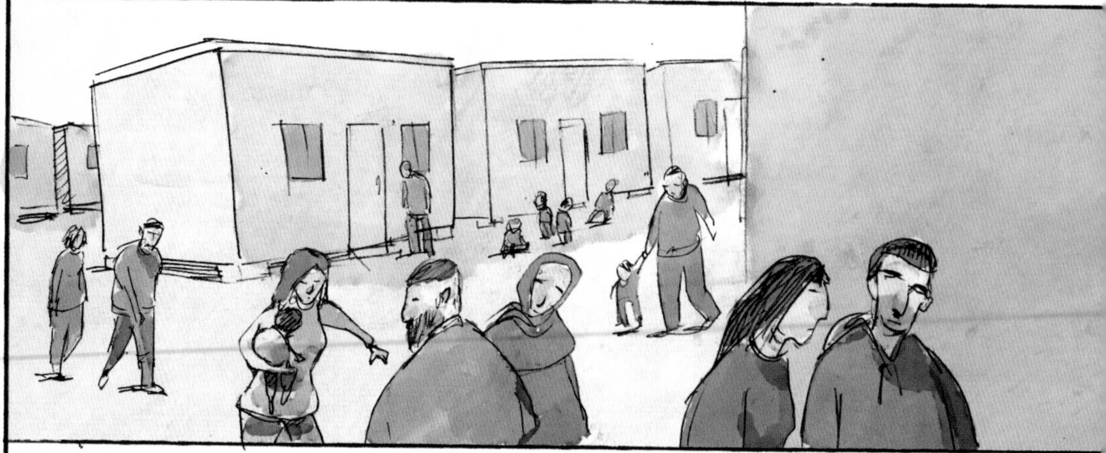

One camp near the Syrian border shelters 14,000 refugees in 2,000 prefabricated metal trailers arranged in straight rows along paved streets. Inside are two small rooms, a bathroom, and built-in heaters/air conditioners. Most have a small sink, a refrigerator, and a hot plate.

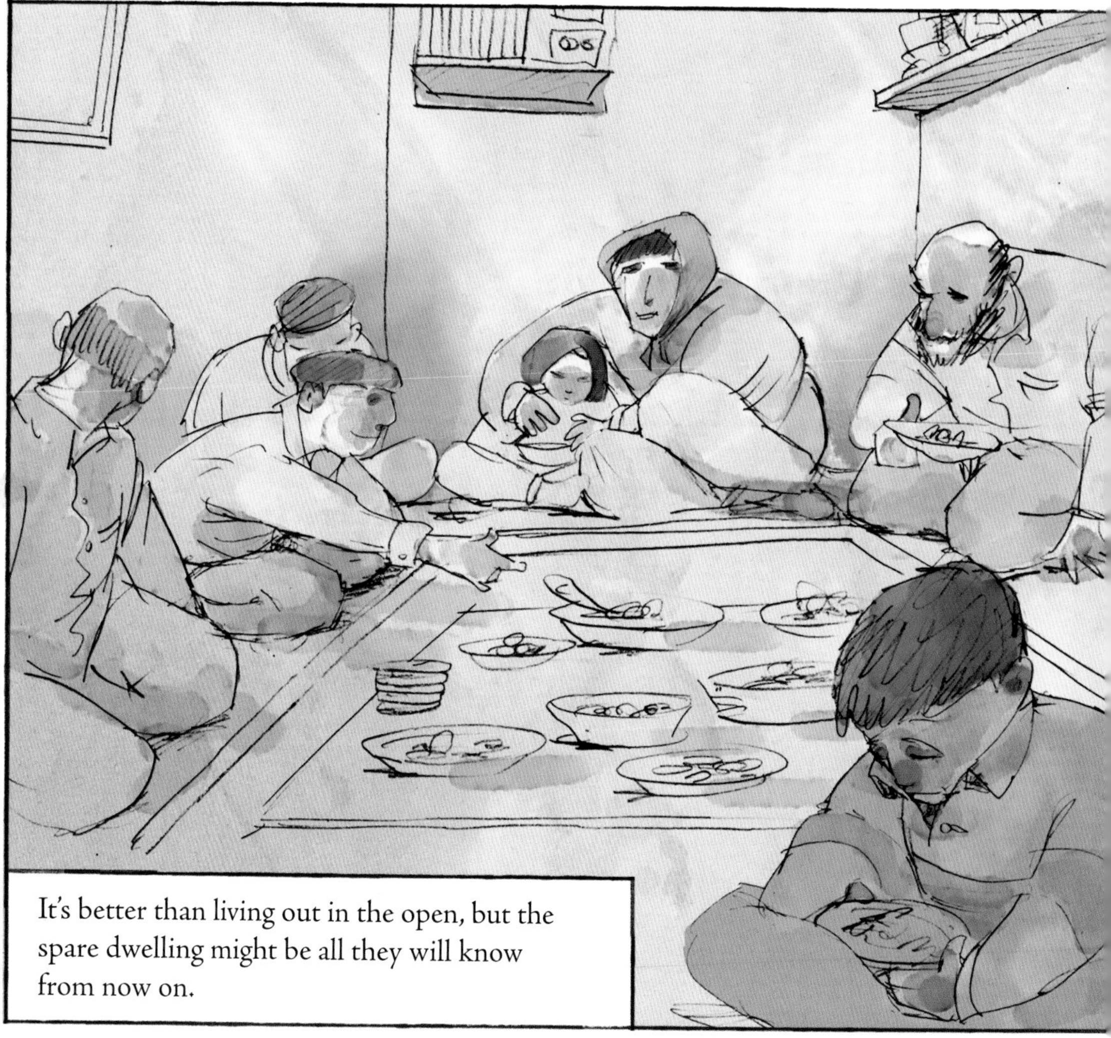
It's better than living out in the open, but the spare dwelling might be all they will know from now on.

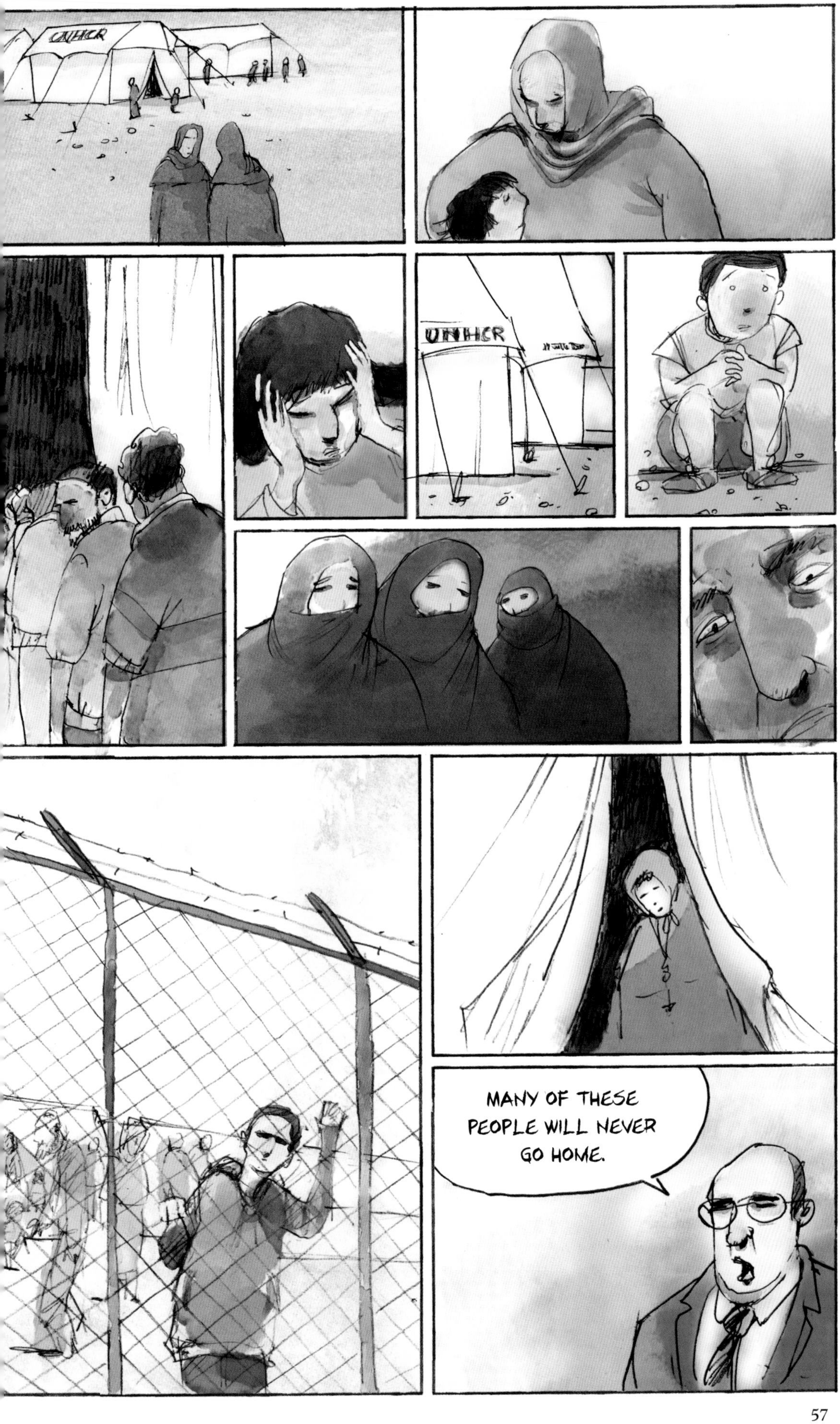
UNHCR
UNHCR
MANY OF THESE PEOPLE WILL NEVER GO HOME.

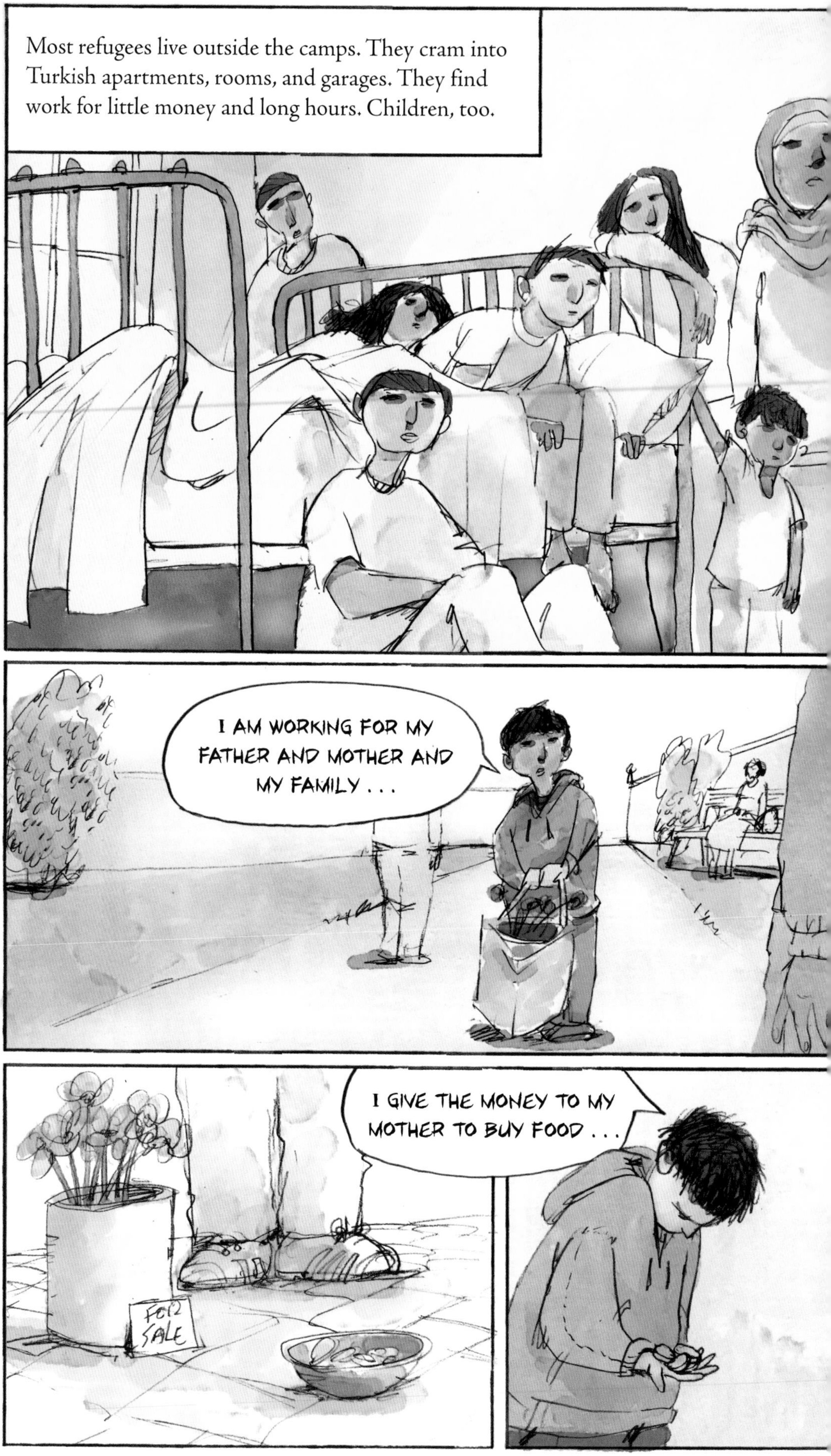
Most refugees live outside the camps. They cram into Turkish apartments, rooms, and garages. They find work for little money and long hours. Children, too.
I AM WORKING FOR MY FATHER AND MOTHER AND MY FAMILY . . .
I GIVE THE MONEY TO MY MOTHER TO BUY FOOD . . .
FOR SALE

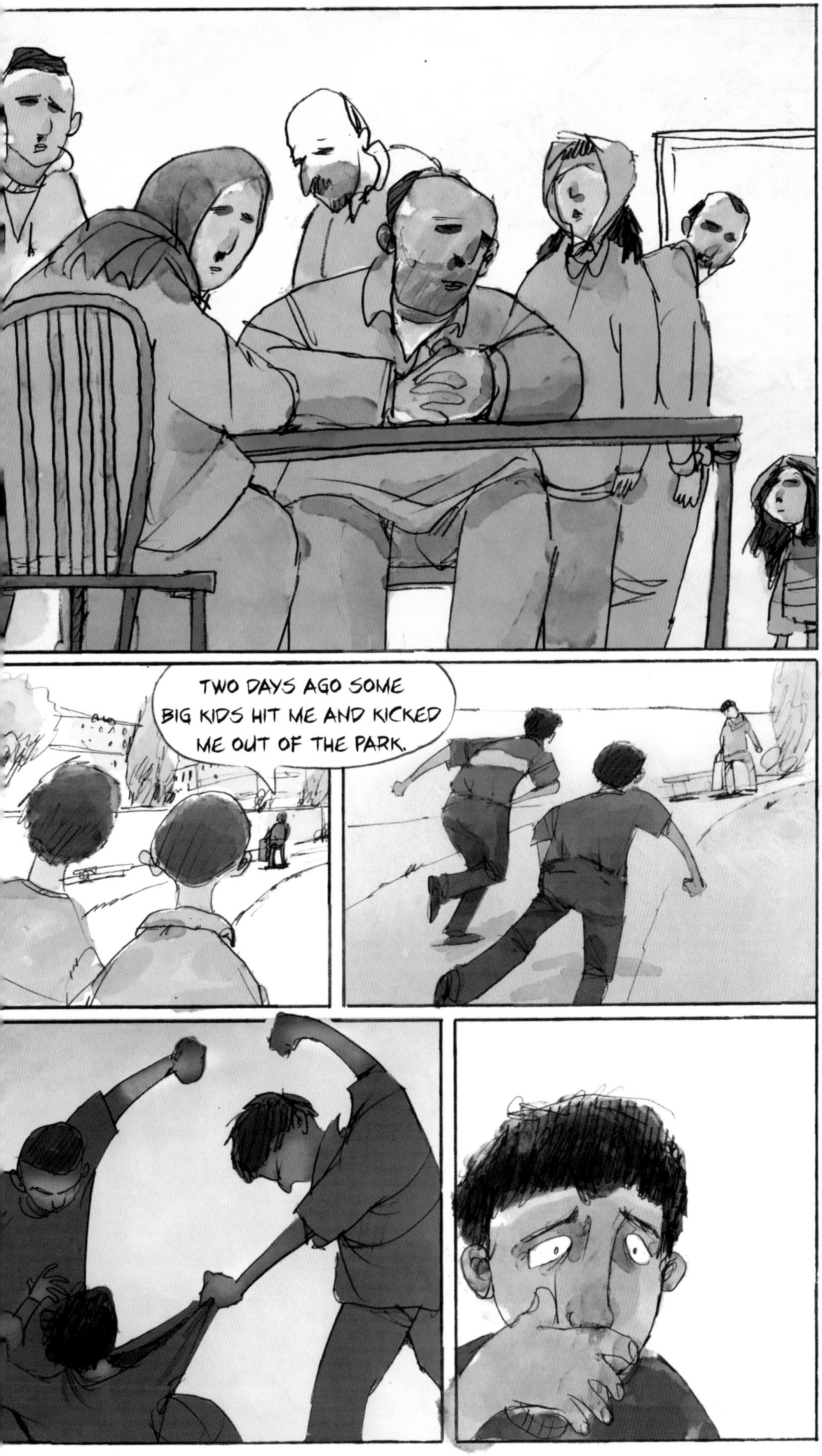
TWO DAYS AGO SOME BIG KIDS HIT ME AND KICKED ME OUT OF THE PARK.

Nearly 4 million Syrians—95 percent of all refugees—find refuge in Turkey, Lebanon, Jordan, Iraq, and Egypt.

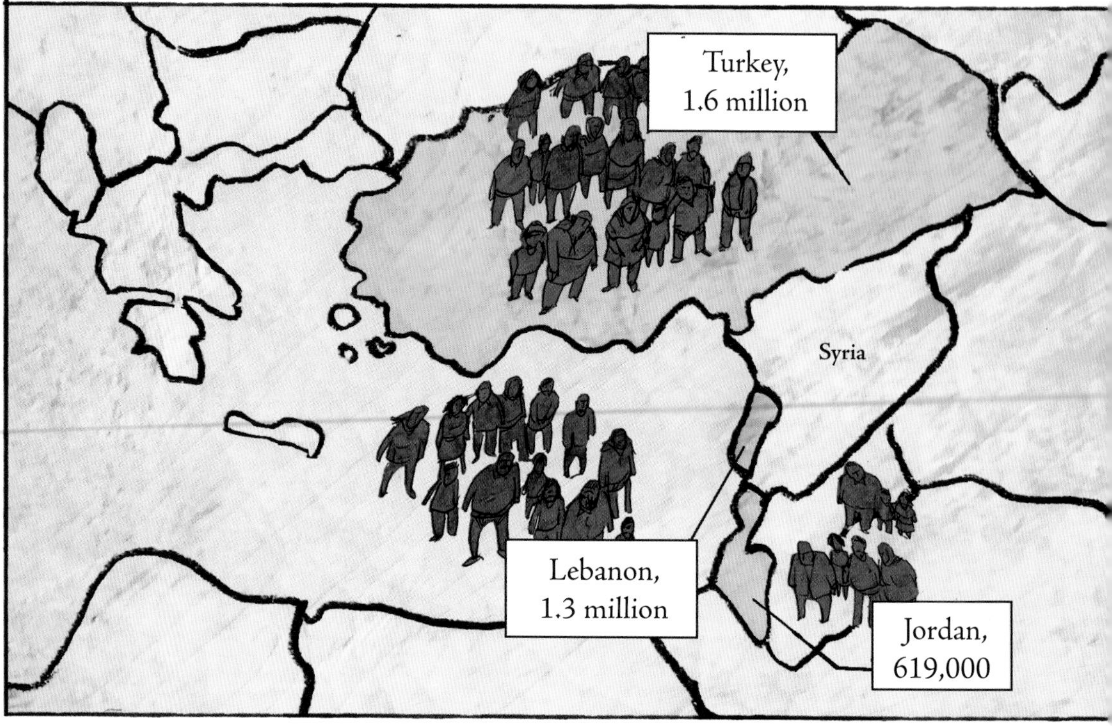
Turkey, 1.6 million
Syria
Lebanon, 1.3 million
Jordan, 619,000

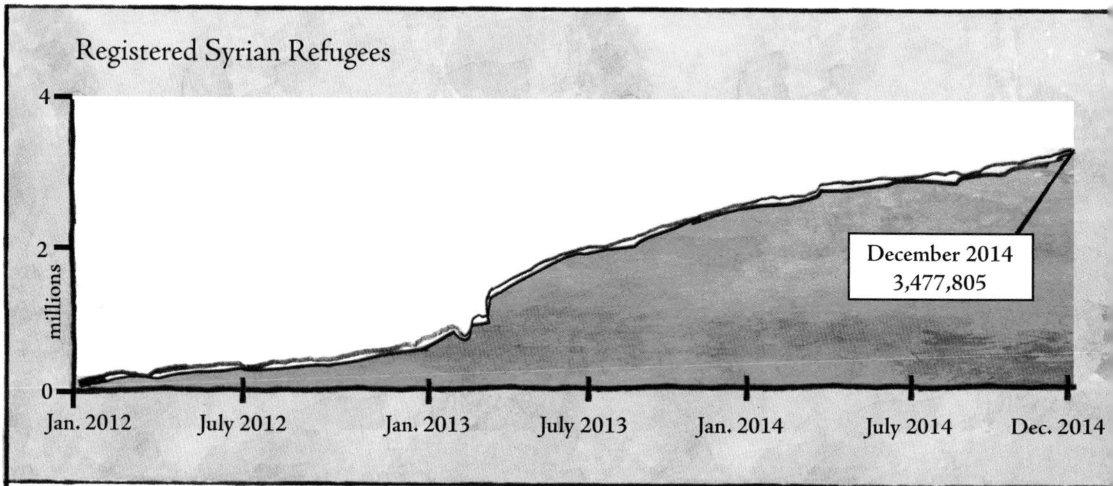
Registered Syrian Refugees
4
2
0
millions
December 2014
3,477,805
Jan. 2012
July 2012
Jan. 2013
July 2013
Jan. 2014
July 2014
Dec. 2014

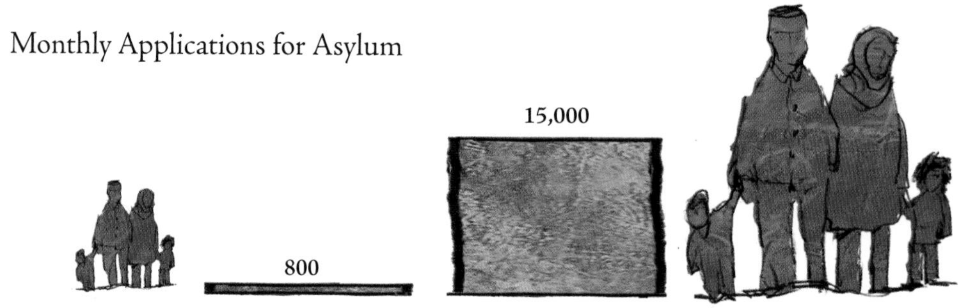
Monthly Applications for Asylum
800
15,000

In December 2011, about 800 people applied for asylum in Europe.

In December 2014, nearly 15,000 people applied for asylum in Europe.

By December 2014, a total of 222,000 people had applied for asylum in Europe.

Before the civil war, the population of Syria is about 22 million people, a bit bigger than Florida's.

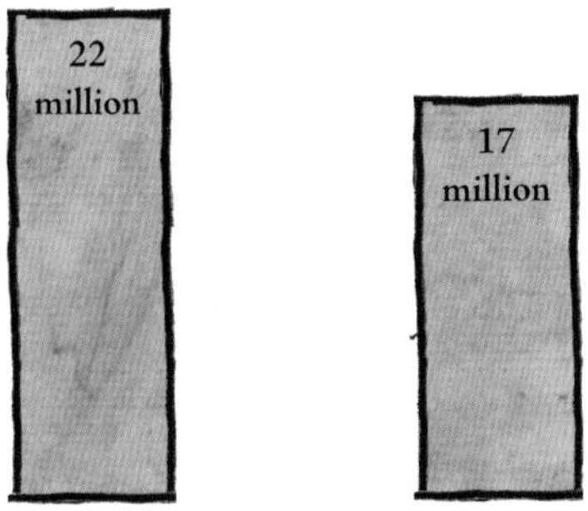
22
million
17
million

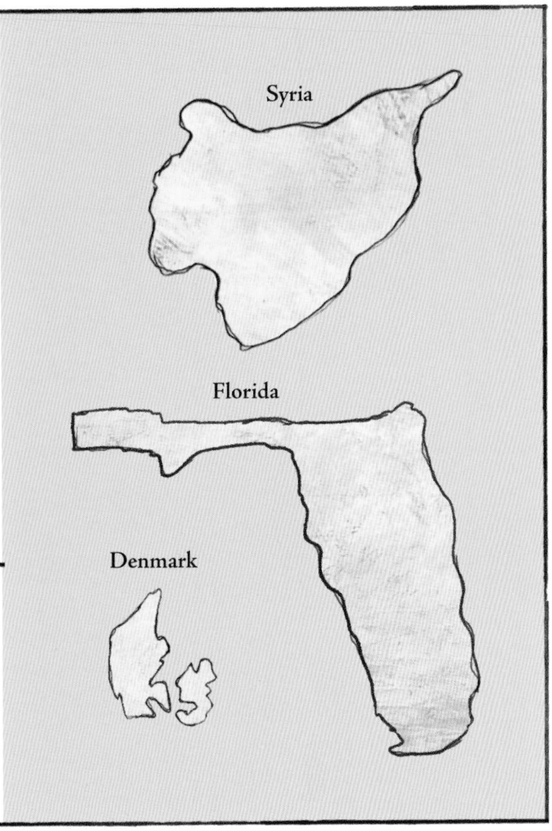
Syria
Florida
Denmark

The flood of refugees reduces the population to about 17 million. The 5.5 million refugees are about equal to the population of Denmark.

Perhaps 200,000 make the dangerous Mediterranean Sea crossing, mostly to Greece and Italy.

In 2014, about 3,500 died or were reported missing.

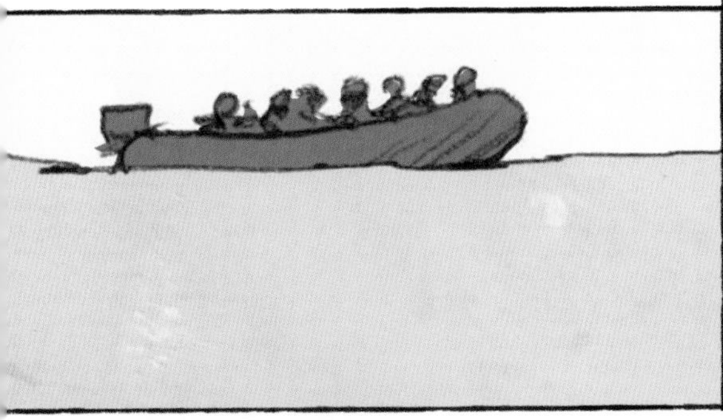

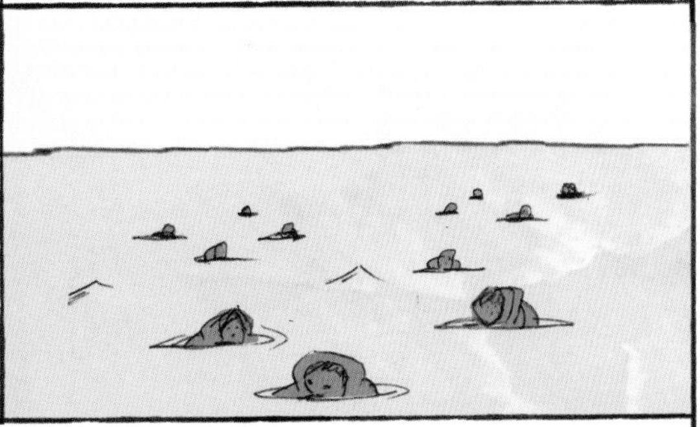

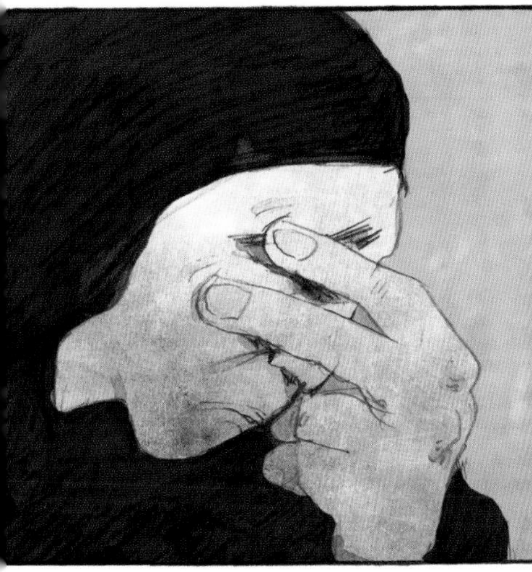

In Syria, about 191,000 people are killed by 2014.

Among the dead are at least 8,800 children and young people under eighteen.

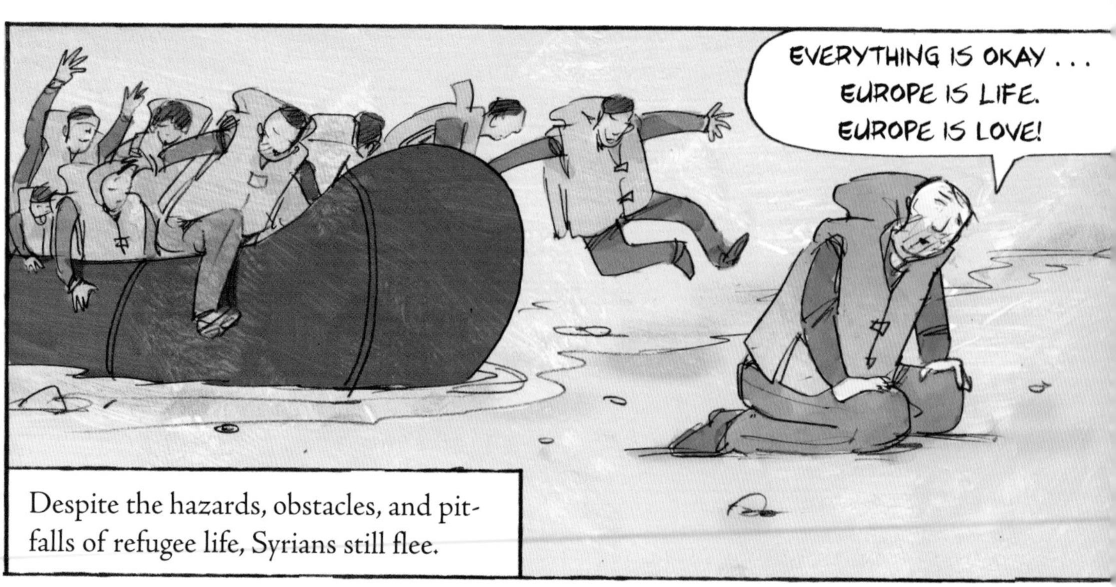
EVERYTHING IS OKAY . . .
EUROPE IS LIFE.
EUROPE IS LOVE!

Despite the hazards, obstacles, and pitfalls of refugee life, Syrians still flee.

But Europe's—and the world's—"love" buckles beneath the huge exodus.

Turkey, Jordan, and Lebanon weary of the drain of food, electricity, and water by the refugees. They complain Syrians steal jobs. Most of the patients in Turkish hospitals are Syrians. Jordan's and Lebanon's economies stumble at the cost of taking in so many new residents.

Lebanese curse the Syrians.

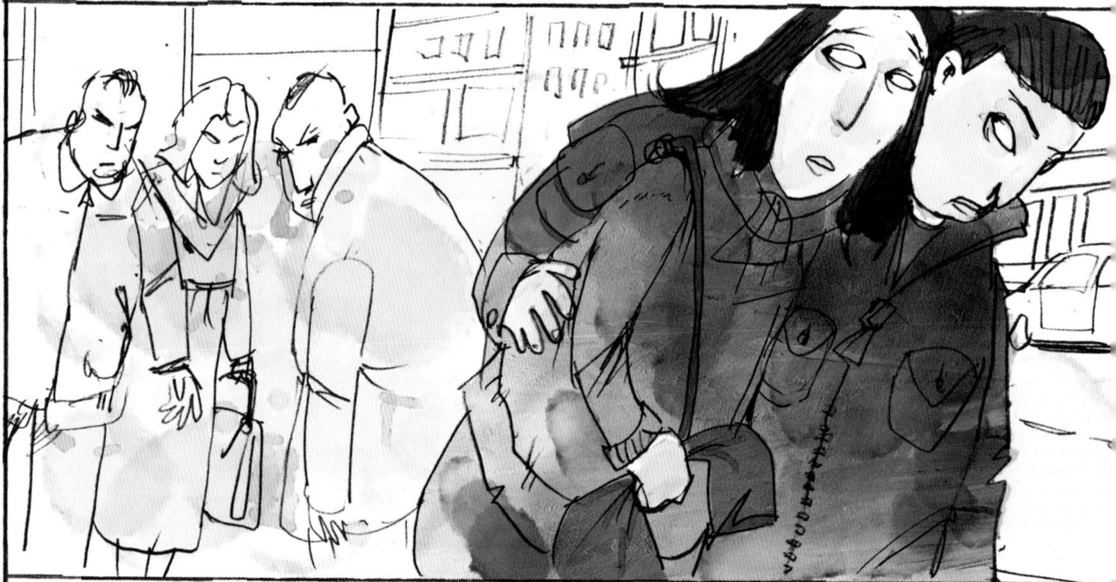

Hungarians fear the thousands of refugees streaming through their country, claiming they threaten jobs and security.

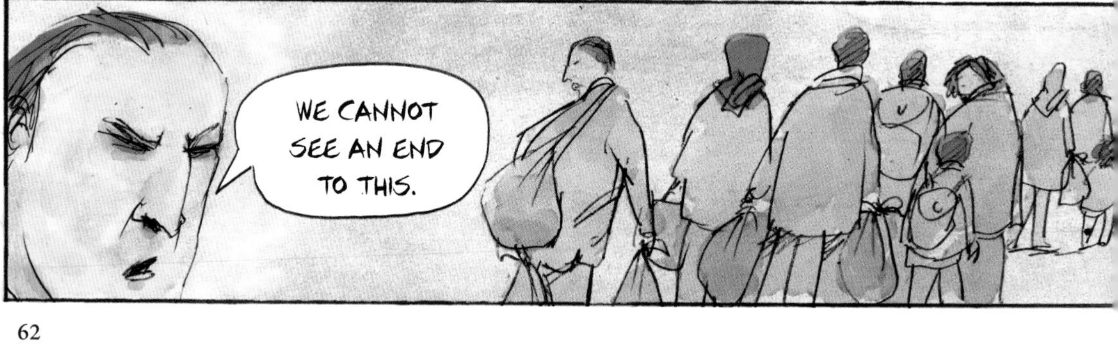
WE CANNOT
SEE AN END
TO THIS.

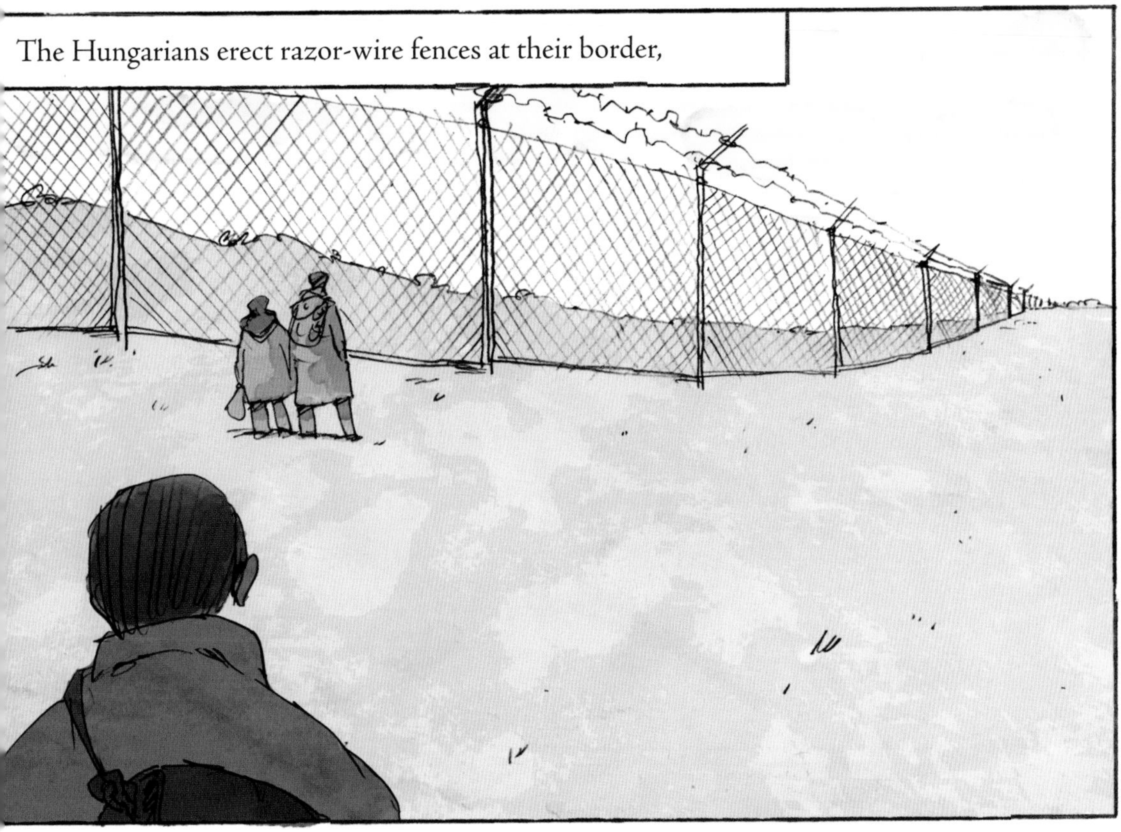
The Hungarians erect razor-wire fences at their border,

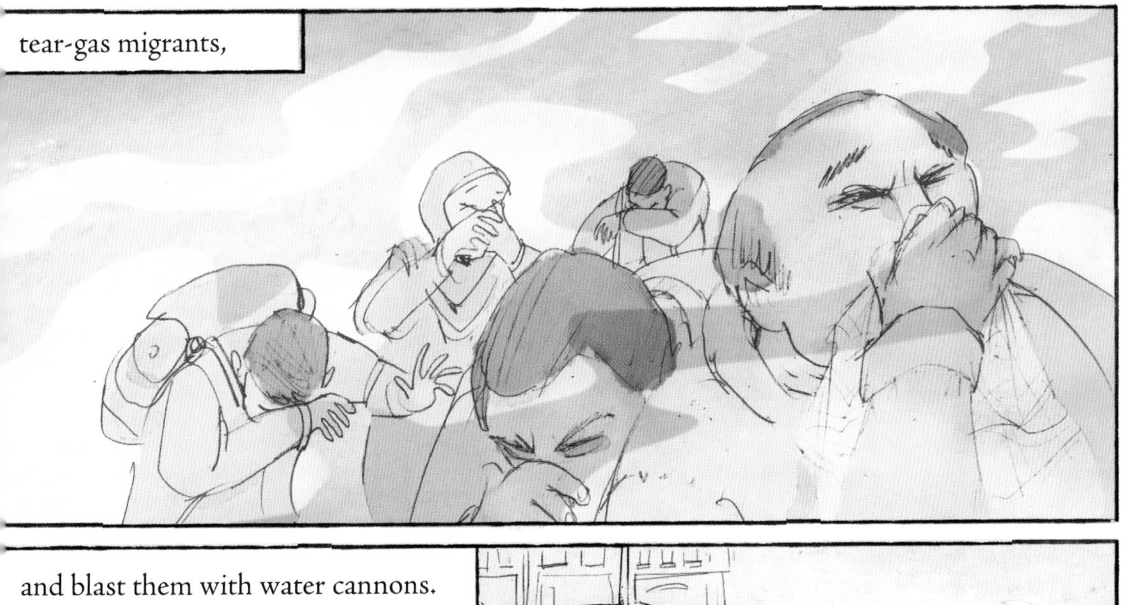
tear-gas migrants,

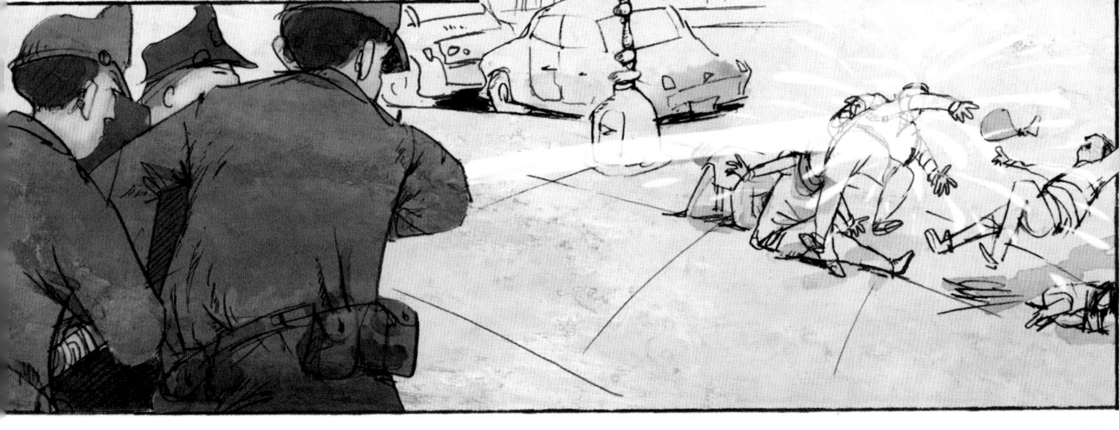
and blast them with water cannons.

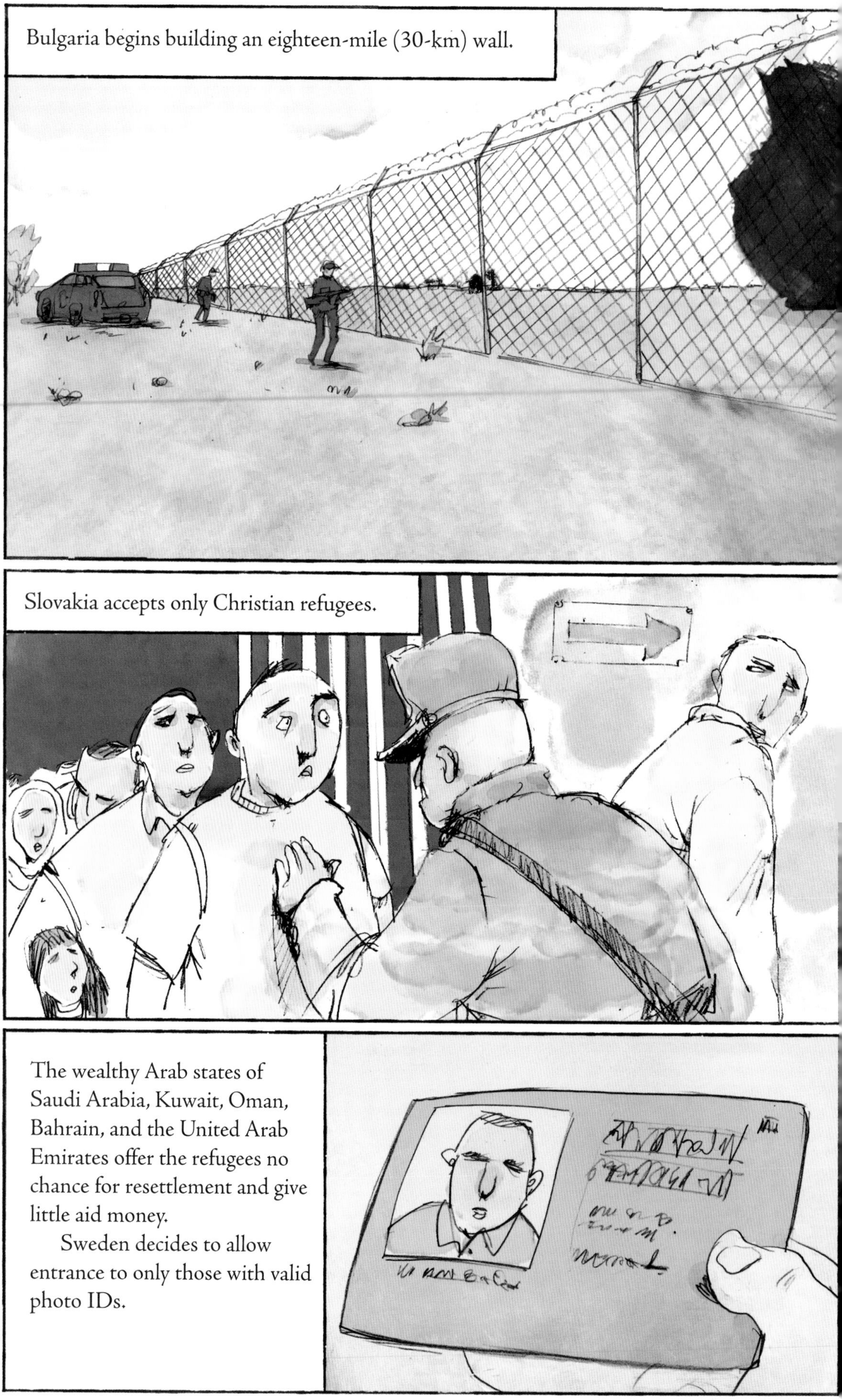
Bulgaria begins building an eighteen-mile (30-km) wall.
Slovakia accepts only Christian refugees.
The wealthy Arab states of Saudi Arabia, Kuwait, Oman, Bahrain, and the United Arab Emirates offer the refugees no chance for resettlement and give little aid money.
Sweden decides to allow entrance to only those with valid photo IDs.

The generous Germans have given refuge to tens of thousands of refugees, but they also move to slow the refugee flood. Shivering Syrians wait in the rain for German officials to process them a handful at a time.

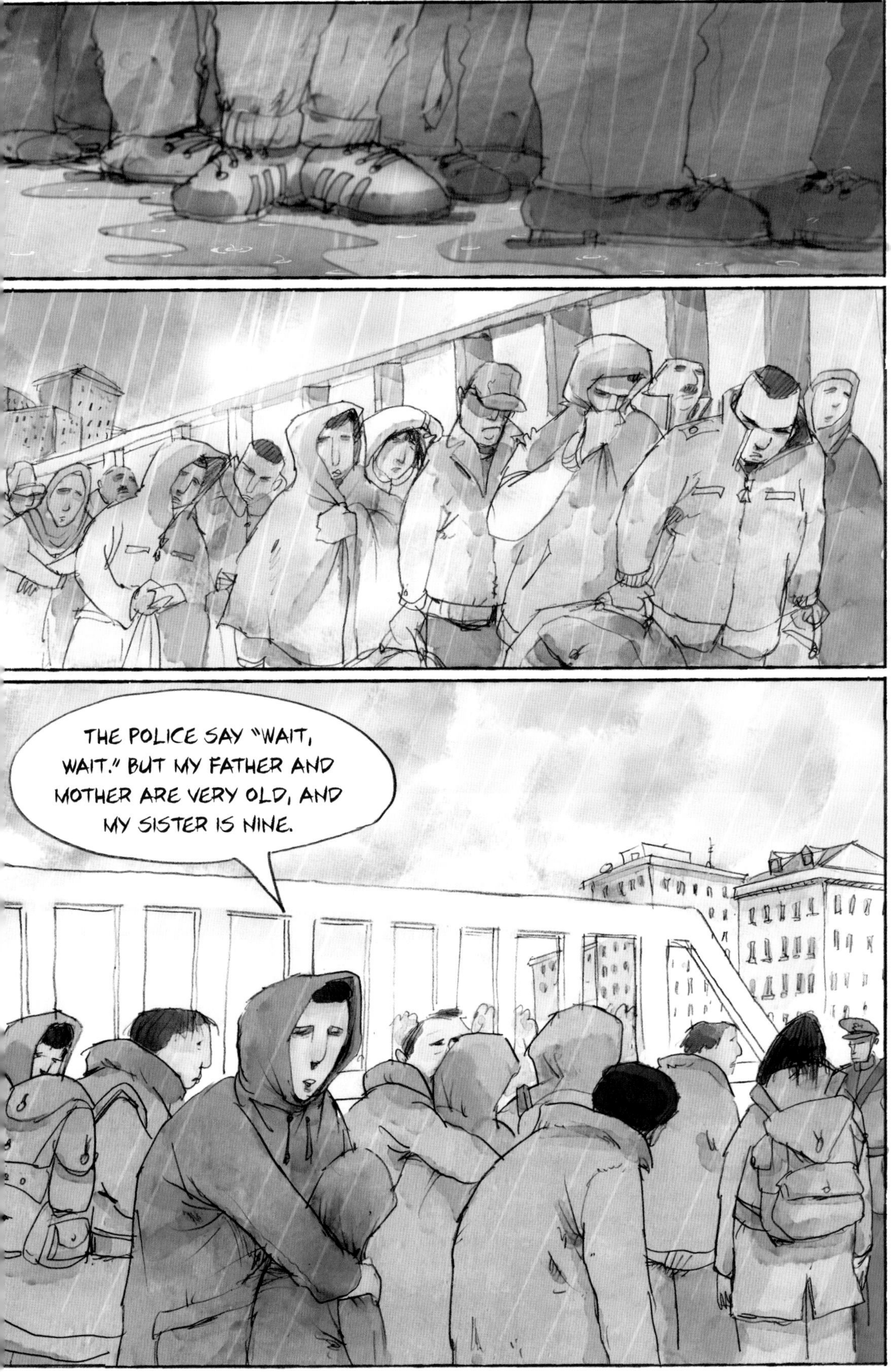
THE POLICE SAY "WAIT, WAIT." BUT MY FATHER AND MOTHER ARE VERY OLD, AND MY SISTER IS NINE.

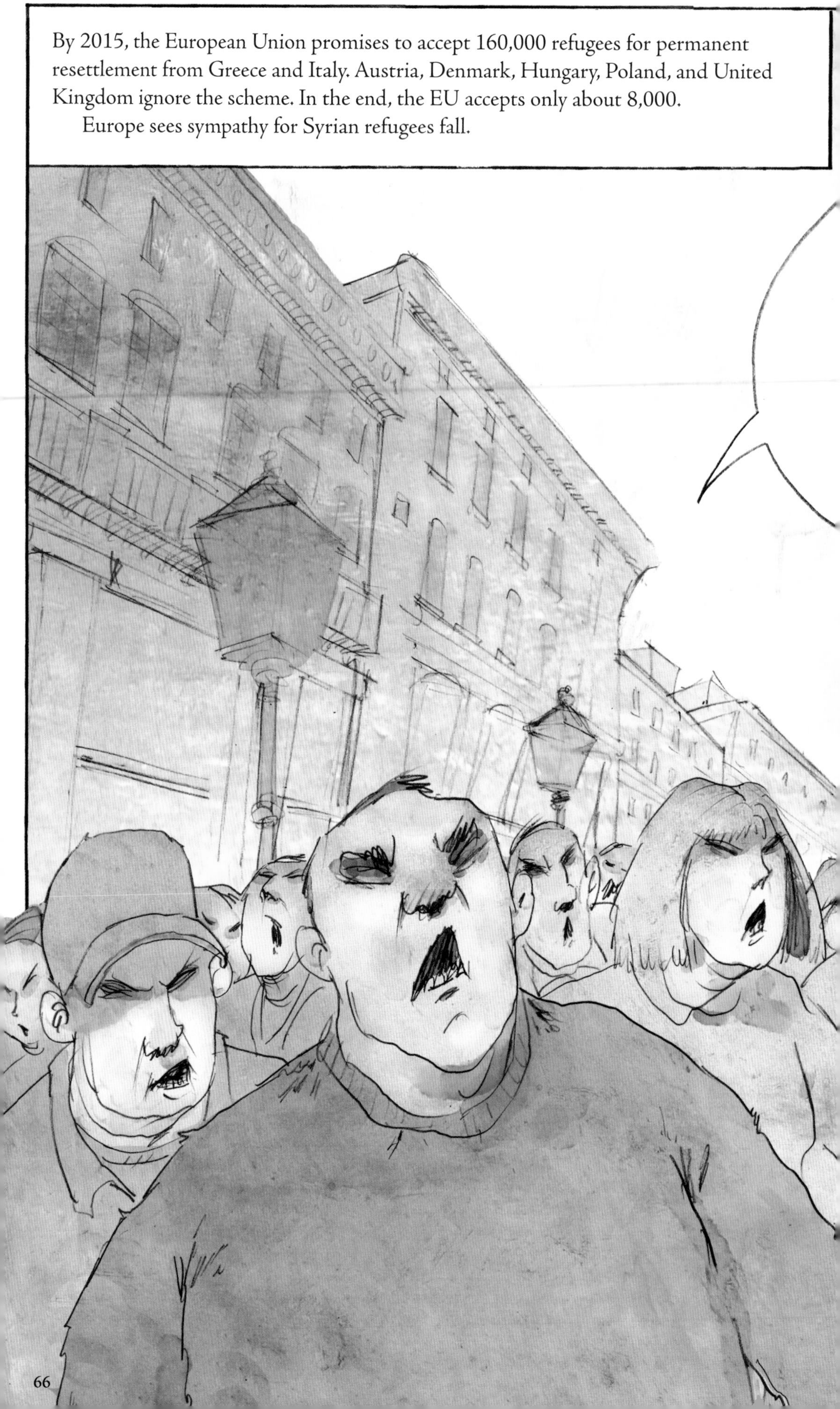
By 2015, the European Union promises to accept 160,000 refugees for permanent resettlement from Greece and Italy. Austria, Denmark, Hungary, Poland, and United Kingdom ignore the scheme. In the end, the EU accepts only about 8,000.
Europe sees sympathy for Syrian refugees fall.

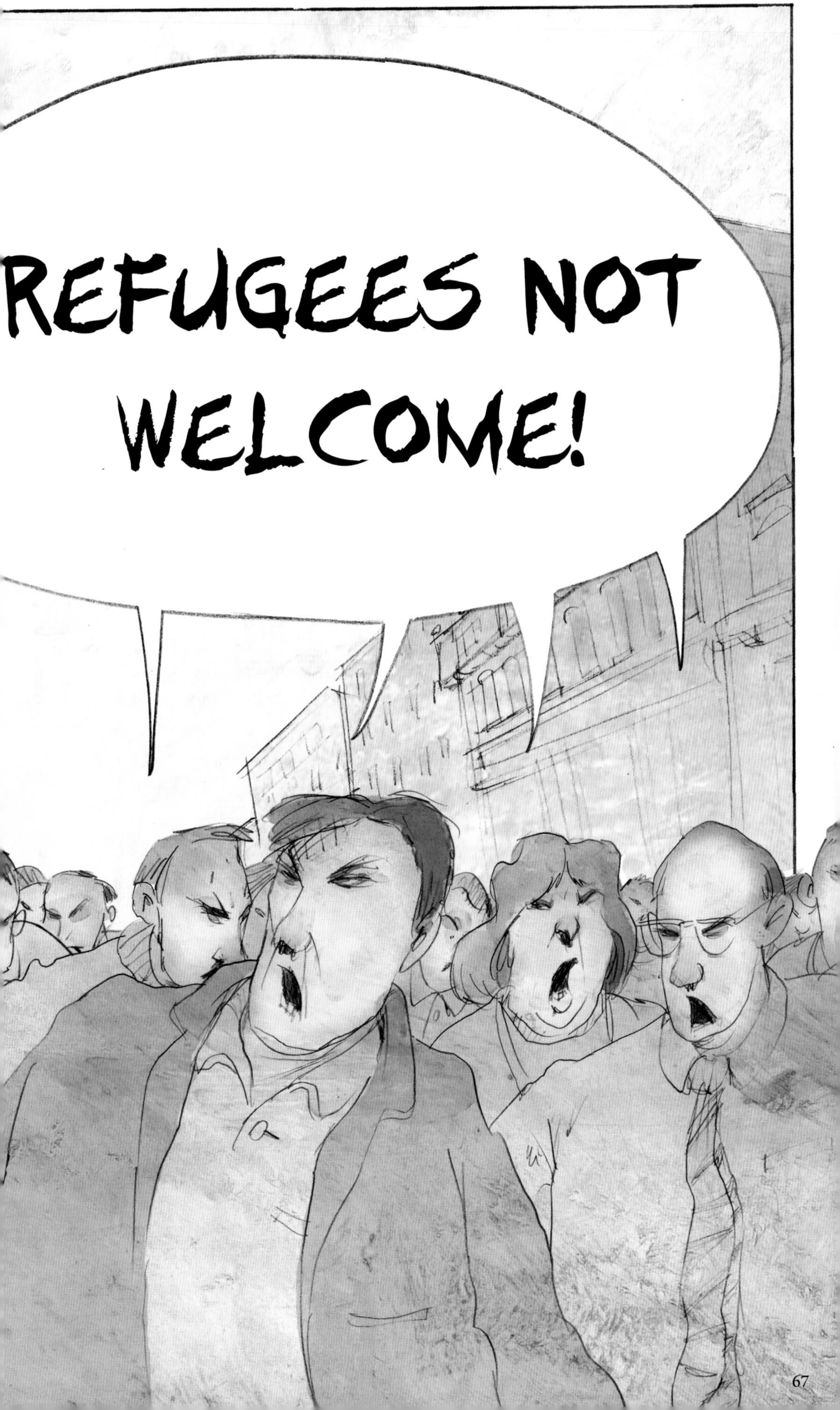
REFUGEES NOT WELCOME!

On November 13, 2015, jihadists murder 130 people in Paris, France. It is the latest act of violence by jihadists who have struck around the world, including the September 11, 2001, attack on the United States. The Paris killers were mostly Belgian and French. Some had fought in Syria and used the refugees' trail to sneak back home.

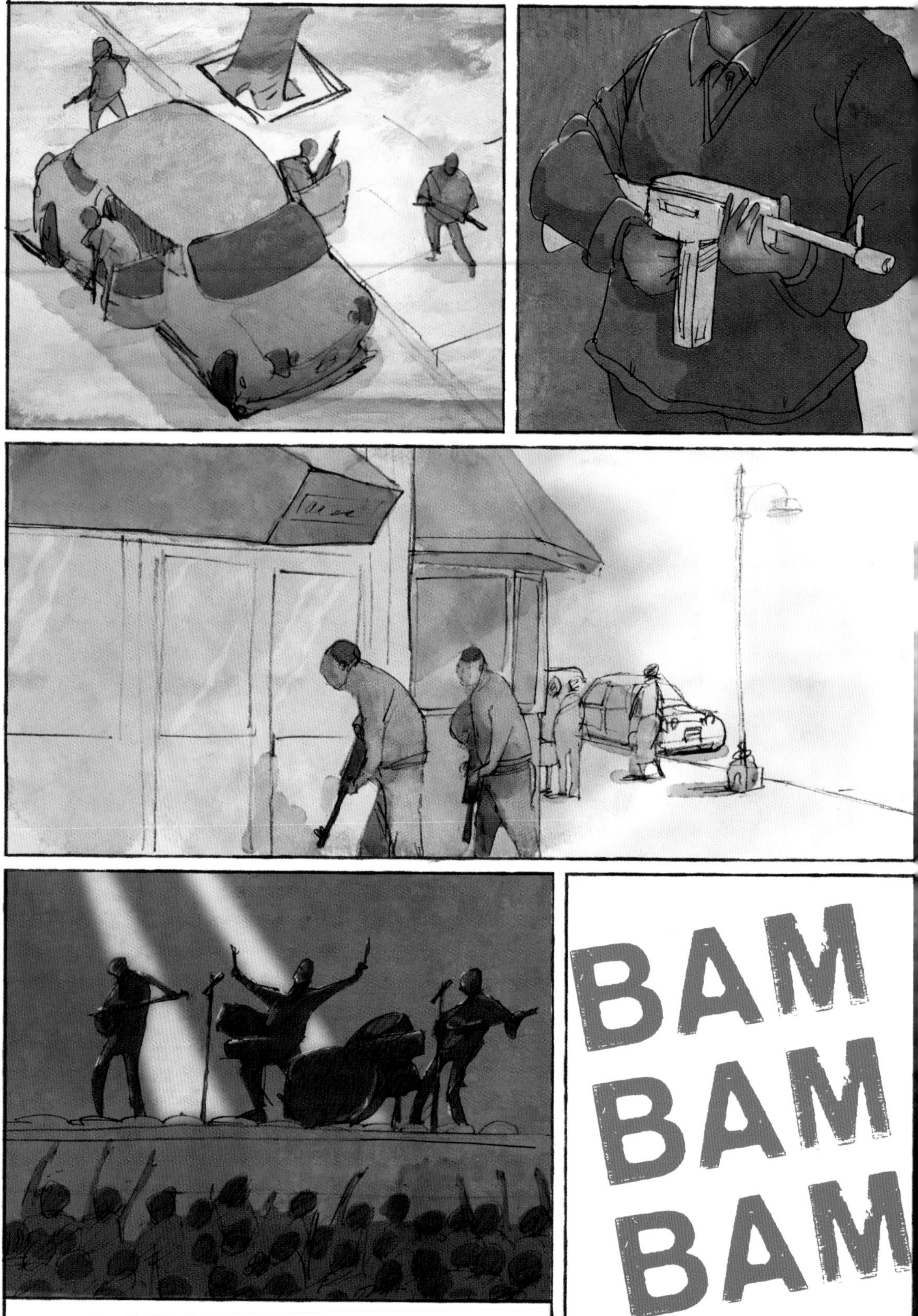
BAM
BAM
BAM

Bataclan Theater

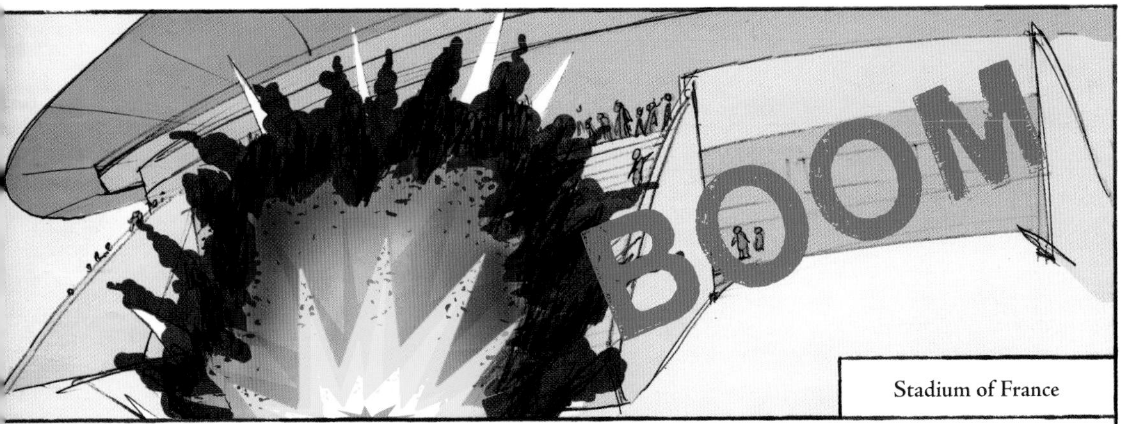
BOOM

Stadium of France

The Paris attack by a ruthless few Muslims sharpens suspicion and fear of *all* followers of Islam. Some people across Europe and America come to believe Syrians and Islam are a threat to their culture and values.

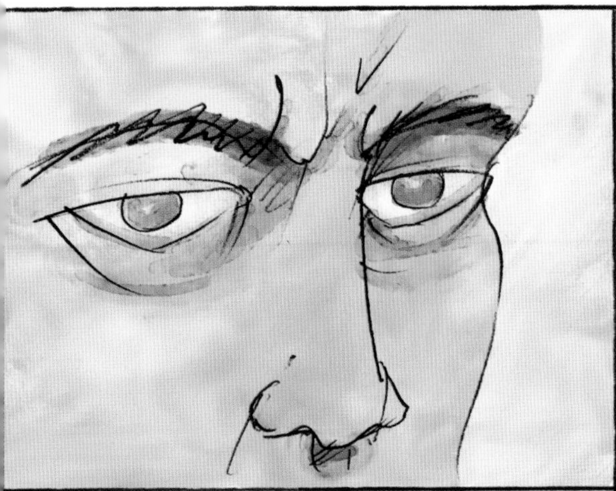

Hungarian prime minister Viktor Orbán: "For us, Europe is at stake today: Europeans' way of life; European values; the survival or demise of European nations, or rather, their transformation beyond recognition."

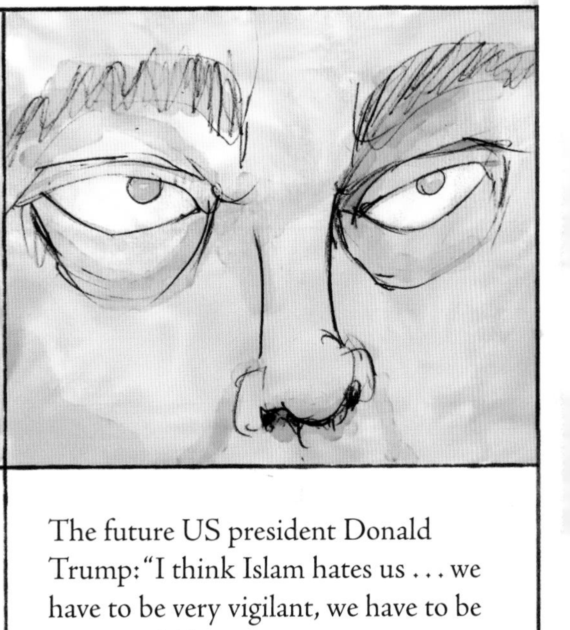

The future US president Donald Trump: "I think Islam hates us . . . we have to be very vigilant, we have to be very careful."

A majority of state governors in America also see danger in the Syrian refugees and oppose their resettlement despite the two years of required screening by the UN, FBI, and Defense Department—among others—before being accepted into the United States.

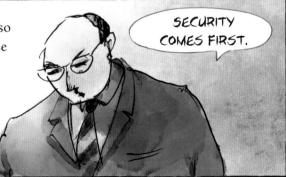

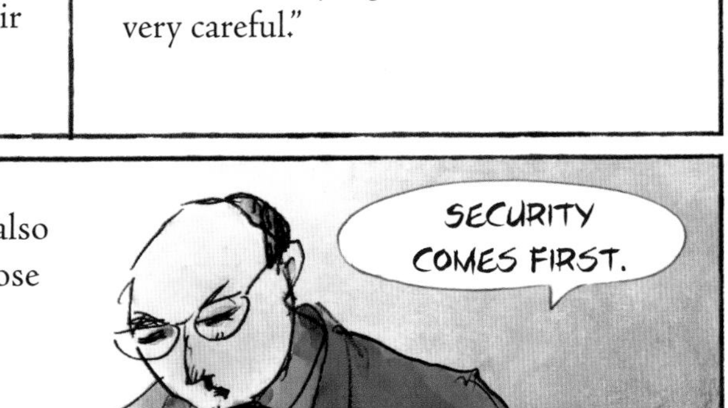
SECURITY COMES FIRST.

Ten thousand refugees—mostly children—are relocated in America, a fraction of the 318,000 Vietnamese and 120,000 Cuban refugees America once welcomed.

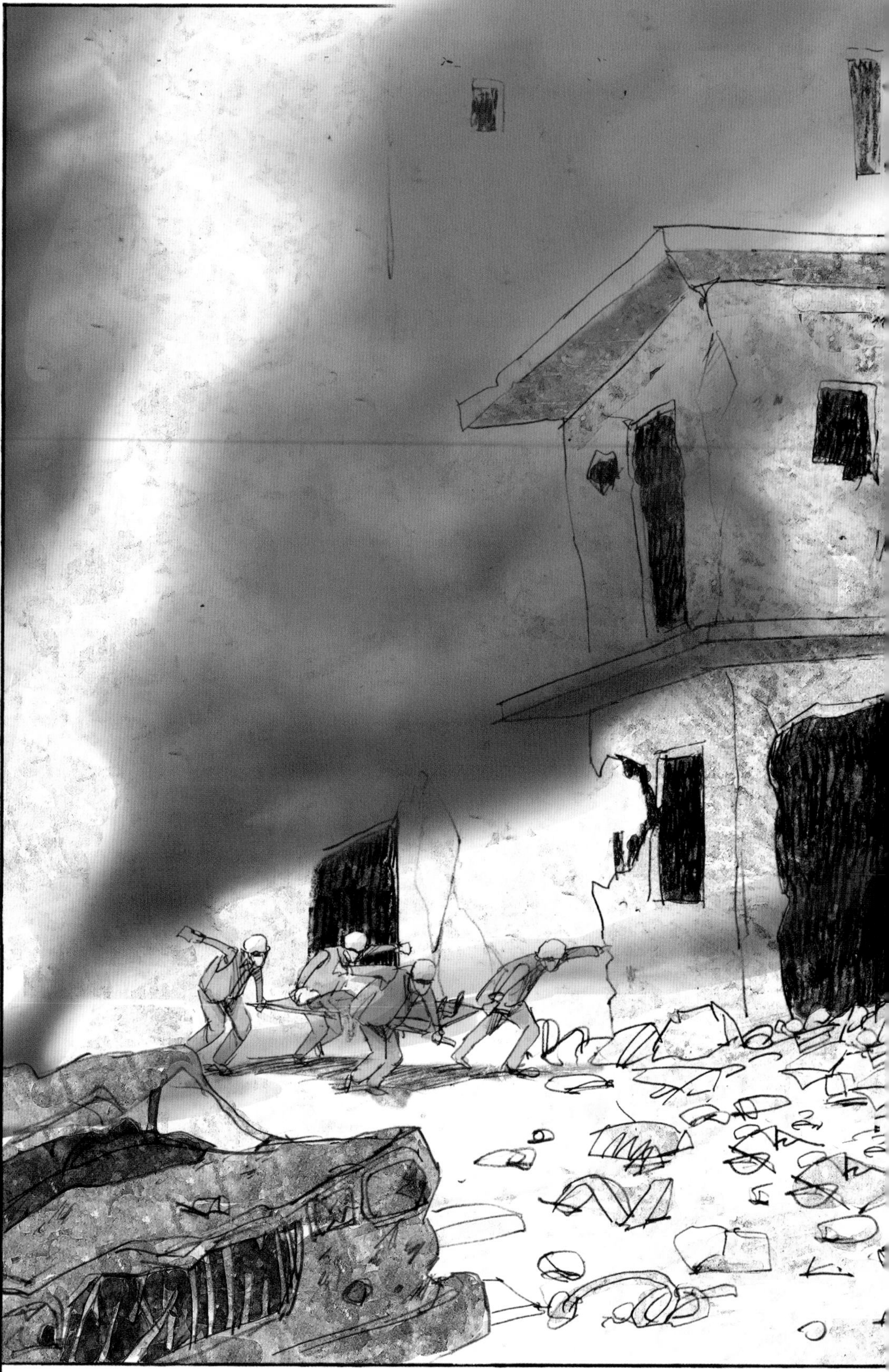

By 2015, Syrian civilians who stayed behind are trapped. Assad drops barrel-bombs and destroys buildings and people while anti-Assad jihadists take time out of fighting to murder any who disagree with them.

People who had hoped to wait out the conflict decide it's time to escape.

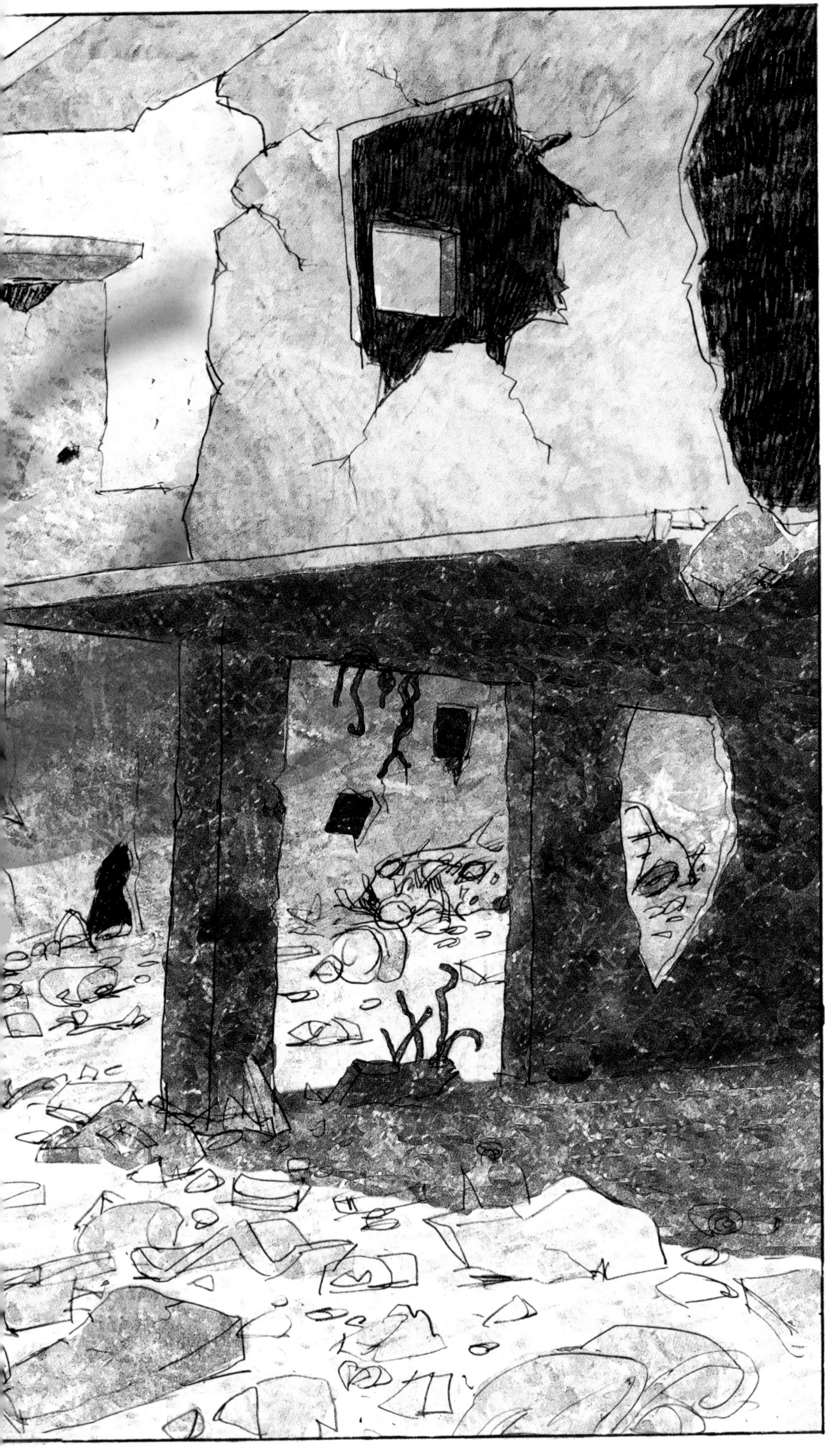

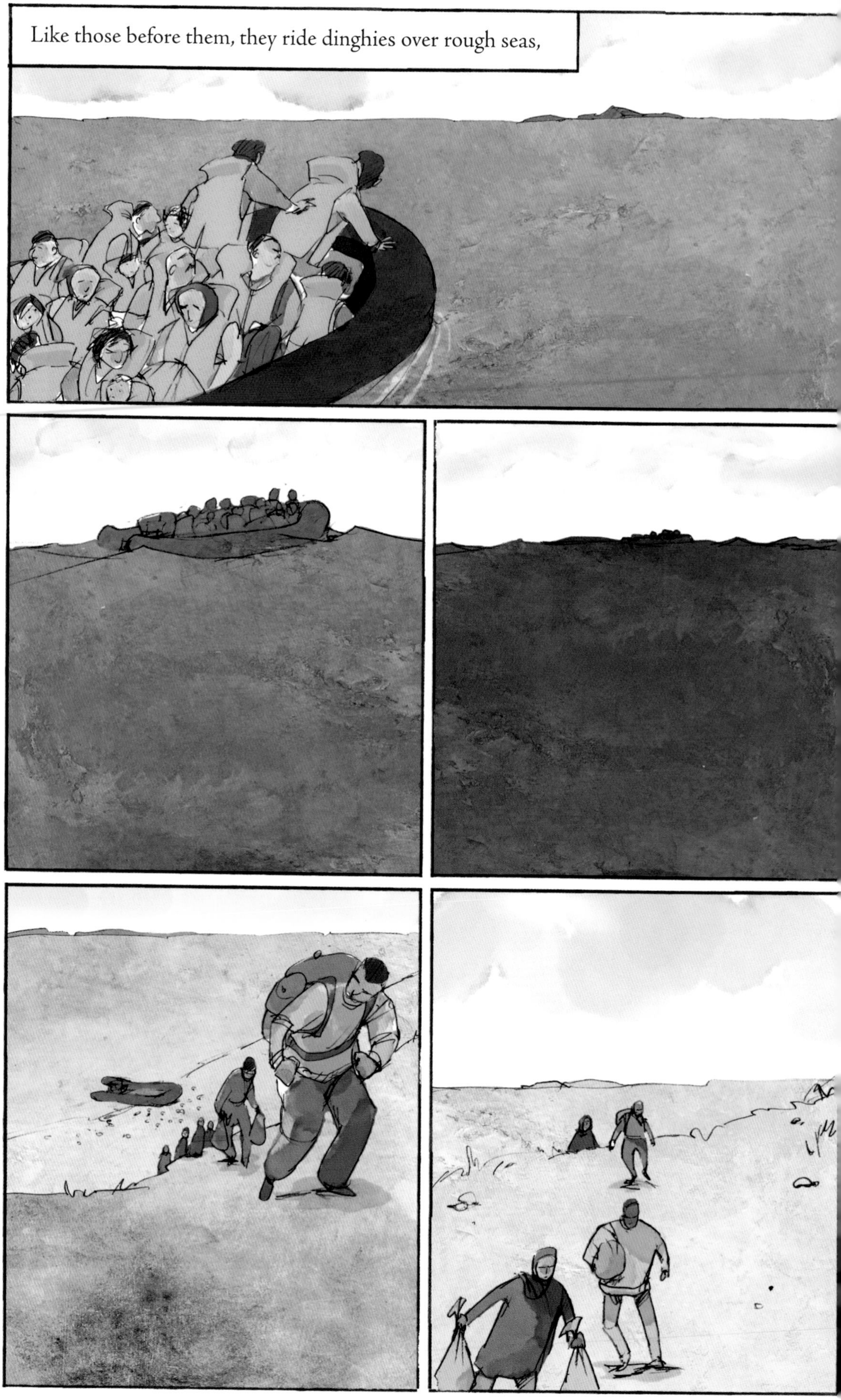
Like those before them, they ride dinghies over rough seas,

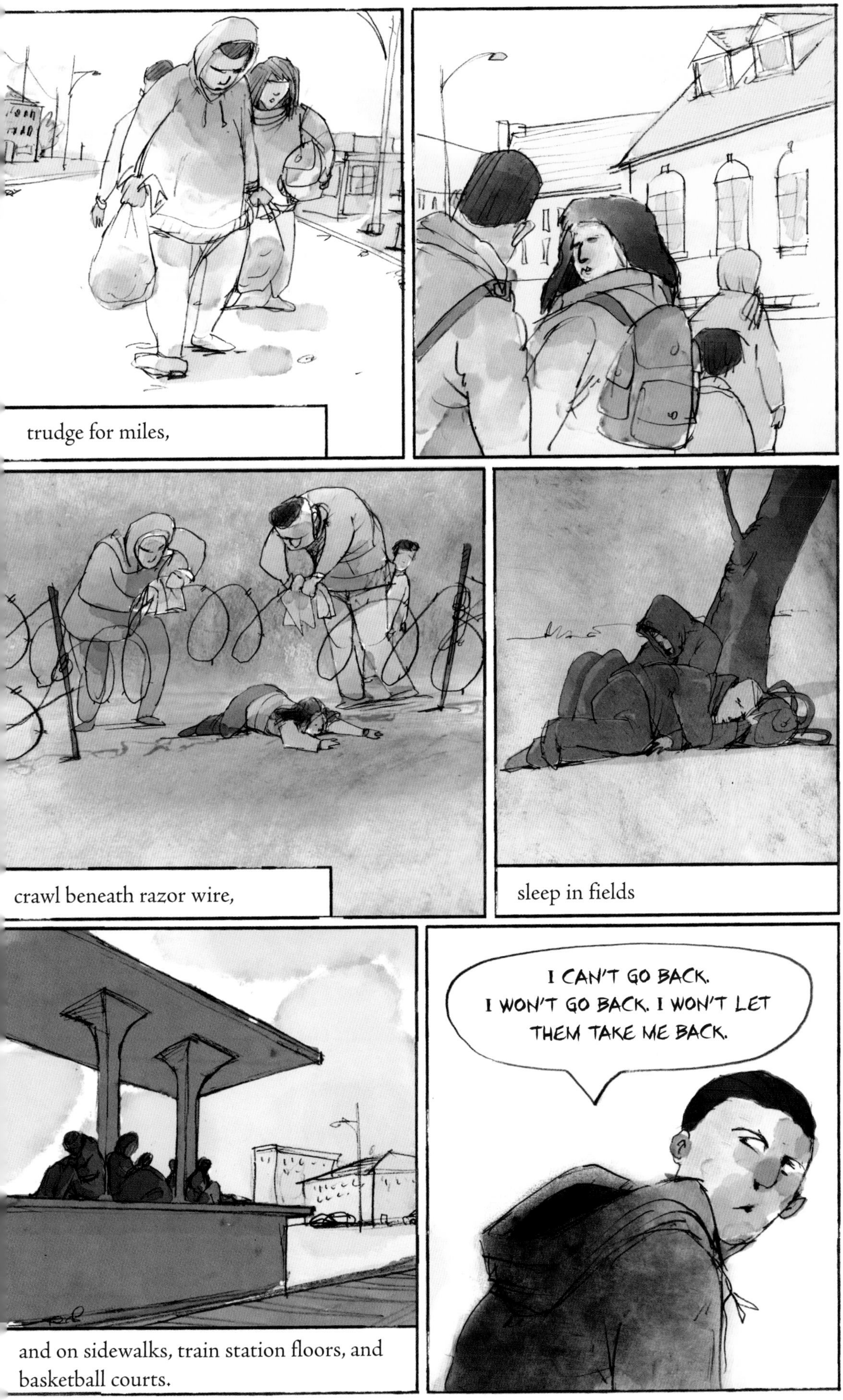
trudge for miles,
crawl beneath razor wire,
sleep in fields
and on sidewalks, train station floors, and basketball courts.
I CAN'T GO BACK. I WON'T GO BACK. I WON'T LET THEM TAKE ME BACK.

In 2016, the European Union and Turkey decide refugees sneaking into Greece by boat from Turkey will be returned to Turkey. The Europeans promise to resettle *officially* registered Syrians from Turkish camps, a tiny fraction of all the refugees in Turkey.

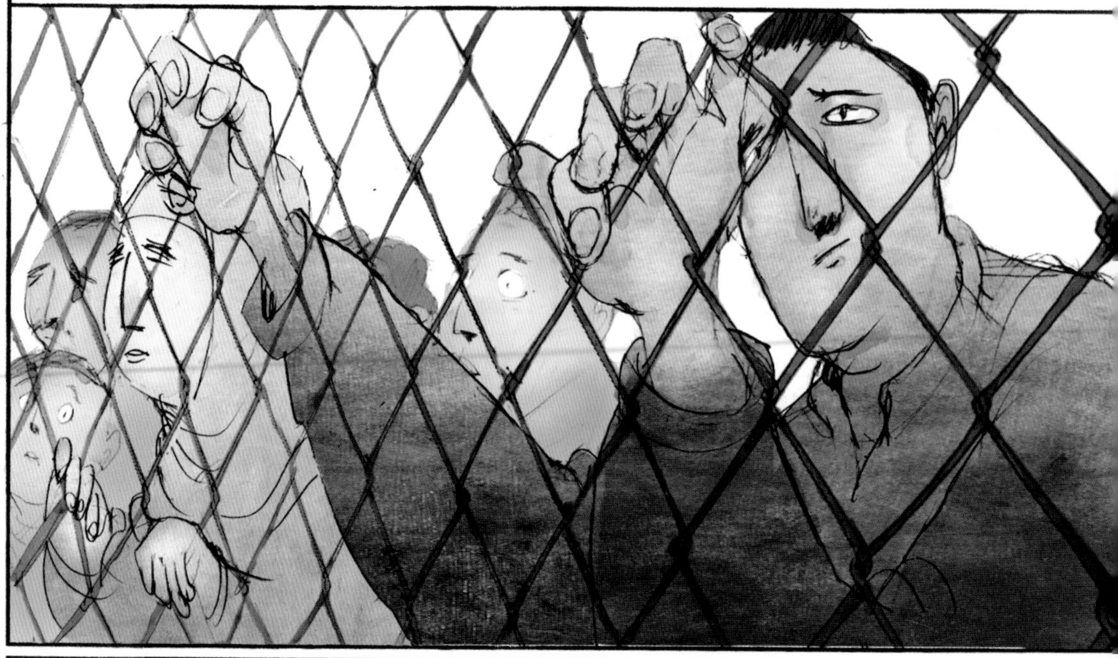

Borders all over Europe tighten or close to refugees.

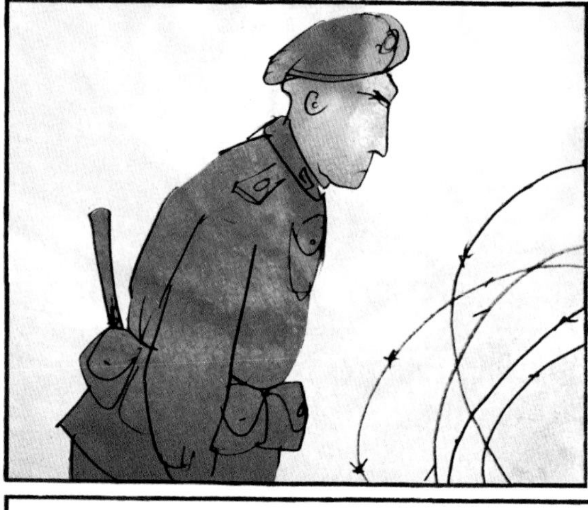

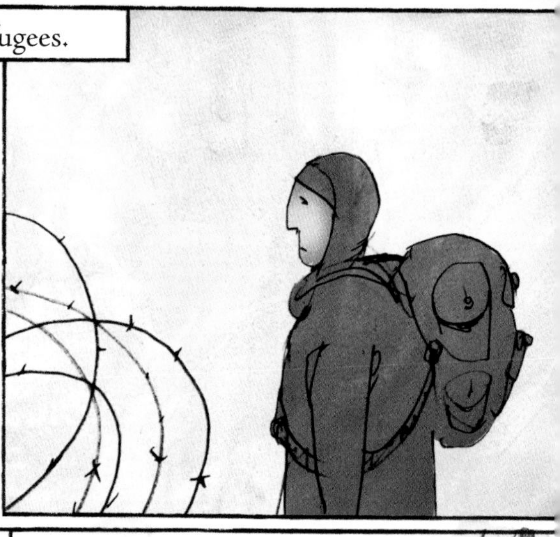

Paths refugees once traveled are now shut.

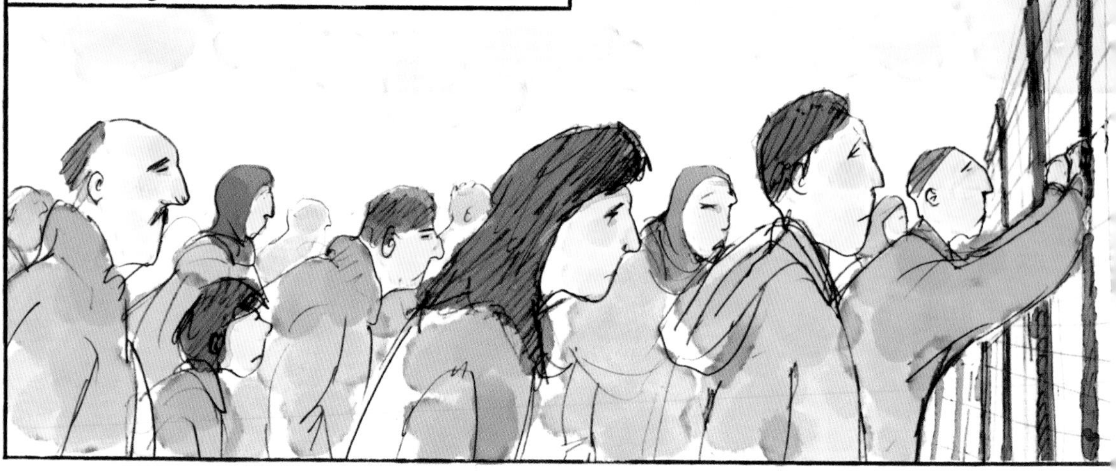

Forty-four thousand are stranded in Greece. It is a "warehouse of souls."

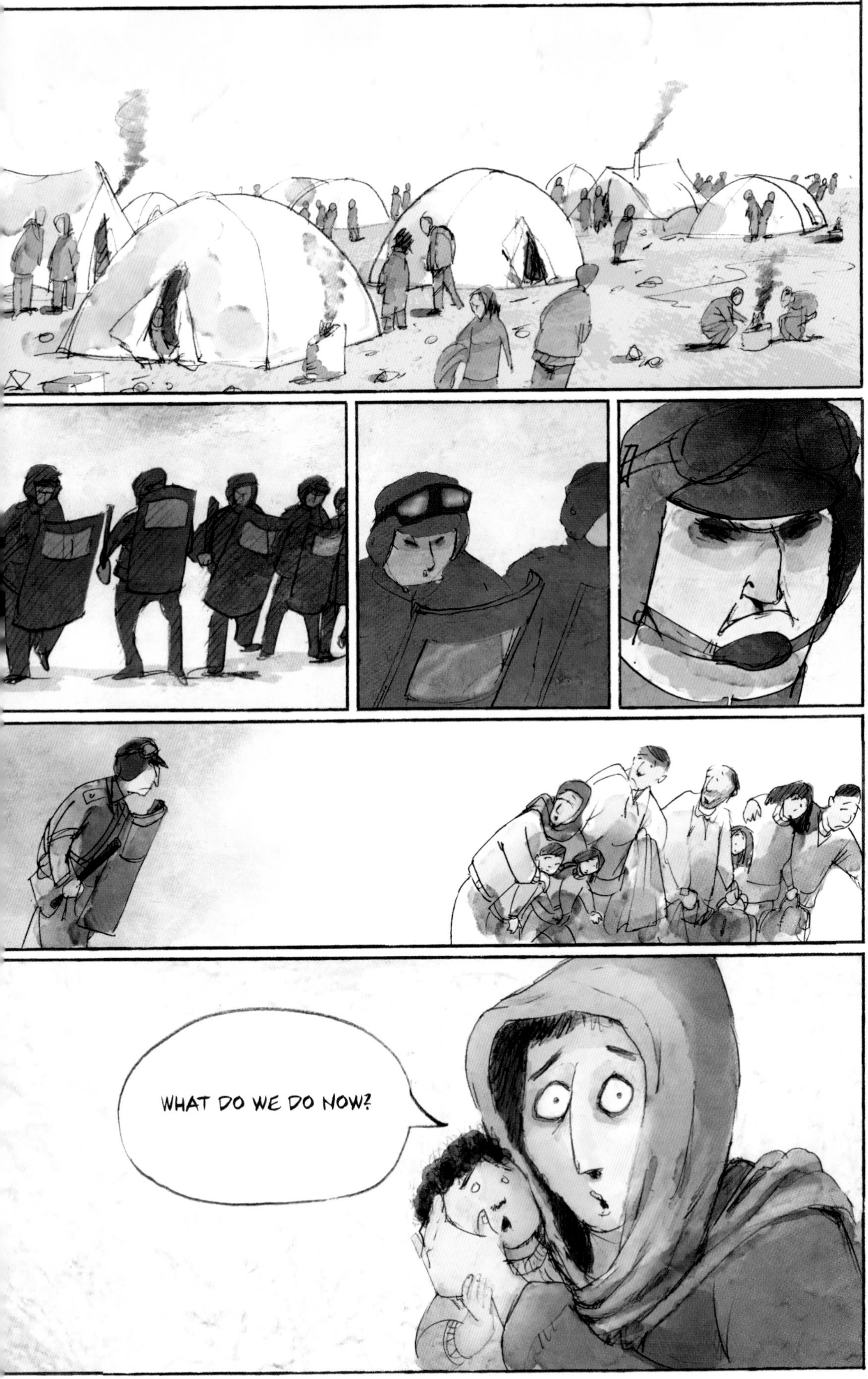

WHAT DO WE DO NOW?

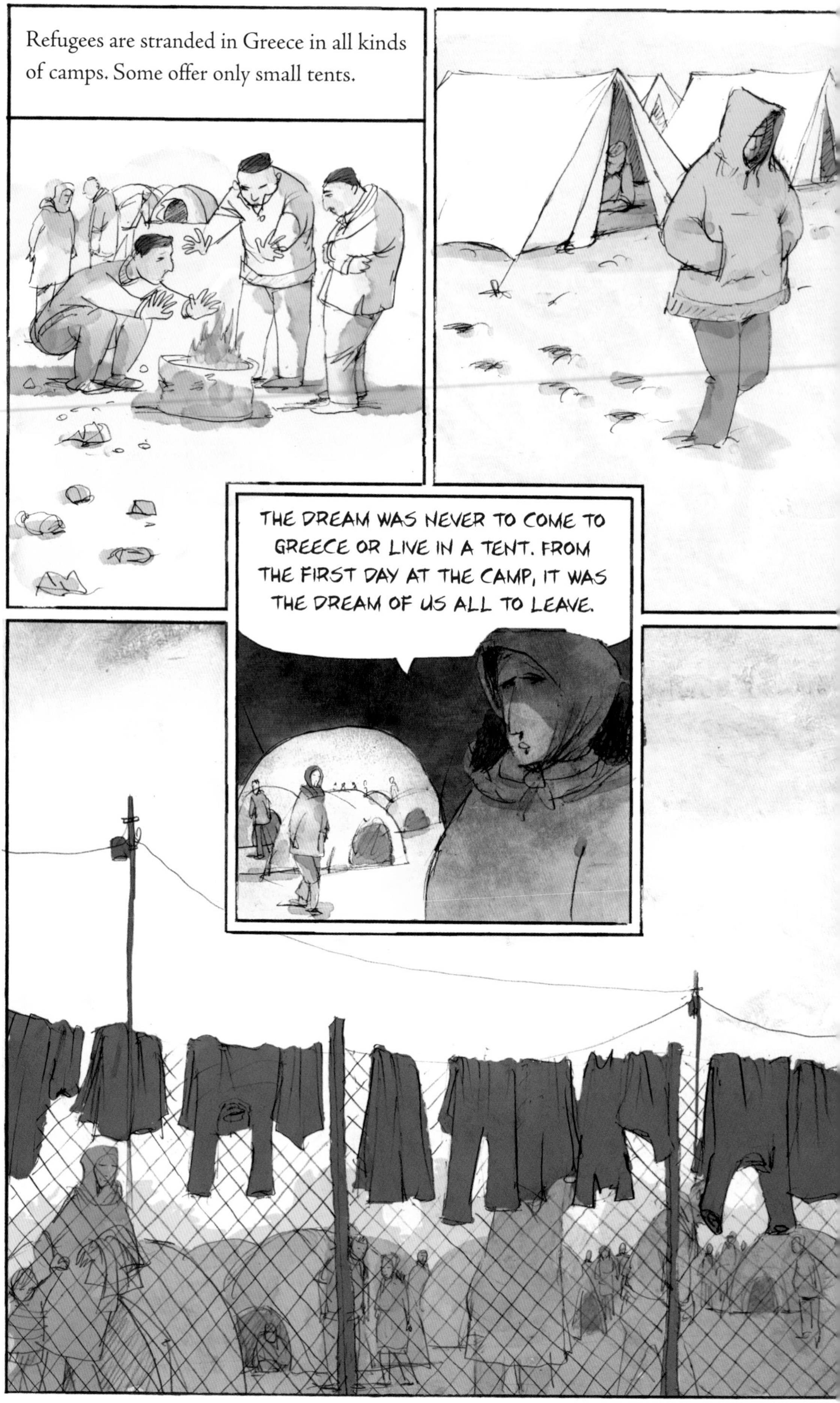
Refugees are stranded in Greece in all kinds of camps. Some offer only small tents.
THE DREAM WAS NEVER TO COME TO GREECE OR LIVE IN A TENT. FROM THE FIRST DAY AT THE CAMP, IT WAS THE DREAM OF US ALL TO LEAVE.

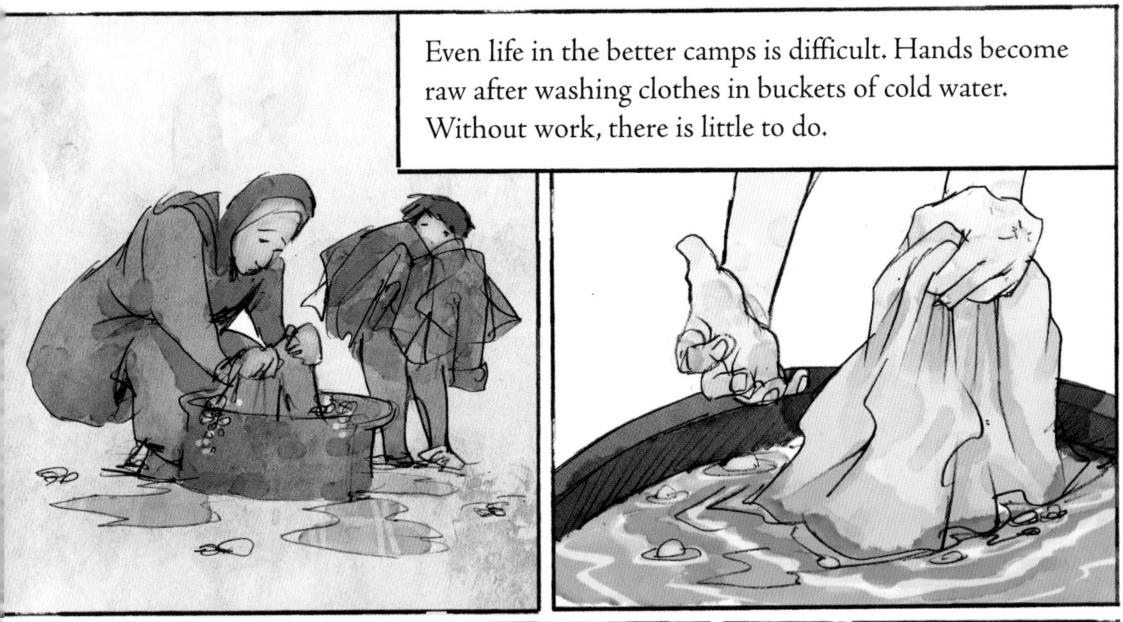
Even life in the better camps is difficult. Hands become raw after washing clothes in buckets of cold water. Without work, there is little to do.

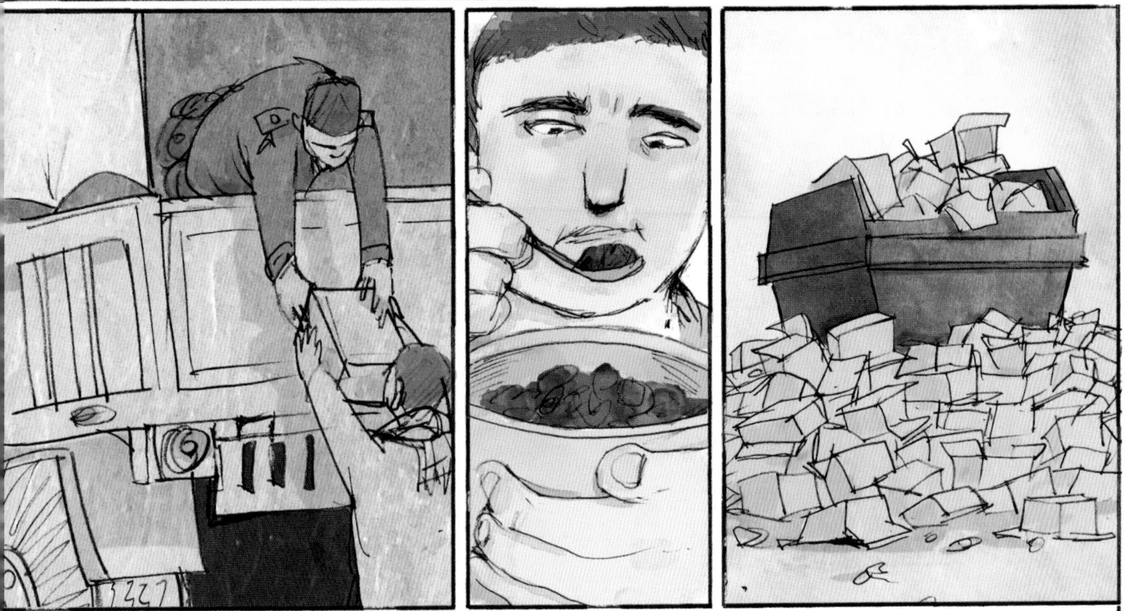

Food provided by the Greek army is monotonous and, at times, rejected by the refugees; hundreds of meals can end up in the garbage.

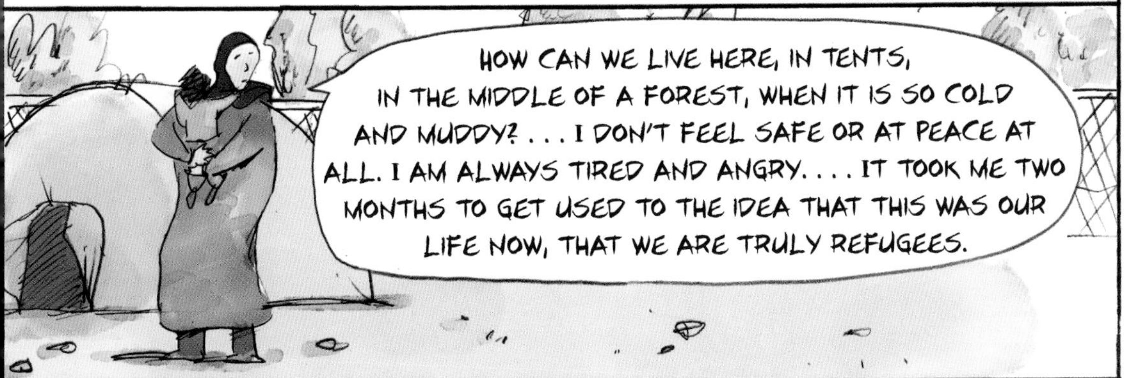
HOW CAN WE LIVE HERE, IN TENTS, IN THE MIDDLE OF A FOREST, WHEN IT IS SO COLD AND MUDDY? . . . I DON'T FEEL SAFE OR AT PEACE AT ALL. I AM ALWAYS TIRED AND ANGRY. . . . IT TOOK ME TWO MONTHS TO GET USED TO THE IDEA THAT THIS WAS OUR LIFE NOW, THAT WE ARE TRULY REFUGEES.

Refugee camps are like small towns and require around-the-clock monitoring. But some of the large charitable organizations running them work only regular nine-to-five business hours and take weekends off.

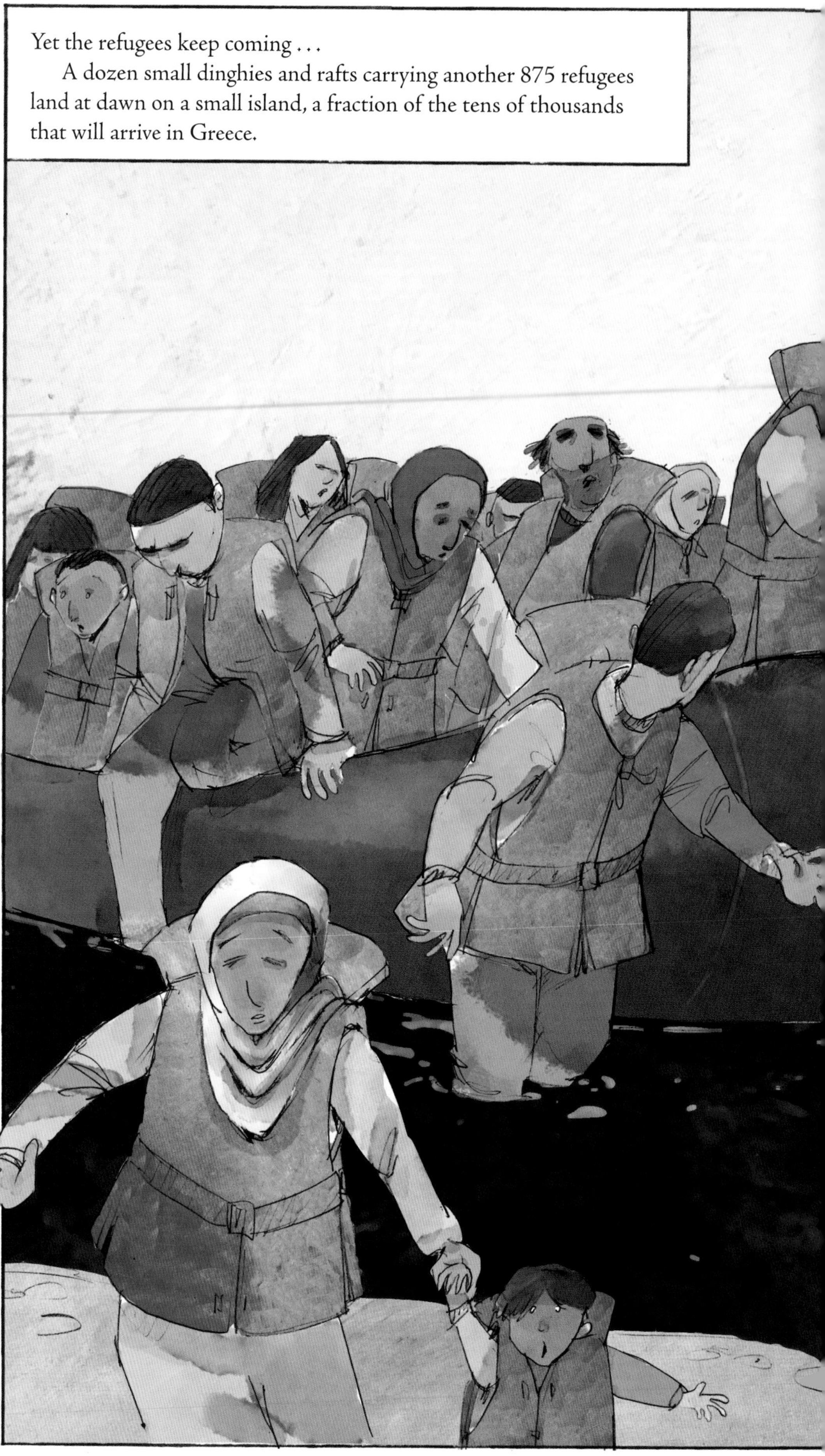
Yet the refugees keep coming . . .
A dozen small dinghies and rafts carrying another 875 refugees land at dawn on a small island, a fraction of the tens of thousands that will arrive in Greece.

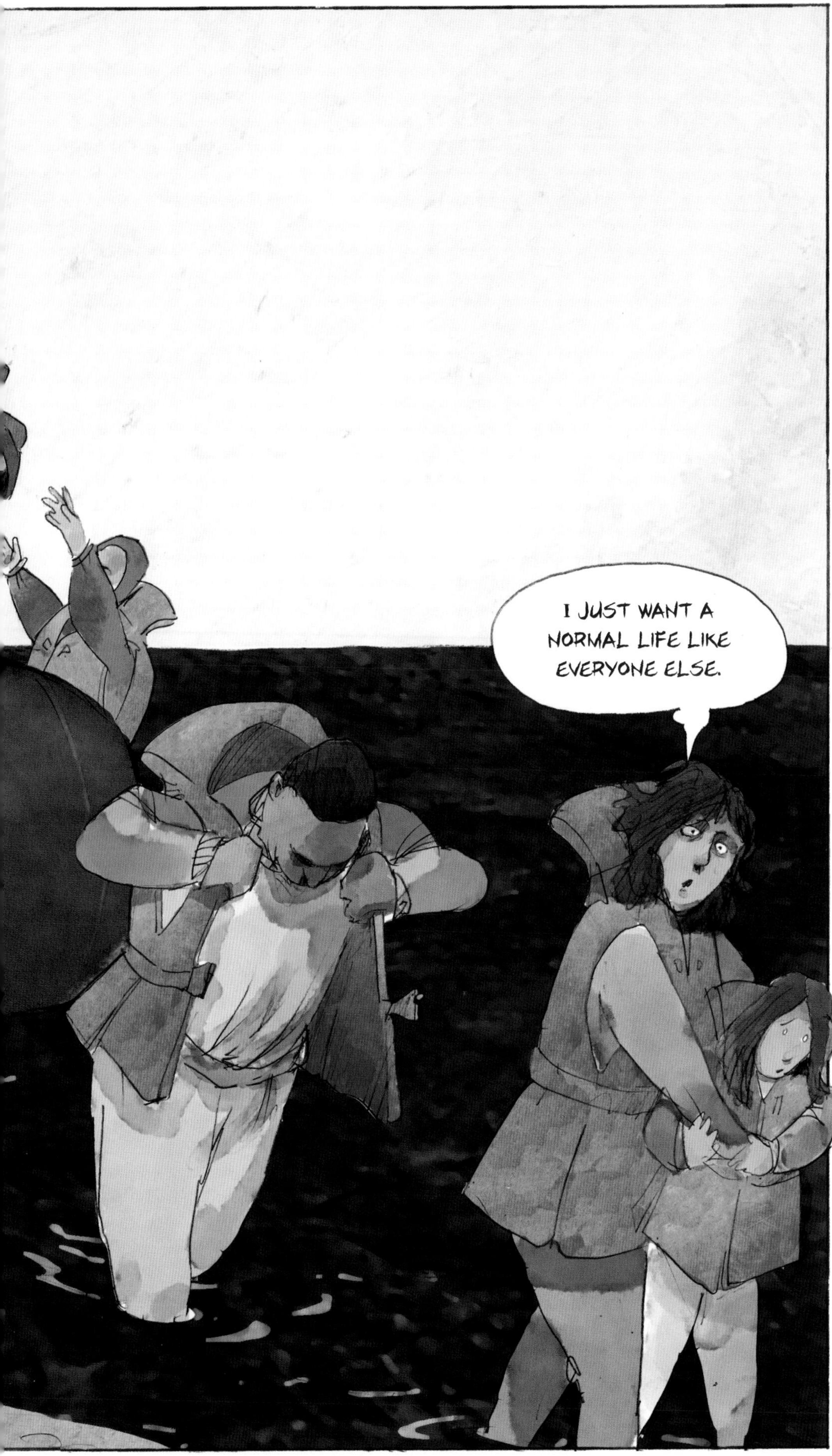
I JUST WANT A NORMAL LIFE LIKE EVERYONE ELSE.

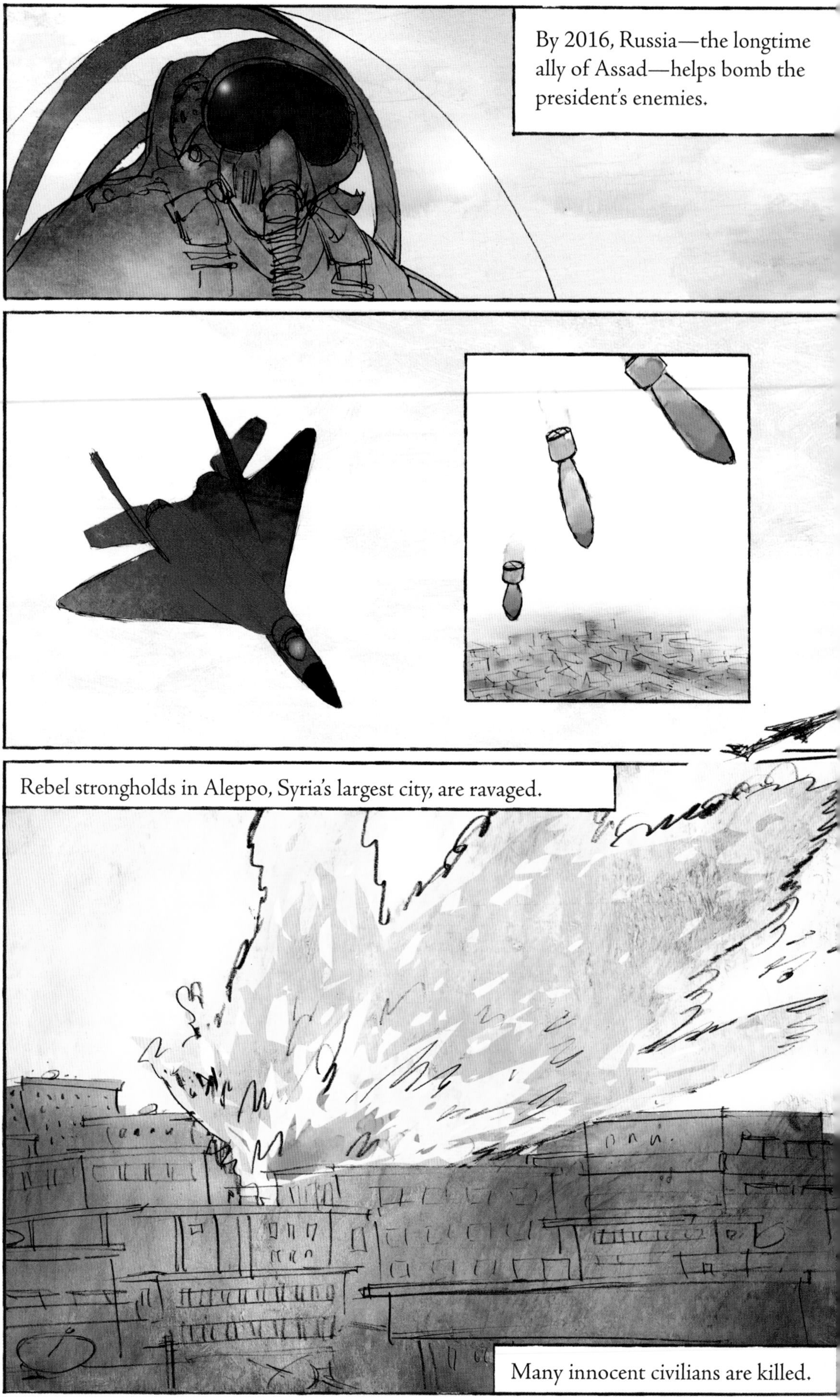
By 2016, Russia—the longtime ally of Assad—helps bomb the president's enemies.
Rebel strongholds in Aleppo, Syria's largest city, are ravaged.
Many innocent civilians are killed.

Thirty-seven thousand people flee Aleppo. Many race to Turkey, but the border is closed. Attempts to sneak across risk death at the hands of Turkish patrols.

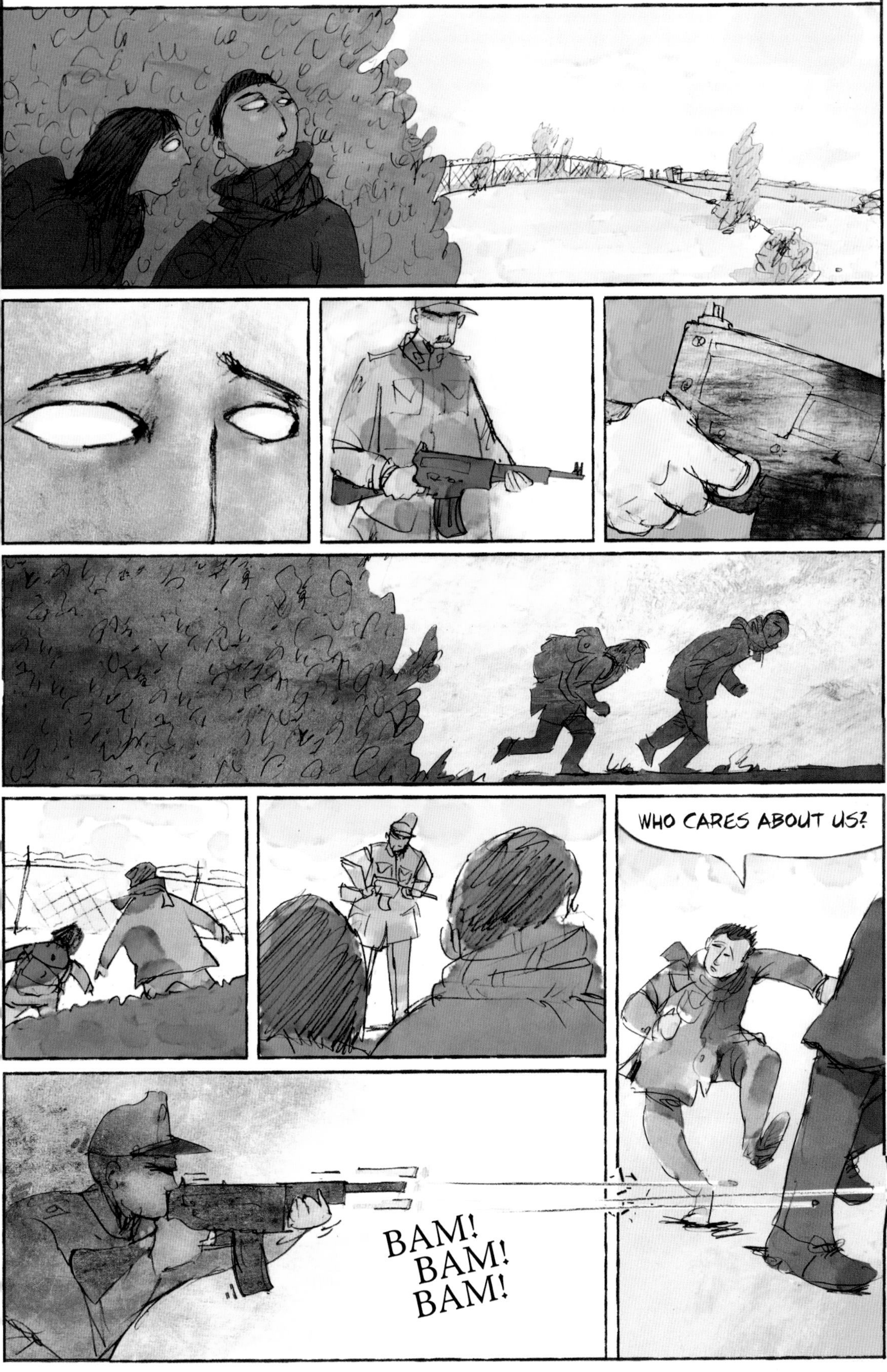
WHO CARES ABOUT US?
BAM! BAM! BAM!

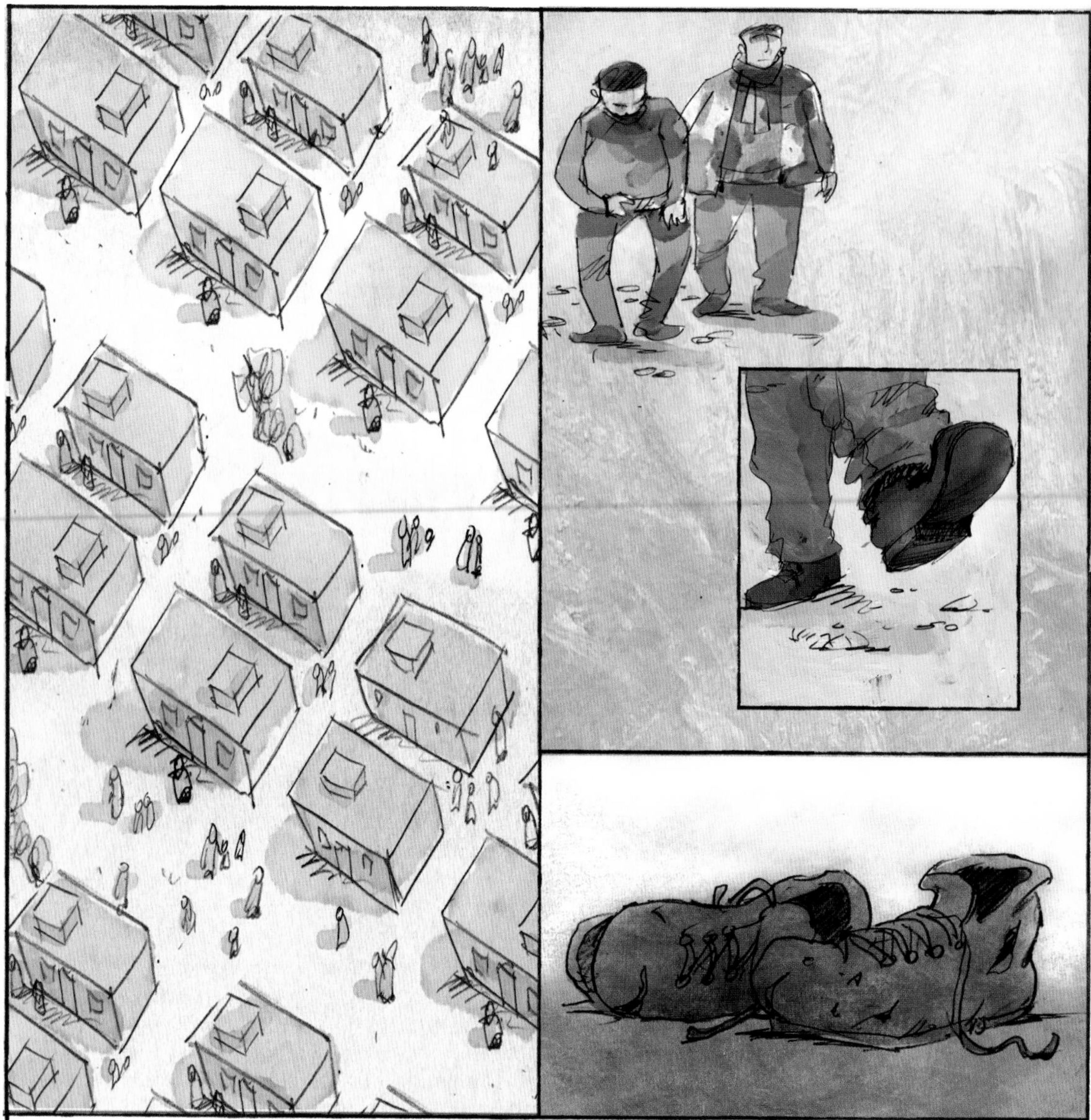

Meanwhile, forty-seven thousand refugees are stranded in Greece, stalled by newly closed borders. In the Greek camps, boredom reigns. With nothing to do, men pace the ground, wearing out their shoes.

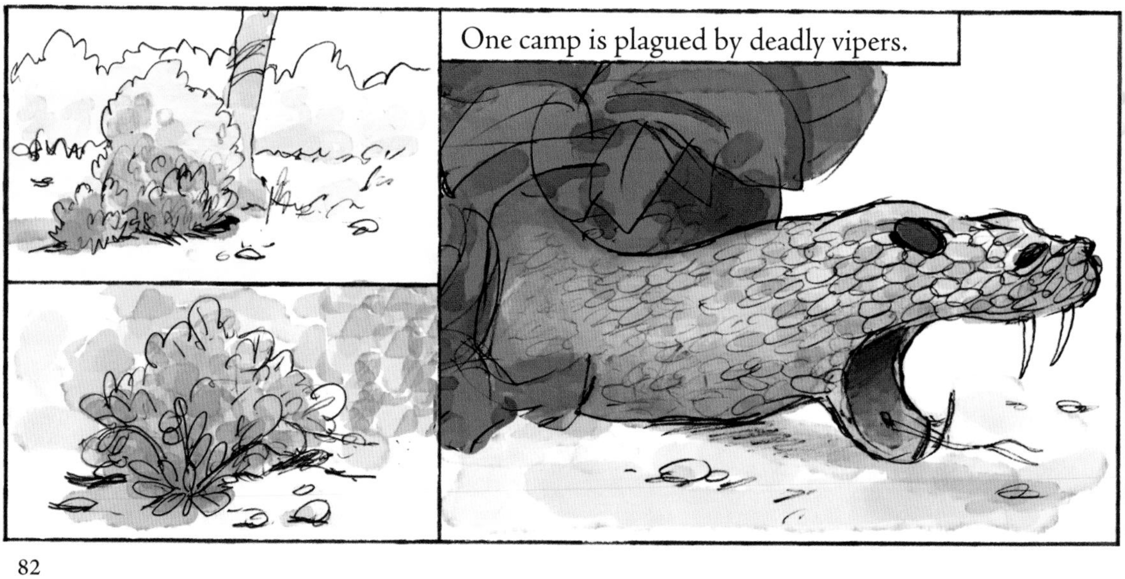
One camp is plagued by deadly vipers.

The Greek government is nearly broke and trash collection is spotty. The piles of garbage are devoured by rats that, in turn, are devoured by the snakes.

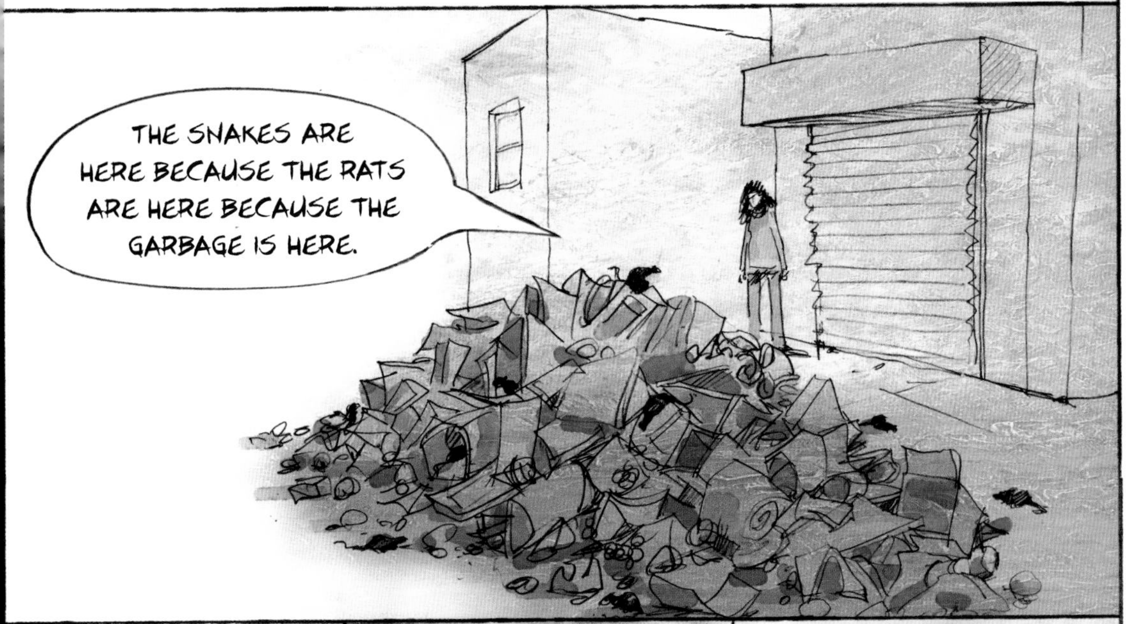
THE SNAKES ARE HERE BECAUSE THE RATS ARE HERE BECAUSE THE GARBAGE IS HERE.

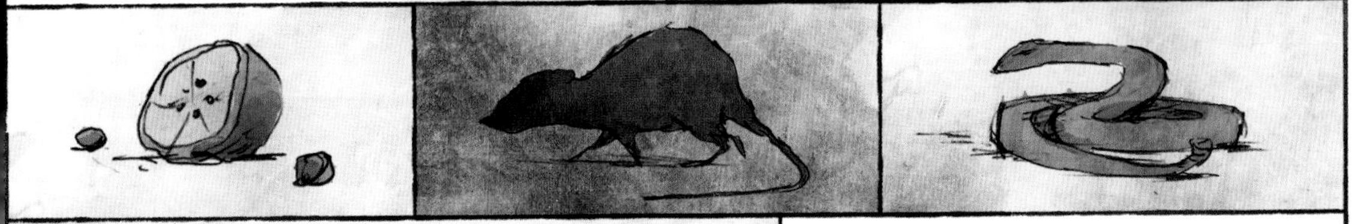

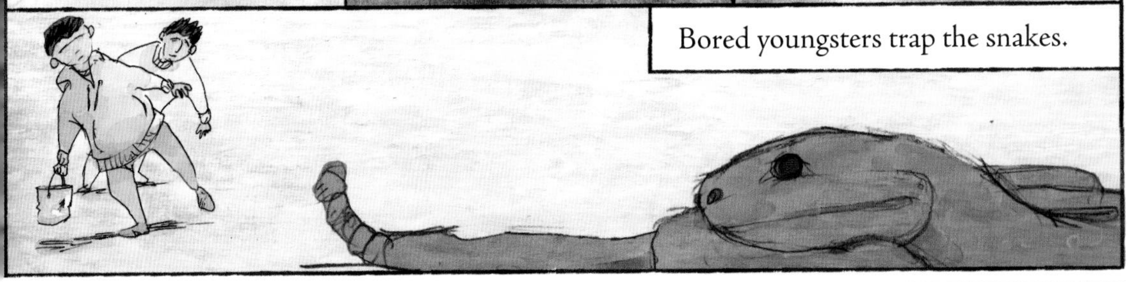
Bored youngsters trap the snakes.

In Lebanon, 1.5 million refugees scrape out a brittle existence with little government help.

Jordan closes the Syrian-Jordanian border, shutting out sixty thousand desperate refugees who are trapped in the desert with few supplies and no medicine.

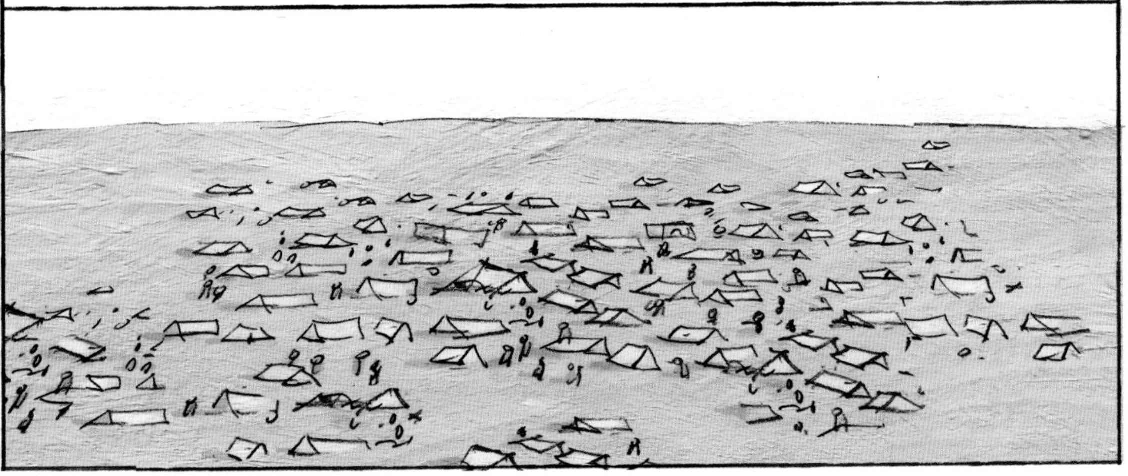

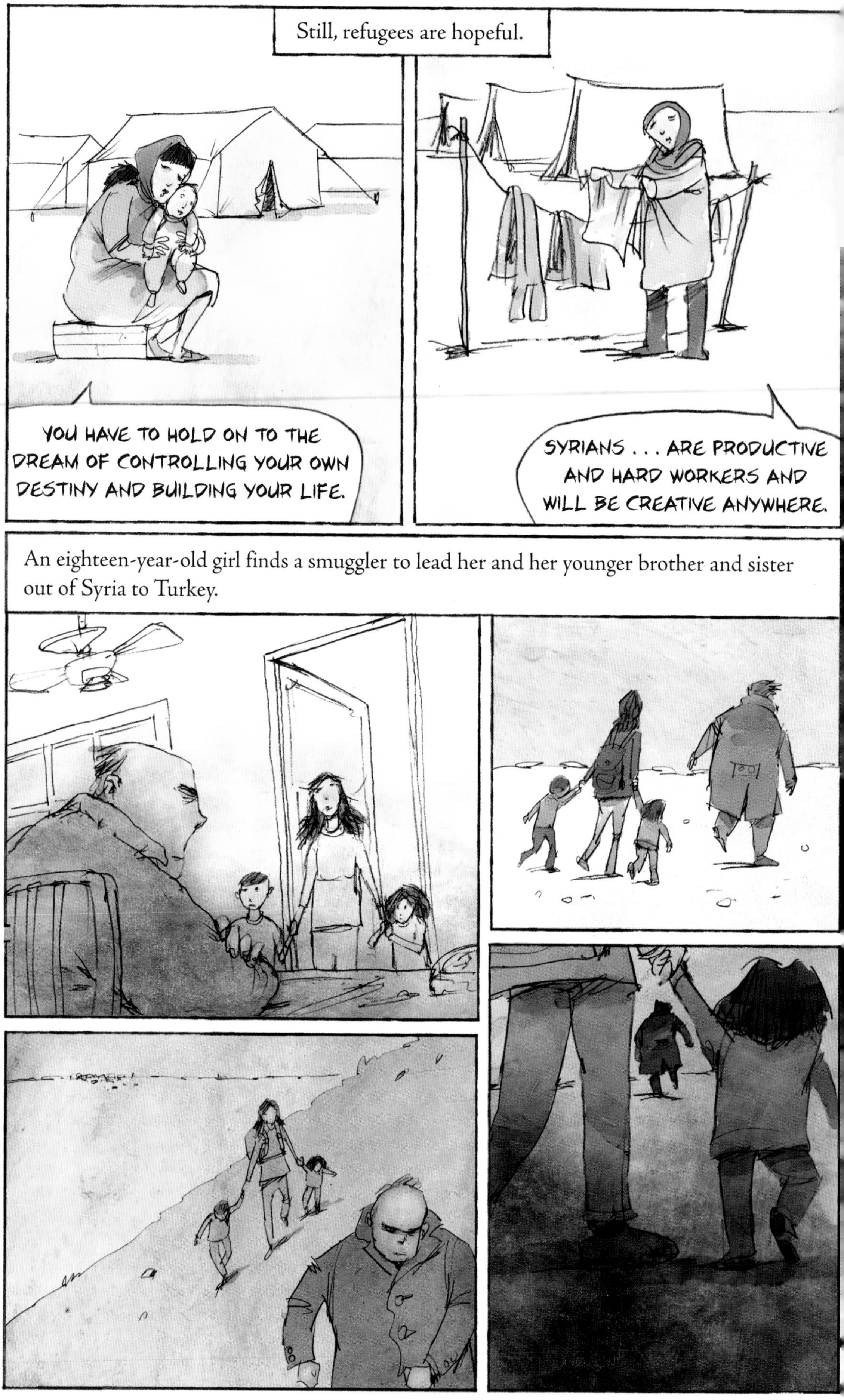
Still, refugees are hopeful.
YOU HAVE TO HOLD ON TO THE DREAM OF CONTROLLING YOUR OWN DESTINY AND BUILDING YOUR LIFE.
SYRIANS . . . ARE PRODUCTIVE AND HARD WORKERS AND WILL BE CREATIVE ANYWHERE.
An eighteen-year-old girl finds a smuggler to lead her and her younger brother and sister out of Syria to Turkey.

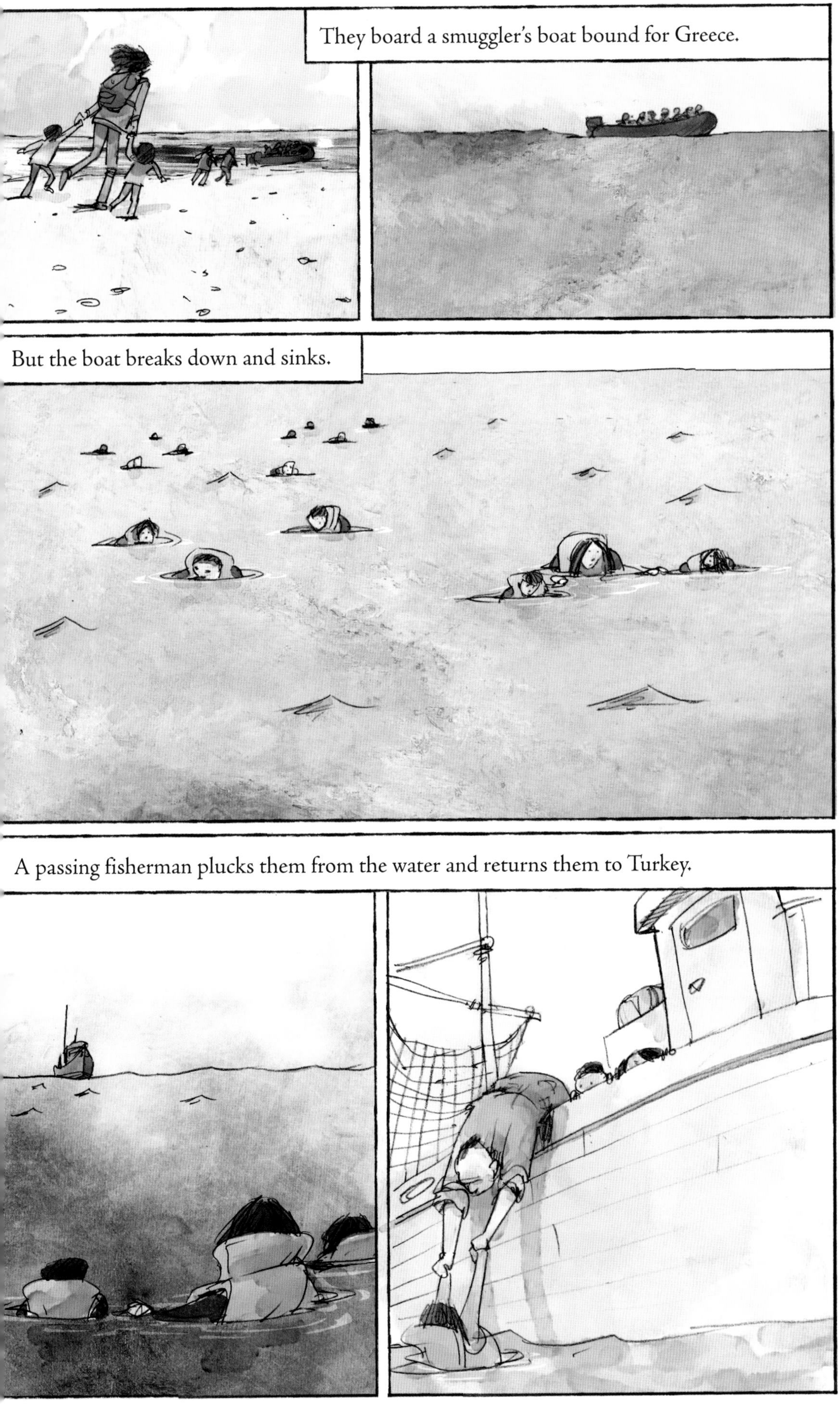
They board a smuggler's boat bound for Greece.
But the boat breaks down and sinks.
A passing fisherman plucks them from the water and returns them to Turkey.

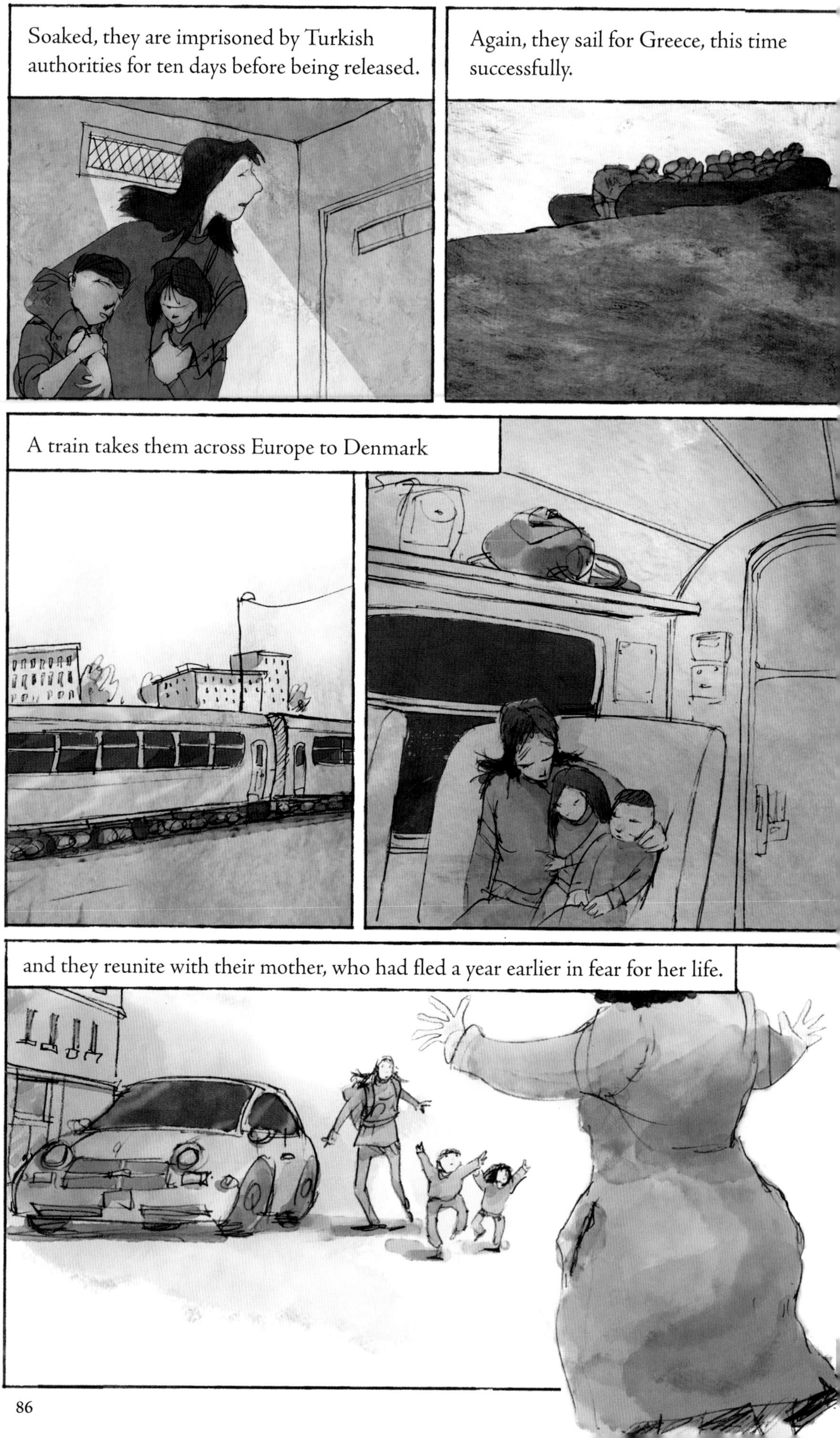
Soaked, they are imprisoned by Turkish authorities for ten days before being released.
Again, they sail for Greece, this time successfully.
A train takes them across Europe to Denmark
and they reunite with their mother, who had fled a year earlier in fear for her life.

The Aleppo pals arrive in Hamburg, Germany, another stop on their way to the Netherlands or Luxembourg. A policeman spots them. They fear their journey is over, and their hearts sink.

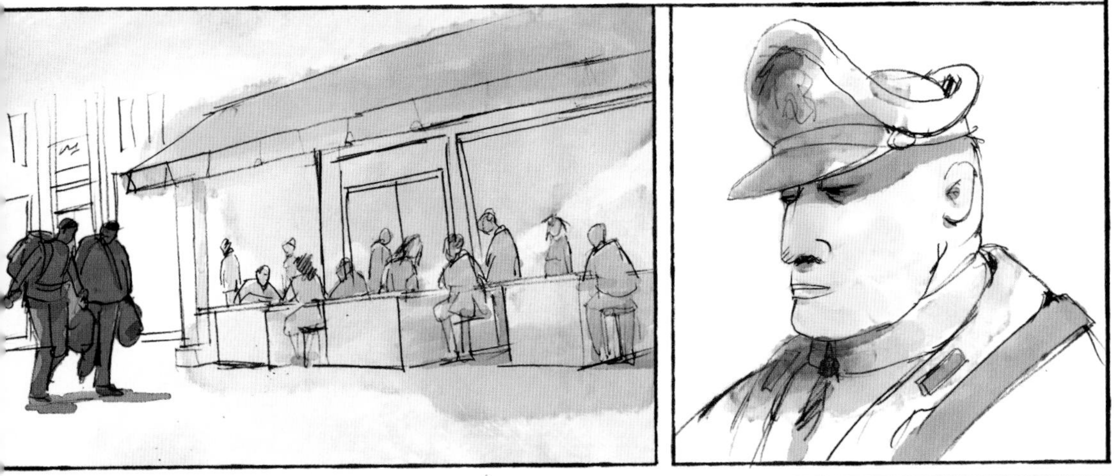

But instead of arresting them, the policeman offers kindness in the shape of an apple and a banana.

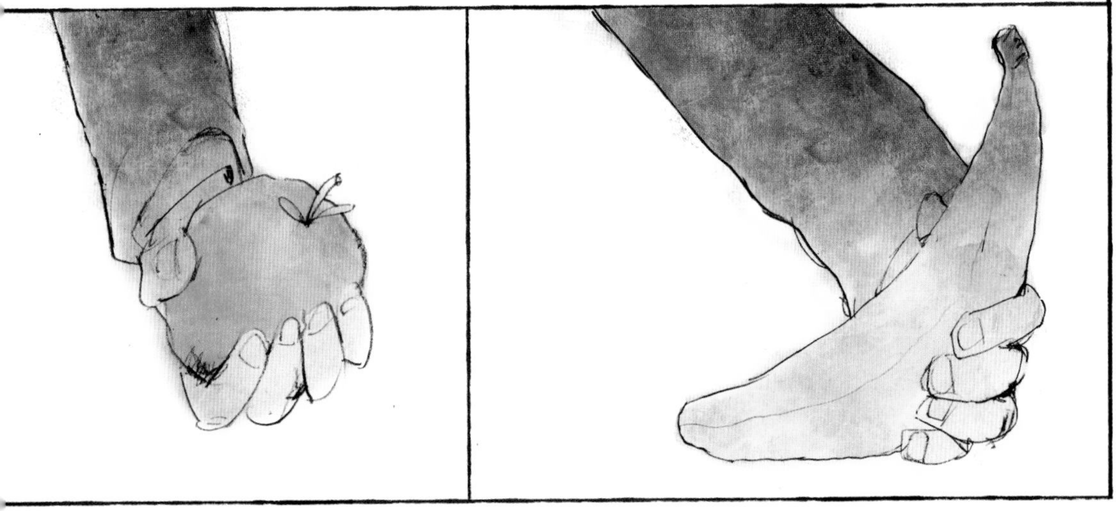

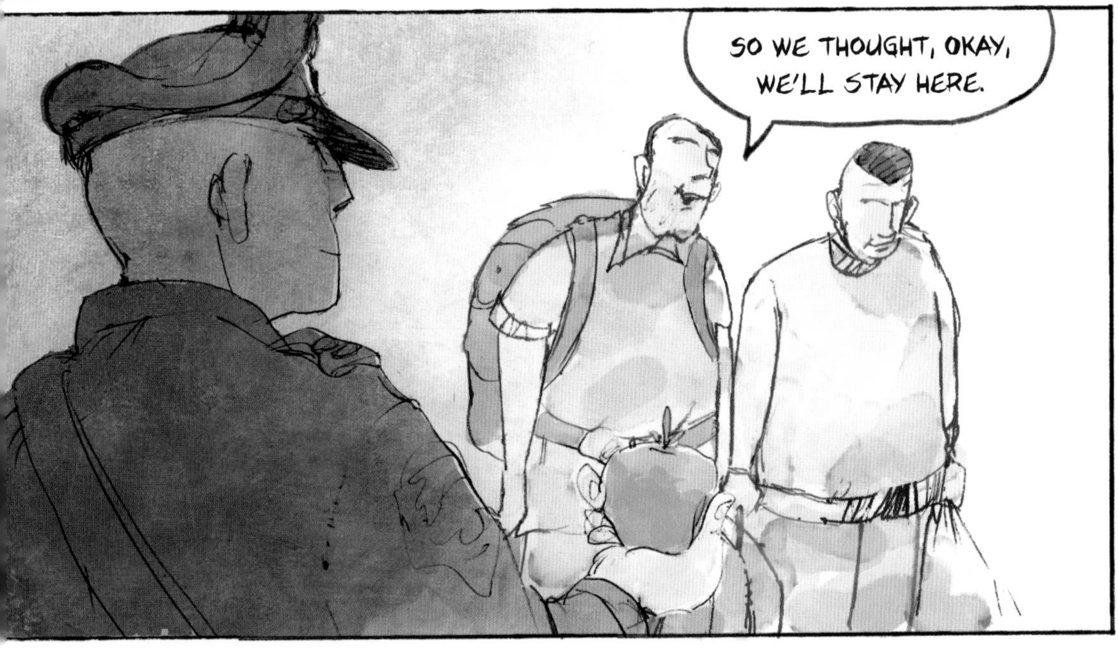
SO WE THOUGHT, OKAY, WE'LL STAY HERE.

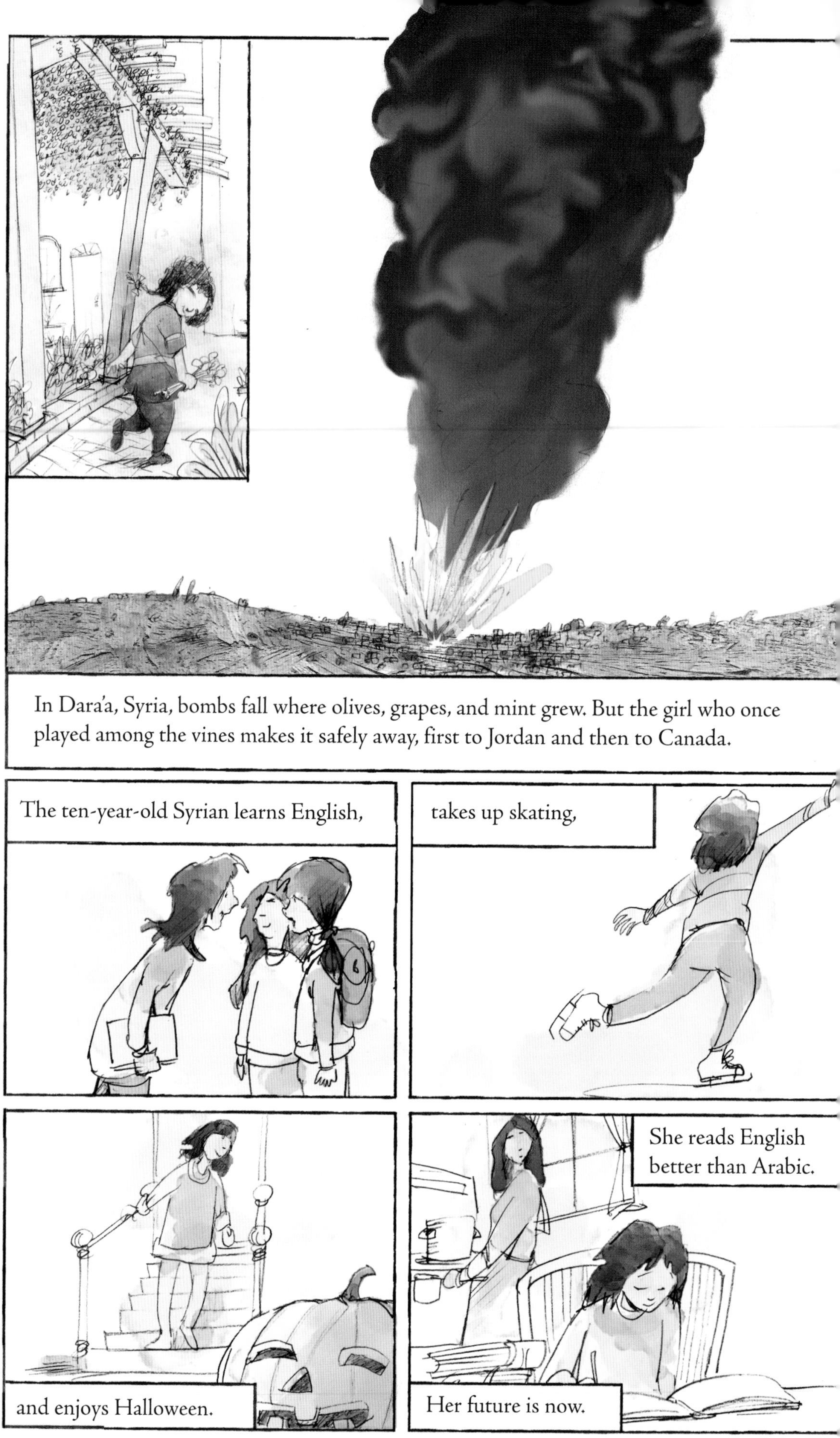
In Dara'a, Syria, bombs fall where olives, grapes, and mint grew. But the girl who once played among the vines makes it safely away, first to Jordan and then to Canada.
The ten-year-old Syrian learns English,
takes up skating,
and enjoys Halloween.
She reads English better than Arabic.
Her future is now.

A family tries three times to leave Syria for Jordan and three times is turned back. Finally, they cross into Jordan and live there for two years before being resettled in Sacramento, California.

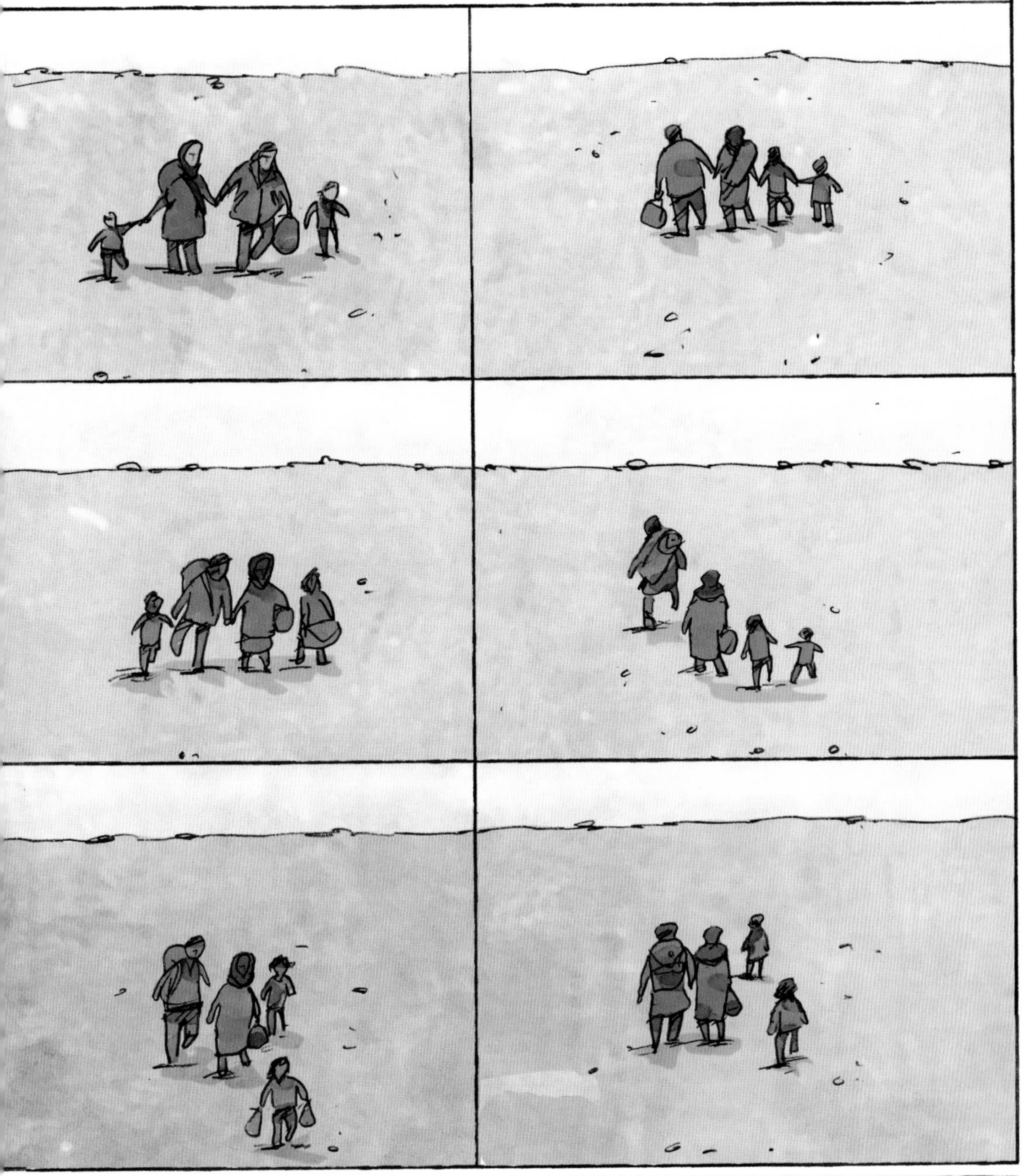

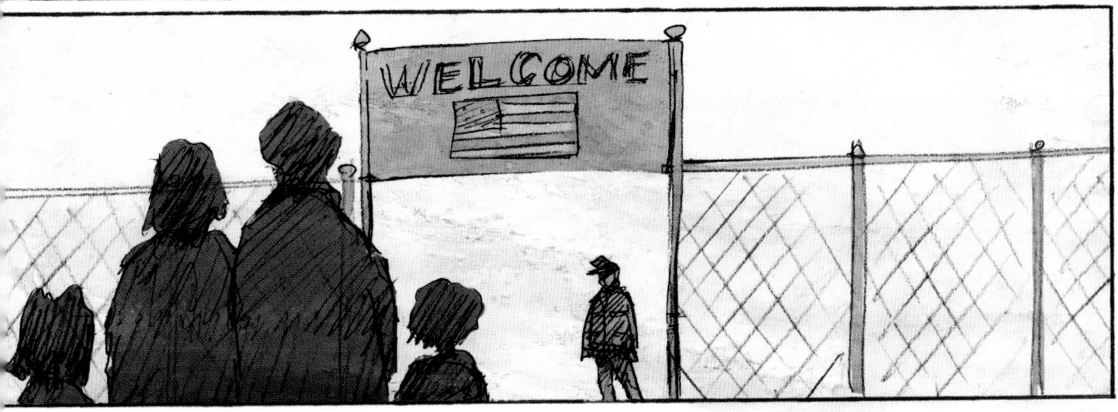
WELCOME

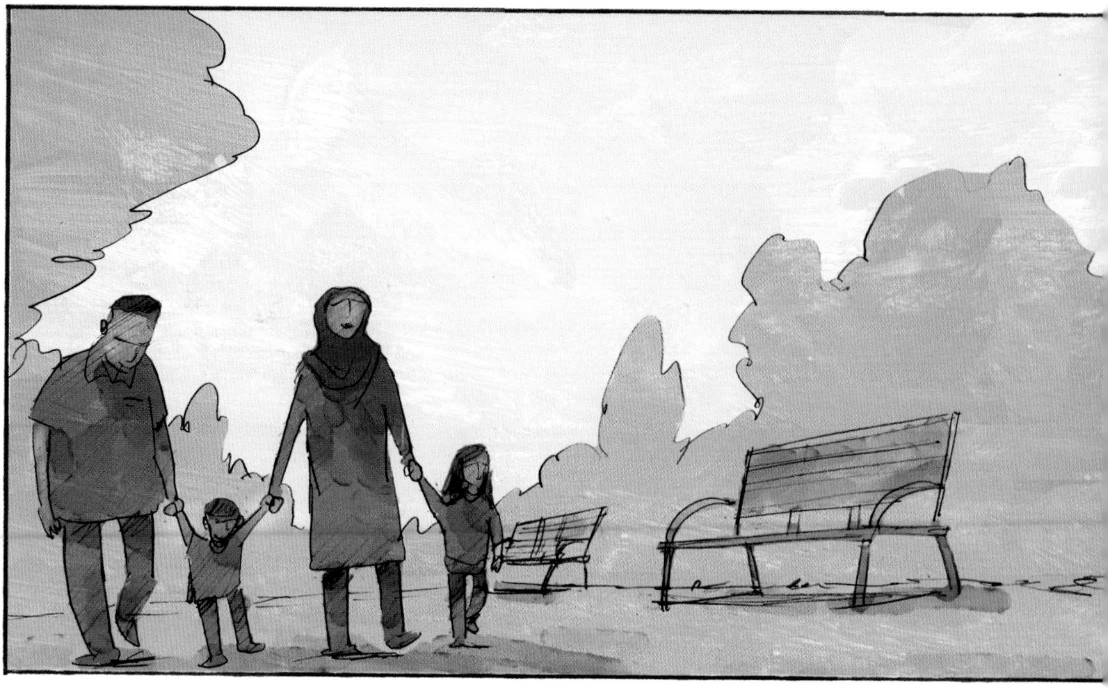

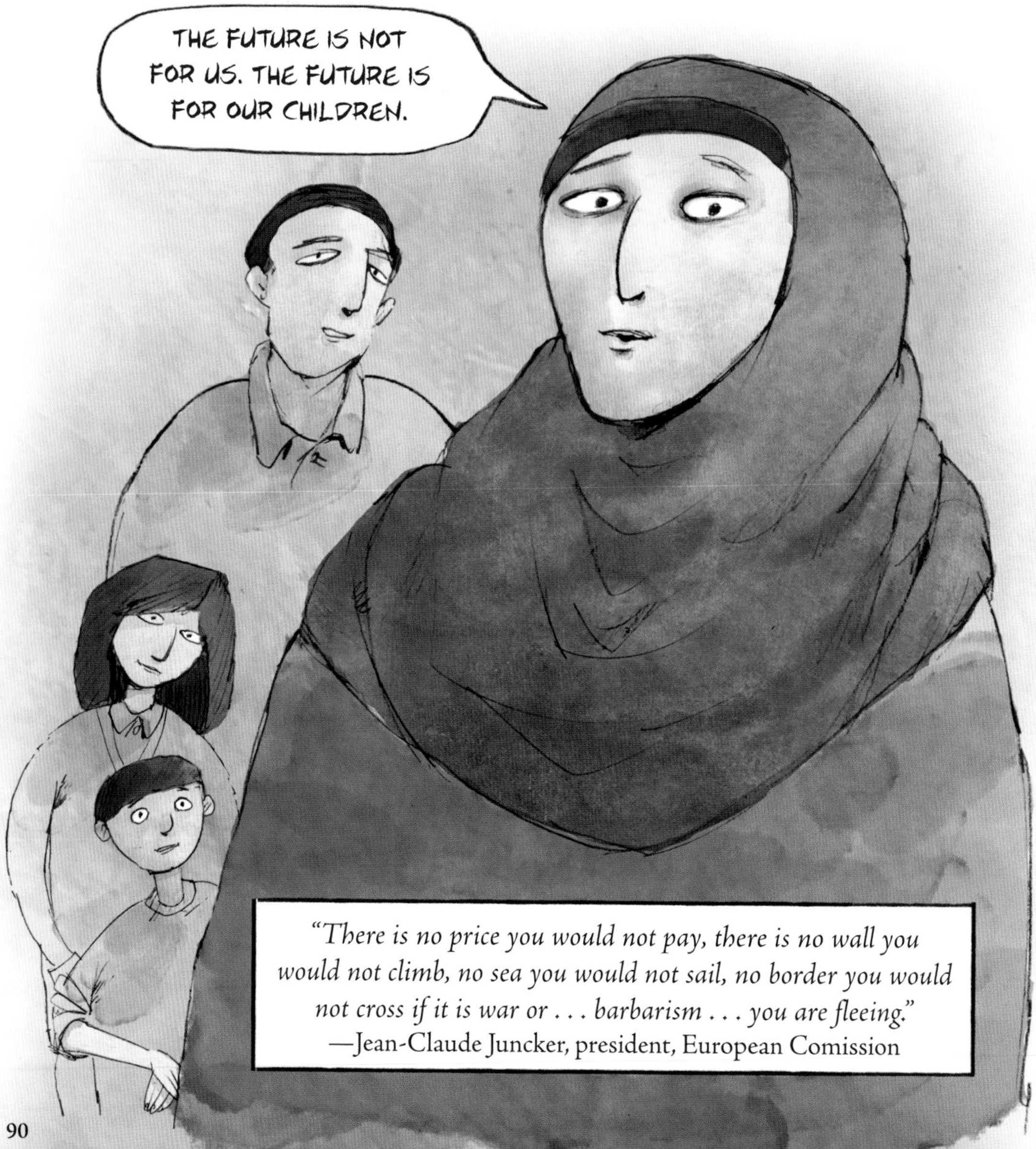
THE FUTURE IS NOT FOR US. THE FUTURE IS FOR OUR CHILDREN.
"There is no price you would not pay, there is no wall you would not climb, no sea you would not sail, no border you would not cross if it is war or . . . barbarism . . . you are fleeing."
—Jean-Claude Juncker, president, European Comission

ABOUT *THE UNWANTED*

Early on, I decided *The Unwanted* would focus on the refugee experience and disregard information beyond that constraint except when necessary for context. I was determined to keep the attention on the refugees—reporting, for example, that a child drowned in the Mediterranean fleeing horrific violence, and not that the child was Shia, Sunni, Kurd, Christian, or Yazidi. To fully portray the complex religious, political, and cultural web that describes Syria—a ruthless Shia-Sunni rivalry dating back to antiquity; undemocratic and unstable governance typical across North Africa and the Middle East; volatile ethnic divisions, such as the striving for an independent homeland by the Kurdish people; the meddling of outside powers for their own geopolitical benefit, to name just a few—would have made for an enormous, sprawling book, one that would not be well served by a graphic novel.

However, I knew that firsthand observation would be important to help highlight the refugees' experience and would add to the accuracy of the book. The following is a journal summary of the refugee camp visits that I made to Greece in May 2017.

RITSONA

In Ritsona, about an hour's drive from Athens, approximately seven hundred Syrians scratch out a hardscrabble life in a refugee camp made from a former Greek air force base. I say approximately seven hundred not to avoid hard-nosed truth but because no one really knows. The camp is open; people come and go as they please, and the census of the camp is always unclear and in dispute—not an unimportant issue when supplies are keyed to head count.

Although the camp is ostensibly under air force control, it's really operated by a hodgepodge of groups, mostly NGOs—nongovernmental organizations. They provide education and arts programs for kids, psychological care, and prenatal and medical care—though health care is haphazard, and residents must do without immediate help on nights and weekends.

Protecting the refugees' dignity is a goal embraced by all the volunteers, and visitors' rules prohibit taking photographs of the refugees without their permission or having up-close examination of their homes—small, boxy shelters that look like compact shipping containers. Before they had the air-conditioned shelters, the refugees lived in tents that, in summer, could heat up to one hundred degrees. A volunteer leads us on a tour of the camp's perimeter, where we can view the shelters at a respectful distance. Here and there, we spot well-tended vegetable gardens.

The UNHCR (United Nations High Commissioner for Refugees)—the most relevant UN agency for the Syrians—visits the camp now and then, overseeing efforts to move residents out of Ritsona to permanent settlement elsewhere. But permanent resettlement is slow and uncertain. Some of Ritsona's residents have been there a year.

None of the refugees want to stay in Greece. The language is hard to learn (no one knows this better than the refugee kids who attend school, where they are taught in Greek), and, more important, there are no jobs. Greek unemployment is at roughly 25 percent . . . a rate the United States last endured during the Great Depression.

The government has stopped providing food at Ritsona and gives the refugees a monthly stipend instead. With it, they shop locally, though others prefer the hour-long bus ride to Athens to buy food more cheaply. Plus, it gives them something to do. Without work, boredom can be crushing.

ELPÍDA

"Elpída" and "Happy Home" are painted over the door of the three-story former factory. "Welcome," "Hello," "Love," and "Hi" are painted in bold red-and-yellow letters above the factory's windows, shout-outs in graffiti to the cars traveling an adjacent highway leaving the crossroads city of Thessaloniki, in northern Greece.

It is home to about one hundred Syrian refugees, mostly women and children.

Elpída—Greek for "hope"—is the brainchild of Amed Khan and Frank Giustra. In 2015, the American financiers helped rescue wet and frightened refugees splashing onto the beaches of the Greek island Lesbos. The experience inspired them to do more, and Elpída is the result.

Before Khan, the Greek government's plan was for refugees to live in tents within the factory. Instead, Khan built rooms in the vacant space, then furnished them with donations. There is a central kitchen for residents to cook meals, a stainless-steel facility reminiscent of a lunchroom kitchen in an American school. There is also a school, really just a clutch of rooms with school supplies strewn about, not for the absence of organization but for the lack of shelving and closets. Self-drawn crayon portraits are taped on the walls, drawings no different from the ones you might find in a classroom in Memphis, Munich, or Marseille. A volunteer teacher from Manchester, England, instructs kids and insists that her students deserve an education and are no different from kids elsewhere.

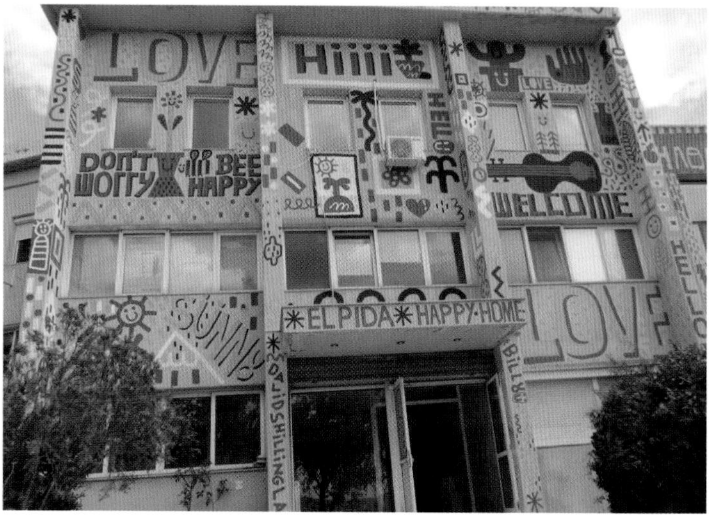
LOVE
Hiiii
DON'T WORRY
BEE HAPPY
WELCOME
*ELPIDA*HAPPY-HOME
LOVE

She isn't entirely correct. Her students *aren't* like kids elsewhere; they've experienced war. Their art projects routinely portray sophisticated weaponry. The wartime experiences have blasted holes in their education, prompting the need for much remedial learning.

The kids' experiences have wounded more than just their education. They're traumatized; some preteens are plagued by stress-induced bed-wetting. Suicide isn't uncommon.

Note: As of this writing, the government has closed all refugee camps in northern Greece and moved their residents to apartments.

LEROS

Leros is a small Greek island overlooked by American tourists, who prefer the gloss of Santorini and Mykonos. From Leros's hills, Turkey is visible on the horizon. Its proximity made Leros a target destination for Syrian refugees. At the height of the crisis, thousands of them crossed to Leros and other nearby Greek islands. They crammed streets as frantic government workers rushed to evacuate them.

At the time of my arrival, only a small camp of refugees remains. It is located on the grounds of a former insane asylum, though the camp's surrounding barbed wire and corner guard towers—now no longer manned—make it resemble a prison. We circle it and notice a couple of the box shelters have been destroyed by fire.

The work of a teenager bent on suicide, we are told.

Its residents are partly tended to by Echo100Plus, one of the NGOs that helped manage the Ritsona camp. Echo was founded by a group of Austrian women who refused to ignore the refugee crisis. Their young and earnest volunteers provide activities for the refugees. They once took them for a beach outing that included swimming. It was only partially successful: some refugees have terror-filled memories of nearly drowning in the same water when they fled Turkey by boat.

This last visit to a camp heightened the discomfort I'd experienced on my first visit—that I was a voyeur to tragedy. The notion of having refugees recount their awful experiences of exodus seemed unnecessary and cruel. After all, those terrible stories are already widely circulated. My unease was hard to shake. In the end, I found value in the visits by their having made me a more sensitive witness to the refugees' dilemma and a more powerful advocate for their salvation.

I hope this book is a confirmation of those beliefs.

POSTSCRIPT

At the time of this writing, the Syrian refugee crisis has sparked a backlash against immigration of all kinds and upended politics across the globe. As a result, the British have decided to exit the European Union. German leader Angela Merkel suffered election setbacks. Hungarian leader Viktor Orbán expanded power via his nativist views. Donald Trump became the president of the United States. Turkey and Greece accepted international agreements to slow the flood of refugees into Western Europe, freezing in place millions of people in refugee camps and facilities for the foreseeable future

The Syrian Civil War drags on. The hope for Bashar al-Assad's defeat has nearly evaporated. His ally, Russia, provides warplanes that help government forces drive rebels from their few, remaining strongholds. Fighting continues to kill and injure a staggering number of children. Assad murders scores of civilians with chemical-gas attacks. America punishes Syria for the attacks with occasional missiles strikes against military sites but with uncertain effect.

There are about 5.7 million registered Syrian refugees. In the first three months of 2018, the United States has accepted eleven for resettlement.

SOURCE NOTES

6 *"Down with the regime"*: #chicagoGirl.

7 *"We want dignity and freedom"*: Fisk, pp.1–4.

9 *"Go home! Disperse! We will shoot"*: Wood.

10 *"It was a peaceful demonstration"*: Wood.

   "They evicted people": Letsch.

11 *"They would usually torture you"*: Rifai.

13 *"It's bomb, bomb, bomb, guns"*: Sacchetti, "Many Migrants."

15 *"We felt maybe it's our turn to die."*: UNHCR, "Syria Emergency."

16 *"If they hear anything"*: Letsch.

17 *"Mum, help! I'm caught!"*: Letsch.

   "Let him become fish food": Letsch.

21 *"Just walk. Don't breathe"*: Salam Neighbor.

   "We gave the babies sleeping pills": Salam Neighbor.

23 *"Don't you know that music"*: Moussaoui.

   "That's when I decided to leave": Moussaoui.

27 *"I had to steer the boat."*: Hull.

   "Safety, a job, and a good life.": Chick.

29 *"Run!"*: Bauer, p. 9.

31 *"Don't let me die"*: Bauer, p. 82.

33 *"I tried to catch my wife"*: Cries from Syria.

34 *"We had two choices"*: Gal, "Mohammed."

39 *"If you stay here"*: Adow.

41 *"Don't come back"*: Chick.

43 *"Here we are dying five thousand times"*: Faiola.

45 *"We heard that Europeans think"*: Gal, "Salah."

   "I am Catholic. Islam, Jewish—I don't care.": Hartocollis, "Budapest Train Station."

52 *"I have a two-year-old brother."*: Wood.

53 *"I became too scared to go to school"*: UNICEF.

   "I want to be a doctor": Lemmon.

55 *"It doesn't even look like planet Earth"*: Sullivan, "New Camp Rises."

57 *"Many of these people will never go home"*: Sullivan, "Changing Region, Changing Lives."

58–59 *"I am working for my father and mother"*: Sullivan, "A Child Goes to Work."

62 *"Everything is okay"*: Sacchetti, "Making the Risky Crossing."

"We cannot see an end to this": Sacchetti, "Many Migrants."

65 "The police say 'Wait, wait.'": Sacchetti, "As They Make Their Way."

67 "Refugees Not Welcome!": Melvin.

69 "For us, Europe is at stake today": Beauchamp, "Hungary's Horrific Treatment"

"I think Islam hates us": DelReal.

"Security comes first": Fantz.

73 "I can't go back.": Sullivan, "Turned Back."

75 "warehouse of souls.": Adow.

"What do we do now?": Yardley.

76 "The dream was never": Gal, "Abeer."

77 "How can we live here,": Gal, "Hala."

79 "I just want a normal life": UNHCR, *Italy: Desperate Rescue at Sea.*

81 "Who cares about us?": Alkousaa.

83 "The snakes are here": Olivier Nasser, volunteer at Ritsona.

84 "You have to hold on": Hart, "Syrian Crisis . . . Besan Tells Her Story."

"Syrians . . . are productive": Salam Neighbor.

87 "So we thought, okay, we'll stay here": Chick.

90 "The future is not for us.": Plus.

"There is no price you would not pay,": Kanter, "E.U. Nations Urged."

105 "Hope Behind the Shadow of Pain!": Noah.

BIBLIOGRAPHY

Achilli, Luigi. Tariq al-Euroba: *Displacement Trends of Syrian Asylum Seekers to the EU*. MPC Research Report. Migration Policy Centre. Florence, Italy: European University Institute, 2016. cadmus.eui.eu/bitstream/handle/1814/38969/ MPCRR_2016_01.pdf?sequence=1&isAllowed=y. Accessed December 7, 2016.

Adow, Mohammed. "The Booming Fake Passport Market for Refugees in Athens." *Reporter's Notebook/ Human Rights* (blog). Al Jazeera. March 3, 2016. www.aljazeera.com/blogs/europe/2016/03/ booming-fake-passport-market-refugees-athens-160304031000398.html. Accessed December 29, 2016.

Alderman, Liz. "Wintry Blast in Greece Imperils Refugees in Crowded Camps." *New York Times*, January 11, 2017. www.nytimes.com/2017/01/11/ world/europe/greece-refugees-crisis-winter-storms. html. Accessed January 12, 2017.

Al-Jawahiry, Warda. "As Winter Blows in Across Lebanon, Refugees Struggle." UNHCR (The UN Refugee Agency). December 23, 2016. www.unhcr. org/en-us/news/latest/2016/12/585cddcf4/ winter-blows-across-lebanon-refugees-struggle. html. Accessed December 27, 2016.

Alkousaa, Riham, and Maximilian Popp. "The Death Strip at the Turkish-Syrian Border." *Spiegel Online*, December 7, 2016. www.spiegel.de/international/ world/death-strip-on-border-between-turkey-and-syria-a-1124706.html. Accessed September 27, 2017.

Almasy, Steve, Pierre Meilhan, and Jim Bittermann. "Paris Massacre." CNN. November 14, 2015. edition.cnn.com/2015/11/13/world/paris-shooting/index.html. Accessed December 8, 2016.

Amnesty International. "EU's Reckless Refugee Returns to Turkey Illegal." June 3, 2016. www.amnesty.org/ en/latest/news/2016/06/eus-reckless-refugee-returns-to-turkey-illegal. Accessed December 15, 2016.

———. "Facts & Figures: Syria Refugee Crisis & International Resettlement." December 5, 2014. www.amnesty.org/en/latest/news/2014/12/ facts-figures-syria-refugee-crisis-international-resettlement. Accessed December 7, 2016.

———. "Refugees, Asylum-Seekers and Migrants." What We Do. www.amnesty.org/en/what-we-do/ refugees-asylum-seekers-and-migrants. Accessed December 7, 2016.

———. *Struggling to Survive*. 2014. www.amnesty.nl/

sites/default/files/public/struggling_to_survive.
pdf. Accessed December 14, 2016.

Amos, Deborah. "Deborah Amos on Syria's Refugee
Crisis." *Moyers & Company*. September 6, 2013.
billmoyers.com/segment/deborah-amos-on-
understanding-syria. Accessed November 22, 2016.

Arango, Tim. "Turkish Public Sours on Syrian Uprising."
New York Times, September 18, 2012. www.
nytimes.com/2012/09/19/world/europe/turks-
weary-of-leaders-support-for-syria-uprising.html.
Accessed November 23, 2016.

Arsu, Sebnem, and Liam Stack. "Syrian Forces Storm
into Restive Town Near Turkey." *New York Times*,
June 10, 2011. www.nytimes.com/2011/06/11/
world/middleeast/11syria.html. Accessed
November 23, 2016.

Associated Press. "Lebanon's President Says Syrian
Refugees Must Return Home." *Seattle Times*,
September 25, 2017. www.seattletimes.com/nation-
world/lebanons-president-says-syrian-refugees-
must-return-home. Accessed October 24, 2017.

———. "Refugee Crisis: 13,000 People Rescued in
Mediterranean in One Week." *Guardian*, May
28, 2016. www.theguardian.com/world/2016/
may/29/refugee-crisis-13000-people-rescued-in-
mediterranean-in-one-week. Accessed November
15, 2016.

Barnard, Anne. "Battle Over Aleppo Is Over, Russia
Says, as Evacuation Deal Reached." *New York
Times*, December 13, 2016. www.nytimes.
com/2016/12/13/world/middleeast/syria-aleppo-
civilians.html. Accessed September 27, 2017.

Basatneh, Alaa. "It's Not Safe to Wear My Hijab Now
That Trump Will Be President." *Splinter* (via
Elisa Rodriguez/*Fusion*), November 15, 2016.
splinternews.com/its-not-safe-to-wear-my-hijab-
now-that-trump-will-be-pr-1793863762. Accessed
December 28, 2016.

Bauer, Wolfgang. *Crossing the Sea: With Syrians on the
Exodus to Europe*. Los Angeles: And Other Stories
Publishing, 2016.

BBC News. "Life and Death in Syria." March 15, 2016.
www.bbc.co.uk/news/resources/idt-841ebc3a-
1be9-493b-8800-2c04890e8fc9. Accessed
September 25, 2017.

———. "Paris Attacks: Who Were the Attackers?"
April 27, 2016. www.bbc.com/news/world-
europe-34832512. Accessed January 31, 2017.

———. "Syria: The Story of the Conflict. March
11, 2016. www.bbc.com/news/world-middle-
east-26116868. Accessed November 22, 2016.

———. "Zaatari Refugee Camp: Rebuilding Lives in the
Desert." September 3, 2013. www.bbc.com/news/
world-middle-east-23801200. Accessed March 30,
2017.

Beauchamp, Zack. "The Dutch Politician Convicted
of Inciting Anti-Immigrant Rage Is Going Up
in the Polls." *Vox*, December 9, 2016. www.vox.
com/world/2016/12/9/13898534/geert-wilders-
convicted-incitement. Accessed December 12, 2016.

———. "Hungary's Horrific Treatment of Refugees, in
One Stunning Video." *Vox*, September 13, 2015.
www.vox.com/2015/9/13/9313371/refugees-
viktor-orban. Accessed December 12, 2015.

Bennett, Brian. "Trump Plans to Slash Refugee
Admissions by More than Half." *Los Angeles Times*,
September 27, 2017. www.latimes.com/politics/
la-na-pol-trump-refugees-20170927-story.html.
Accessed September 29, 2017.

Berman, Russell. "Can Terrorists Really Infiltrate the
Syrian Refugee Program?" *Atlantic*, November
18, 2015. www.theatlantic.com/politics/
archive/2015/11/can-terrorists-really-infiltrate-
the-syrian-refugee-program/416475. Accessed
November 21, 2016.

Bohlen, Celestine. "In Paris, Longing for Damascus." *New
York Times*, December 21, 2012. www.nytimes.
com/2012/12/22/world/europe/22iht-letter22.
html. Accessed November 23, 2016.

Bonessi, Dominique. "Better Life? Syrian Kids in Turkey
Must Go to Work, Not School." *USA Today*,
October 15, 2016. www.usatoday.com/story/news/
world/2016/10/15/better-life-syrian-kids-turkey-
must-go-work-not-school/92009490. Accessed
March 31, 2017.

Booth, William. "Europe Gets Ready to Ship Refugees
Stuck in Greece Back to Turkey." *Washington Post*,
April 1, 2016. www.washingtonpost.com/world/
europe/europe-gets-ready-to-ship-refugees-stuck-
in-greece-back-to-turkey/2016/04/01/06a79270-

f5d1-11e5-958d-d038dac6e718_story.html?utm_term=.ac7acec7050c. Accessed September 27, 2017.

Borger, Julian. "Refugee Arrivals in Greece Exceed 100,000 in Less Than Two Months." *Guardian*, February 23, 2016. www.theguardian.com/world/2016/feb/23/number-of-refugee-arrivals-in-greece-passes-100000-in-less-than-two-months. Accessed December 15, 2016.

Boyle, Darren. "A Frozen Shower." *Daily Mail Online*, December 26, 2016. www.dailymail.co.uk/news/article-4066404/A-frozen-shower-Syrian-migrants-wash-open-air-makeshift-Belgrade-camp-thousands-refugees-continue-journey-Europe.html?ITO=1490. Accessed December 28, 2016.

Bremmer, Ian. "These 5 Facts Explain America's Shameful Reaction to Syrian Refugees." *Time*, November 30, 2015. time.com/4126371/these-5-facts-explain-americas-shameful-reaction-to-syrian-refugees. Accessed November 21, 2016.

Carstensen, Jeanne. "Syrian Refugees Are Now Paying Smugglers to Take Them Back." *GlobalPost Investigations*, November 2, 2016. gpinvestigations.pri.org/syrian-refugees-are-now-paying-smugglers-to-take-them-back-6fa9ef8242e3#.gzblvh5o1. Accessed November 15, 2016.

Cecco, Leyland, and Annie Sakkab. "Syrian Seamstress Becomes a Part of Community Fabric." UNHCR (The UN Refugee Agency). December 15, 2016. www.unhcr.org/en-us/news/stories/2016/12/584e6ad04/syrian-seamstress-becomes-part-community-fabric.html. Accessed December 27, 2016.

#chicagoGirl: The Social Network Takes on a Dictator. Film. Directed by Joe Piscatella. 2013.

Chick, Kristen. "Two Syrian Refugees: A 1,500-Mile Journey of Hope and Hardship." *Christian Science Monitor*, July, 19, 2015. www.csmonitor.com/World/Europe/2015/0719/Two-Syrian-refugees-a-1-500-mile-journey-of-hope-and-hardship. Accessed January 3, 2017.

Collett, Elizabeth. "The Paradox of the EU-Turkey Refugee Deal." Migration Policy Institute. March 2016. www.migrationpolicy.org/news/paradox-eu-turkey-refugee-deal. Accessed November 15, 2016.

Connolly, Kate. "EU-Turkey Deal Begins as Syrian Refugees Arrive in Germany and Finland." *Guardian*, April 4, 2016. www.theguardian.com/world/2016/apr/04/eu-turkey-deal-syrian-refugees-germany-istanbul-hanover. Accessed September 25, 2017.

Cries from Syria. Film. Directed by Evgeny Afineevsky. An Afineevsky-Tolmor Production. March 10, 2017.

Cumming-Bruce, Nick, and Steven Erlanger. "U.N. Calls Lag in Syria Aid Worst Funding Crisis in Recent Memory." *New York Times*, March 15, 2013. www.nytimes.com/2013/03/16/world/middleeast/un-calls-lag-in-syria-aid-worst-funding-crisis-in-recent-memory.html. Accessed November 23, 2016.

David, Jenny. "Turkey: Syrian Refugees Will Not Be Granted Work Permits, Minister Says." Bloomberg BNA. August 31, 2015. www.bna.com/turkey-syrian-refugees-n17179935355. Accessed March 30, 2017.

DelReal, Jose A. "Trump: 'I Think Islam Hates Us.'" *Washington Post*, March 9, 2016. www.washingtonpost.com/news/post-politics/wp/2016/03/09/trump-i-think-islam-hates-us/?tid=a_inl&utm_term=.100490d104a4. Accessed December 13, 2016.

Doctors without Borders (Medecins sans Frontieres). *Greece in 2016: Vulnerable People Get Left Behind*. MSFGreece. October 2016. www.msf.org/sites/msf.org/files/report_vulnerable_people_201016_eng.pdf. Accessed November 15, 2016.

European Commission. *Relocation and Resettlement—State of Play*. December 6, 2016. ec.europa.eu/dgs/home-affairs/what-we-do/policies/european-agenda-migration/background-information/docs/20161208/update_of_the_factsheet_on_relocation_and_resettlement_en.pdf. Accessed December 13, 2016.

Fagotto, Matteo. "Cold Comfort: The Syrian Refugees Trying to Make a New Life in Sweden." *Guardian*, April 29, 2014. www.theguardian.com/world/2014/apr/29/syrian-refugees-sweden-new-life. Accessed December 15, 2016.

Fahim, Kareem, and Hwaida Saad. "A Faceless Teenage Refugee Who Helped Ignite Syria's War." *New York Times*, February 8, 2013. www.nytimes.

com/2013/02/09/world/middleeast/a-faceless-teenage-refugee-who-helped-ignite-syrias-war.html. Accessed November 22, 2016.

Faiola, Anthony. "One Family's Journey from Aleppo to Austria." *Washington Post*, June 26, 2015. www.washingtonpost.com/graphics/world/exodus/black-route. Accessed January 24, 2017.

Fantz, Ashley, and Ben Brumfield. "More Than Half the Nation's Governors Say Syrian Refugees Not Welcome." CNN. November 19, 2015. www.cnn.com/2015/11/16/world/paris-attacks-syrian-refugees-backlash/index.html. Accessed December 12, 2016.

Fisk, Robert, Patrick Cockburn, Kim Sengupta, and the *Independent. Syria: Descent into the Abyss*. Miami: Mango Media, 2016.

Fleming, Melissa. "Crossings of Mediterranean Sea Exceed 300,000, Including 200,000 to Greece." UNHCR (The UN Refugee Agency). August 28, 2015. www.unhcr.org/news/latest/2015/8/55e06a5b6/crossings-mediterranean-sea-exceed-300000-including-200000-greece.html. Accessed September 25, 2017.

———. *A Hope More Powerful Than the Sea*. New York: Flatiron Books, 2017.

Fox News. "Syrian Refugees Now Enrolling in Schools." October 20, 2016. www.foxnews.com/us/2016/10/20/syrian-refugees-now-enrolling-in-schools.html. Accessed December 13, 2016.

Francis, Enjoli, David Muir, and Christine Romo. "Syrian Refugee Children Forced to Work." ABC News. September 2, 2014. abcnews.go.com/International/childhood-interrupted-syrian-refugee-children-forced-work/story?id=25221155. Accessed March 31, 2017.

Gal, Shayanne. Interview. January 19, 2017.

Gal, Shayanne, and Clara Veale. "Abeer"; "Salah"; "Mohammed"; "Aida"; "Hala." *Voices of Refugees* (blog). voicesofrefugees.net. Accessed January 17, 2017.

Gelling, Peter. "Becoming a Refugee: Essays by Young Syrians." *GlobalPost Investigations*, May 30, 2016. gpinvestigations.pri.org/becoming-a-refugee-

essays-by-young-syrians-f7338a3f1650#.cvfedx5fx. Accessed November 15, 2016.

Gettleman, Jeffrey. "Escaping Syria to a Barren Plain of Sweat and Grit." *New York Times*, July 30, 2012. www.nytimes.com/2012/07/31/world/middleeast/syrian-refugees-escape-to-a-barren-plain-of-sweat-and-grit-in-turkey.html. Accessed November 23, 2012.

Glass, Charles. *Syria Burning: A Short History of a Catastrophe*. London: Verso, 2016.

Gumrukcu, Tuvan, Daren Butler, and Kevin Liffey. "Turkey to Set Up Tent City for up to 80,000 Refugees Fleeing Aleppo: Deputy PM." Reuters. December 13, 2016. www.reuters.com/article/us-mideast-crisis-syria-turkey-refugees-idUSKBN1422HO. Accessed December 29, 2016.

Güsten, Susanne. "As Refugees Flood Turkey, Asylum System Nears Breakdown." *New York Times*, September 26, 2012. www.nytimes.com/2012/09/27/world/middleeast/as-refugees-flood-turkey-asylum-system-nears-breakdown.html. Accessed November 23, 2016.

Haq, Husna. "Syrian Refugees Are Quietly Trickling into the US; How Many, and Where?" *Christian Science Monitor*, October 21, 2015. www.csmonitor.com/World/Global-News/2015/1021/Syrian-refugees-are-quietly-trickling-into-the-US-How-many-and-where-video. Accessed December 12, 2016.

Hart, Marion. "Syrian Crisis: How Syrian Children Cope—Ammar Tells His Story." UNICEF USA. March 16, 2016. www.unicefusa.org/stories/how-syrian-children-cope-%E2%80%94-ammar-tells-his-story/30100. Accessed December 16, 2016.

———. "Syrian Crisis: How Syrian Children Cope—Besan Tells Her Story." UNICEF USA. March 17, 2016. www.unicefusa.org/stories/how-syrian-children-cope-%E2%80%94-besan-tells-her-story/30108. Accessed December 16, 2016.

———. "Syrian Crisis: How Syrian Children Cope—Maya Tells Her Story." UNICEF USA. March 15, 2016. www.unicefusa.org/stories/how-syrian-children-cope-%E2%80%94-maya-tells-her-story/30087. Accessed December 16, 2016.

———. "Syrian Crisis: How Syrian Children Cope—Saja Tells Her Story." UNICEF USA. March 15, 2016.

www.unicefusa.org/stories/how-syrian-children-cope-%E2%80%94-saja-tells-her-story/30094. Accessed December 16, 2016.

Hartocollis, Anemona. "Budapest Train Station Haunted by Ethnic Division." Reporter's Notebook: Traveling in Europe's River of Migrants (series). *New York Times*, September 2, 2015. www.nytimes.com/interactive/projects/cp/reporters-notebook/migrants/hungary-treatment-refugees. Accessed December 12, 2016.

———. "A Family Waits for a Chance to Reach Sweden." Reporter's Notebook: Traveling in Europe's River of Migrants (series). *New York Times*, September 7, 2015. www.nytimes.com/interactive/projects/cp/reporters-notebook/migrants/hungary-treatment-refugees. Accessed December 12, 2016.

———. "Greek Island of Kos, Overwhelmed with Migrants, Tries to Move Them Along." *New York Times*, August 13, 2015. www.nytimes.com/2015/08/14/world/europe/greece-kos-migrants-refugees-syria.html. Accessed November 22, 2016.

———. "Helping Hands on the Road to Vienna." Reporter's Notebook: Traveling in Europe's River of Migrants (series). *New York Times*, September 8, 2015. www.nytimes.com/interactive/projects/cp/reporters-notebook/migrants/hungary-treatment-refugees. Accessed December 12, 2016.

———. "Migrants in Serbia Create Makeshift Charging Stations for Smartphones." Reporter's Notebook: Traveling in Europe's River of Migrants (series). *New York Times*, August 30, 2015. www.nytimes.com/interactive/projects/cp/reporters-notebook/migrants/hungary-treatment-refugees. Accessed December 12, 2016.

———. "Refugees in Budapest Use TV Satellite Truck to Recharge Their Phones." Reporter's Notebook: Traveling in Europe's River of Migrants (series). *New York Times*, September 8, 2015. www.nytimes.com/interactive/projects/cp/reporters-notebook/migrants/hungary-treatment-refugees. Accessed December 12, 2016.

———. "Syrian Family Overcomes Hardships of War, but Finds Path Blocked in Denmark." Reporter's Notebook: Traveling in Europe's River of Migrants (series). *New York Times*, September 11, 2015. www.nytimes.com/interactive/projects/cp/reporters-notebook/migrants/hungary-treatment-refugees. Accessed December 12, 2016.

———. "Wearing the Journey Lightly." Reporter's Notebook: Traveling in Europe's River of Migrants (series). *New York Times*, September 7, 2015. www.nytimes.com/interactive/projects/cp/reporters-notebook/migrants/hungary-treatment-refugees. Accessed December 12, 2016.

Heefner, Colette. Echo100Plus volunteer. Interview. January 16, 2017.

History.com. "April 20, 1980: Castro Announces Mariel Boatlift." This Day in History. www.history.com/this-day-in-history/castro-announces-mariel-boatlift. Accessed December 8, 2016.

Horowitz, Evan. "Understanding the Migrant Crisis." *Boston Globe*, September 10, 2015. www.bostonglobe.com/news/world/2015/09/10/understanding-migrant-crisis/7TaDfbQYv1kVciOEjHOCUK/story.html. Accessed December 8, 2016.

Hubbard, Ben. "Syrian War Drags On, but Assad Future Looks as Secure as Ever." *New York Times*, September 25, 2017. www.nytimes.com/2017/09/25/world/middleeast/syria-assad-war.html. Accessed September 27, 2017.

Hull, Jonah. "Travelling to Athens with a Syrian Refugee." *Reporter's Notebook/Syria's Civil War* (blog). Al Jazeera. August 21, 2016. www.aljazeera.com/blogs/europe/2015/08/travelling-athens-syrian-refugee-150821123741872.html. Accessed December 15, 2016.

International Organization for Migration. "Mediterranean Migrant Arrivals in 2016 Near 155,000; Deaths Reach 467." Press Room. March 18, 2016. www.iom.int/news/mediterranean-migrant-arrivals-2016-near-155000-deaths-reach-467. Accessed September 27, 2017.

———. "Over 600,000 Displaced Syrians Returned Home in First 7 Months of 2017." Press Room. August 11, 2017. www.iom.int/news/over-600000-displaced-syrians-returned-home-first-7-months-2017. Accessed September 27, 2017.

Jebreal, Rula. "How to Treat Refugees with Dignity: A Lesson from Turkey." *New York Times*, September 27, 2017. www.nytimes.com/2017/09/27/opinion/turkey-syrian-refugees.html?. Accessed September 27, 2017.

Kanter, James. "E.U. Nations Urged to Accept 160,000 Migrants." *New York Times*, September 9, 2015. www.nytimes.com/2015/09/10/world/europe/europe-migrant-crisis-jean-claude-juncker.html. Accessed December 28, 2016.

———. "European Union Reaches Deal with Turkey to Return New Asylum Seekers." *New York Times*, March 18, 2016. www.nytimes.com/2016/03/19/world/europe/european-union-turkey-refugees-migrants.html. Accessed September 27, 2017.

Kantor, Jodi, and Catrin Einhorn. "Refugees Encounter a Foreign Word: Welcome." *New York Times*, July 1, 2016. www.nytimes.com/2016/07/01/world/americas/canada-syrian-refugees.html?hp&action=click&pgtype=Homepage&clickSource=story-heading&module=photo-spot-region&region=top-news&WT.nav=top-news. Accessed December 17, 2016.

———. "What Does It Mean to Help One Family?" *New York Times*, October 22, 2016. www.nytimes.com/interactive/2016/10/22/world/americas/canada-refugees-syria.html?hp&action=click&pgtype=Homepage&clickSource=story-heading&module=photo-spot-region&region=top-news&WT.nav=top-news. Accessed December 17, 2016.

———. "Wonder and Worry, as a Syrian Child Transforms." *New York Times*, December 17, 2016. www.nytimes.com/2016/12/17/world/americas/syrian-refugees-canada.html?hp&action=click&pgtype=Homepage&clickSource=story-heading&module=photo-spot-region&region=top-news&WT.nav=top-news. Accessed December 17, 2016.

Kirkpatrick, David D., and Hwaida Saad. "Exodus Out of Syria Grows, U.N. Says." *New York Times*, September 5, 2012. query.nytimes.com/gst/fullpage.=9E07E4D61E3CF936A3575A C0A9649D8B63. Accessed November 23, 2016.

Lageman, Thessa. "The Cemetery of Unknown Refugees from the Mediterranean." Features. Al Jazeera. December 29, 2016. www.aljazeera.com/indepth/features/2016/11/tunisia-cemetery-unknown-refugees-161112103347956.html. Accessed December 29, 2016.

Lemmon, Gayle Tzemach. "Syrian Refugees: Desperate Just to Go to School." CNN. March 2, 2016. www.cnn.com/2016/03/01/opinions/syrian-refugees-turkey-education-lemmon/index.html. Accessed March 31, 2017.

Letsch, Constanze, and Phoebe Greenwood. "Syrian Refugees: In Their Own Words." *Guardian*, April 2, 2012. www.theguardian.com/world/2012/apr/02/syrian-refugees-their-own-words. Accessed November 16, 2016.

Liptak, Kevin, and Jim Acosta. "Obama Slams Republicans over Refugee Stance." CNN. November 18, 2015. www.cnn.com/2015/11/17/politics/obama-syria-refugees-paris-attacks. Accessed December 12, 2016.

Lister, Tim. "Eating Toothpaste, Avoiding Gangs: Why Migrants Head to Mediterranean." CNN. April 22, 2015. www.cnn.com/2015/04/21/europe/mediterranean-boat-migrants-lister/index.html. Accessed December 13, 2016.

MapFight. "Washington (US) Is 1.0 Times as Big as Syria." mapfight.appspot.com/us.wa-vs-sy/washington-us-syria-size-comparison. Accessed September 25, 2017.

Melvin, Don, and Greg Botelho. "Police Clash with Protestors Angry about Cologne Sex Attacks." CNN. January 29, 2016. www.cnn.com/2016/01/09/europe/germany-new-year-violence/index.html. Accessed December 14, 2017.

Migration Policy Centre. *Syrian Refugees: A Snapshot of the Crisis—in the Middle East and Europe.* Florence, Italy: European University Institute. Updated September 2016. syrianrefugees.eu/timeline. Accessed December 7, 2016.

Mitscherlich, Johanna. "Crisis in Syria: Life in Darkness." *CARE Blog,* January 27, 2014. www.care.org/blog/crisis-syria-life-darkness. Accessed March 31, 2017.

Monsted, Anders, and Caroline Bach. "Syrian Mother Reunites with Children She Feared Had

Drowned." UNHCR (The UN Refugee Agency). December 13, 2016. www.unhcr.org/en-us/news/stories/2016/12/583571364/syrian-mother-reunites-children-feared-drowned.html. Accessed December 13, 2016.

Moussaoui, Rana. "His Piano Burned, Musician Joins Migrant Tide." *Daily Star*, September 21, 2015. www.dailystar.com.lb/News/Middle-East/2015/Sep-21/316005-his-piano-burned-musician-joins-migrant-tide.ashx. Accessed November 30, 2016.

Mullen, Jethro, and Ashley Fantz. "Hundreds of Migrant Deaths at Sea: What Is Europe Going to Do?" CNN. April 20, 2015. www.cnn.com/2015/04/20/africa/italy-migrant-boat-capsizes/index.html. Accessed December 13, 2016.

Nasr, Joseph. "Germany's Syrian Refugees Celebrate Merkel Win but Fear Rise of Far-Right." Reuters. *New York Times*, September 24, 2017. www.nytimes.com/reuters/2017/09/24/world/europe/24reuters-germany-election-migrants.html?partner=IFTTT&_r=0. Accessed September 25, 2017.

Nebehay, Stephanie, and Gabriela Baczynska. "Europe Seen on Cusp of New Humanitarian Crisis at Greece-Macedonia Border." Reuters. March 1, 2016. www.reuters.com/article/us-europe-migrants-unhcr-idUSKCN0W344I. Accessed December 15, 2016.

Noah, Sahir. "Hope Behind the Shadow of Pain!" Original poem.

Novacic, Ines. "Syrian Refugees Find Obstacles in U.S., but Also Hope." CBS News. September 9, 2015. www.cbsnews.com/news/syria-refugee-crisis-mothers-find-obstacles-in-us-but-also-hope. Accessed January 3, 2017.

Orange, Richard, Jamie Merrill, and Sophie Hardach. "Refugee Crisis: Three Stories from Syrians Who Have Made a New Life in the West." *Independent*, September 11, 2015. www.independent.co.uk/news/world/europe/refugee-crisis-three-stories-from-syrians-who-have-made-a-new-life-in-the-west-10497136.html. Accessed December 29, 2016.

Ou, Ed. "Syrian Refugees Languish in Turkey." *New York Times*, November 15, 2011. www.nytimes.com/slideshow/2011/11/15/world/middleeast/20111115_REFUGEES.html. Accessed November 23, 2016.

Plus, AJ. "Syrian Refugees: Starting Over in the US." Al Jazeera America. March 14, 2015. america.aljazeera.com/articles/2015/3/14/syrian-refugees-find-a-home-in-the-us.html. Accessed January 3, 2017.

Price, Megan, Anita Gohdes, and Patrick Ball. *Updated Statistical Analysis of Documentation of Killings in the Syrian Arab Republic*. Human Rights Data Analysis Group. Office of the UN High Commissioner for Human Rights. August 2014. www.ohchr.org/Documents/Countries/SY/HRDAGUpdatedReportAug2014.pdf. Accessed September 27, 2017.

Rankin, Jennifer. "EU Met Only 5% of Target for Relocating Refugees from Greece and Italy." *Guardian*, December 8, 2016. www.theguardian.com/world/2016/dec/08/eu-met-only-5-of-target-for-relocating-refugees-from-greece-and-italy. Accessed December 13, 2016.

Redden, Jack. "A Million Children Are Now Refugees from Syria Crisis." UNHCR (The UN Refugee Agency). August 23, 2013. www.unhcr.org/news/latest/2013/8/521621999/million-children-refugees-syria-crisis.html. Accessed December 6, 2016.

Ridgwell, Henry. "Syrian Refugees Struggle in Squalid Conditions on Lebanese Border." *Voice of America*, January 31, 2012. www.voanews.com/a/syrian-refugees-struggle-in-squalid-conditions-on-lebanese-border-138508554/151435.html. Accessed October 25, 2017.

Rifai, Bassam S. "Syrian Refugees Tell Their Harrowing Stories in Their Own Words." *New York Daily News*, September 13, 2015. www.nydailynews.com/opinion/syrian-refugees-harrowing-stories-article-1.2358726. Accessed November 16, 2016.

Sacchetti, Maria. "After Perilous Crossing, More Dangers Lie Ahead for Migrants." Desperate Journey (occasional series). *Boston Globe*, September 18, 2015. apps.bostonglobe.com/graphics/2015/09/refugees. Accessed December 8, 2016.

———. "As They Make Their Way into Germany, the Future Is Still Uncertain for Many Migrants." Desperate Journey (occasional series). *Boston Globe*,

September 28. 2015. apps.bostonglobe.com/
graphics/2015/09/refugees. Accessed December 8,
2016.

———. "Chaos at the Crossing." Desperate Journey
(occasional series). *Boston Globe*, September 19,
2015. apps.bostonglobe.com/graphics/2015/09/
refugees. Accessed December 8, 2016.

———. "Dispatches from Lesbos." Desperate Journey
(occasional series). *Boston Globe*, September 17,
2015. apps.bostonglobe.com/graphics/2015/09/
refugees. Accessed December 8, 2016.

———. "Making the Risky Crossing." Desperate Journey
(occasional series). *Boston Globe*, September 14,
2015. apps.bostonglobe.com/graphics/2015/09/
refugees. Accessed December 8, 2016.

———. "Many Migrants, Refugees Relieved to Reach
Austria as They Make Trek North." Desperate
Journey (occasional series). *Boston Globe*,
September 23. 2015. apps.bostonglobe.com/
graphics/2015/09/refugees. Accessed December 8,
2016.

———. "Toll of Migration Hits Mothers, Children
Hard." Desperate Journey (occasional series). *Boston
Globe*, September 21, 2015. apps.bostonglobe.com/
graphics/2015/09/refugees. Accessed December 8,
2016.

Salam Neighbor. Film. Directed by Zach Ingrasci. 1001
Media Group, 2015.

Shadid, Anthony. "Syrian Unrest Stirs New Fear of
Deeper Sectarian Divide." *New York Times*, June
13, 2011. www.nytimes.com/2011/06/14/world/
middleeast/14syria.html. Accessed November 23,
2016.

Simpson, John. "Who Are the Winners and Losers from
the Arab Spring?" BBC News. November 12, 2014.
www.bbc.com/news/world-middle-east-30003865.
Accessed March 30, 2017.

Smale, Alison, and Stephen Castle. "Migrant Influx
Prompts Macedonia, Britain and France to Increase
Security." *New York Times*, August 20, 2015.
www.nytimes.com/2015/08/21/world/europe/
macedonia-detains-migrants-from-greece-at-
border.html. Accessed November 22, 2016.

Solomon, Ben. "TimesCast: Syrians Flee to Turkey." *New
York Times*, June 9, 2011. www.nytimes.com/video/
world/middleeast/100000000857478/timescast-
syrians-flee-to-turkey.html. Accessed November 23,
2016.

Stack, Liam. "For Refugees from Syria, a Visit with No
Expiration Date." *New York Times*, November 14,
2011. www.nytimes.com/2011/11/15/world/
middleeast/refugees-from-syria-settle-in-for-long-
wait-in-turkey.html. Accessed November 23, 2016.

Sullivan, Kevin. "Changing Region, Changing
Lives." Refuge: 18 Stories of the Syrian
Exodus (series). *Washington Post*, December
3, 2013. www.washingtonpost.com/sf/syrian-
refugees/2013/12/03/refuge-stories-from-the-
syrian-exodus. Accessed December 16, 2016.

———. "A Child Goes to Work." Refuge: 18 Stories
of the Syrian Exodus (series). *Washington Post*,
December 2, 2013. www.washingtonpost.com/
sf/syrian-refugees/2013/12/02/child-worker.
Accessed December 16, 2016.

———. "New Camp Rises" Refuge: 18 Stories of the
Syrian Exodus (series). *Washington Post*, December
2, 2013. www.washingtonpost.com/sf/syrian-
refugees/2013/12/02/new-camp-rises. Accessed
December 16, 2016.

———. "Stitching a Life." Refuge: 18 Stories of the
Syrian Exodus (series). *Washington Post*, December
2, 2013. www.washingtonpost.com/sf/syrian-
refugees/2013/12/02/stitching-a-life. Accessed
December 7, 2016.

———. "Turned Back." Refuge: 18 Stories of the Syrian
Exodus (series). *Washington Post*, December
2, 2013. www.washingtonpost.com/sf/syrian-
refugees/2013/12/02/turned-back. Accessed
December 16, 2016.

Syria Campaign. "Care about Syrian Refugees? Listen to
Them." *Huffington Post*, December 7, 2015. www.
huffingtonpost.com/the-syria-campaign/what-
syrian-refugees-in-europe-want_b_8692520.html.
Accessed December 15, 2016.

Tagaris, Karolina. "EU-Turkey Deal Fails to Stem
Refugee Flight to Greece." Reuters. March 20, 2016.
www.reuters.com/article/us-europe-migrants-
greece-idUSKCN0WM0AC. Accessed December
15, 2016.

Tharoor, Ishaan. "The Arab World's Wealthiest Nations Are Doing Next to Nothing for Syria's Refugees." *Washington Post*, September 4, 2015. www.washingtonpost.com/news/worldviews/wp/2015/09/04/the-arab-worlds-wealthiest-nations-are-doing-next-to-nothing-for-syrias-refugees/?utm_term=.303b99bf4a6a. Accessed December 12, 2016.

———. "Slovakia Will Take in 200 Refugees, but They Have to Be Christian." *Washington Post*, August 19, 2015. www.washingtonpost.com/news/worldviews/wp/2015/08/19/slovakia-will-take-in-200-syrian-refugees-but-they-have-to-be-christian/?utm_term=.6abfbbf7896b. Accessed December 12, 2016.

———. "Trump and Pence's Opposition to Syrian Refugees Is Based on a Huge Lie." *Washington Post*, October 5, 2016. www.washingtonpost.com/news/worldviews/wp/2016/10/05/the-huge-lie-at-the-heart-of-trump-and-pences-opposition-to-syrian-refugees/?utm_term=.a3b5a103b8fa. Accessed December 13, 2016.

Thorpe, Nick. "Hungary Races to Build Border Fence as Migrants Keep Coming." BBC News. August 6, 2015. www.bbc.com/news/world-europe-33802453. Accessed November 22, 2016.

UNHCR (The UN Refugee Agency). *Desperate Journeys*. January–June 2017. data2.unhcr.org/en/documents/download/58838. Accessed September 25, 2017.

———. *Europe Monthly Report*. August 2017. data2.unhcr.org/en/documents/download/59081. Accessed September 25, 2017.

———. *Italy: Desperate Rescue at Sea*. Film. YouTube.com. July 24, 2014. www.youtube.com/watch?v=tiCx93dReic. Accessed December 13, 2016.

———. "Mediterranean Situation." data2.unhcr.org/en/situations/mediterranean. Accessed September 25, 2017.

———. "Meet Bushra." www.unrefugees.org/2013/03/photos-meet-bushra-the-one-millionth-syrian-refugee. Accessed December 14, 2016.

———. "Syria Emergency." www.unhcr.org/en-us/syria-emergency.html. Accessed November 22, 2016.

———. "Syria Regional Refugee Response." data.unhcr.org/syrianrefugees/regional.php. Accessed March 30, 2017.

UNICEF. "Basement Schools Provide Safety and Vital Continuity for Syrian Children Under Siege." At a Glance: Syrian Arab Republic. March 14, 2017. www.unicef.org/infobycountry/syria_95096.html. Accessed March 31, 2017.

Violations Documentation Center in Syria. *The Monthly Statistical Report on Victims*. November 2016. vdc-sy.net/Website/wp-content/uploads/2016/12/November-report-Eng.pdf. Accessed December 27, 2016.

Walsh, Deirdre, and Ted Barrett. "House Passes Bill That Could Limit Syrian Refugees." CNN. November 19, 2015. www.cnn.com/2015/11/19/politics/house-democrats-refugee-hearings-obama. Accessed December 12, 2016.

Weaver, Matthew. "Syrian Refugees: More Than 5M in Neighbouring Countries Now, Says UN." *Guardian*, March 30, 2017. www.theguardian.com/world/2017/mar/30/syrian-refugee-number-passes-5m-mark-un-reveals. Accessed September 27, 2017.

Winsor, Ben. "Here's Which Countries Are Helping Syria's Refugee Crisis—and Which Ones Are Refusing." *Business Insider*, September 11, 2014. www.businessinsider.com/the-countries-taking-syrias-refugees-2014-9?op=1. Accessed December 7, 2016.

Wood, Paul. "This Is the Life of a Syrian Refugee." *GlobalPost Investigations*, September 23, 2015. gpinvestigations.pri.org/a-daily-hustle-to-survive-this-is-the-life-of-a-syrian-refugee-55d411a7d234#.2y0fwjkpo. Accessed November 15, 2016.

Yardley, Jim. "A 'High Degree of Miserable' in a Refugee-Swollen Greece." *New York Times*, March 17, 2016. www.nytimes.com/2016/03/18/world/europe/greece-idomeni-refugees.html. Accessed October 25, 2017.

Yazbek, Samar. *The Crossing: My Journey to the Shattered Heart of Syria*. London: Ebury Publishing, 2015.

ACKNOWLEDGMENTS

Gabriella Dixon and Catharina Kahane, Echo100Plus (www.echo100plus.com)

Amed Khan, Elpída Home (elpidahome.org)

Shayanne Gal and Clara Veale, *Voices of Refugees* (www.voicesofrefugees.net)

Liz Alderman, *New York Times*

Volunteers with Echo and Elpída: Colette Heefner, Vaggelis Xafinis, Dina Rokic, Dayna Fondell, Joanne Coalesx, Jumana Abo Oxa, Felix Heins, Oliver Nasser, and Katie Hearsum

My wife, Deborah Nadel. Her insights and observations were invaluable.

ACROSS THE WORLD, MORE THAN 65 MILLION PEOPLE HAVE BEEN FORCED FROM THEIR HOMES, HALF OF WHOM ARE UNDER EIGHTEEN YEARS OLD. THIS BOOK IS DEDICATED TO THEM.

hmhco.com

The illustrations are pen & ink with digital paint.

The text type was set in Adobe Jenson Pro.

The speech bubble type was set in CC Tim Sale Brush.

Library of Congress Cataloging-in-Publication Data

Names: Brown, Don, 1949– author.

Title: The unwanted : stories of the Syrian refugees / by Don Brown.

Description: Boston : Houghton Mifflin Harcourt, [2018] | Audience: Age: 14+ | Audience: Grade 9 to 12. | Includes bibliographical references.

Identifiers: LCCN 2017024785 | ISBN 9781328810151 (alk. paper)

Subjects: LCSH: Syria—History—Civil War, 2011—Refugees—Juvenile literature.

Classification: LCC DS98.6 .B76 2018 | DDC 956.9104/231—dc23

LC record available at https://lccn.loc.gov/2017024785

Manufactured in China

SCP 10 9 8 7 6 5 4 3 2 1

4500715623

HOPE BEHIND THE SHADOW OF PAIN!

I will draw my dreams
on the wall of hope . . .
A hope of finding home . . .
Hope of going to school . . .
Hope of holding my parents'
hands and walking through the darkness without feeling scared . . .
It seems hard, but from the
heart of disaster I will be waiting
for somehow everything
to come to an end . . .
And see the light behind the darkness . . .
And remember always,
when life gives you all reasons
to give up . . . Don't.
Don't let the stumbles on the round stop the journey.
Stay strong and think
of that word . . . which they
call "HOPE."

"Hope Behind the Shadow of Pain!" by Sahir Noah

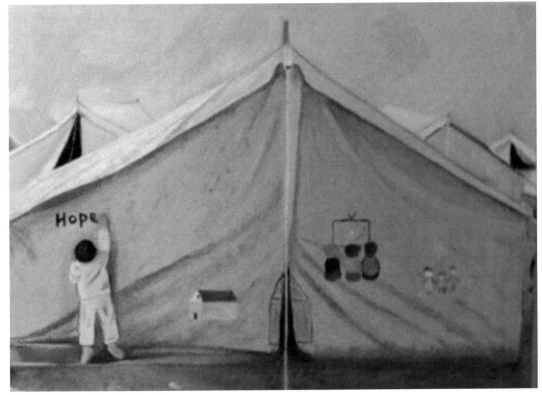

"Hope" by Salam Noah